THE SCARECROW AUTHOR BIBLIOGRAPHIES

MAXWELL ANDERSON:

an annotated bibliography of primary and secondary works

by
ALFRED S. SHIVERS

Scarecrow Author Bibliographies, No. 72

The Scarecrow Press, Inc.
Metuchen, N.J., & London
1985

Library of Congress Cataloging in Publication Data

Shivers, Alfred S.
    Maxwell Anderson : an annotated bibliography of
primary and secondary works.

    (Scarecrow author bibliographies ; no. 72)
    Includes indexes.
    1. Anderson, Maxwell, 1888-1959--Bibliography.
I. Title. II. Series.
Z8035.5.S53 1985   [PS3501.N256] 016.813'52 85-14227
ISBN 0-8108-1833-7

Dedicated to

DR. CHARLES EUGENE MOUNTS

　　　teacher
　　　poet
　　　mentor
　　　friend

remembering those wonderful years
we had at the University of
Florida

■ CONTENTS

That Maxwell Anderson (1888-1959) belongs among the ranks of the foremost American playwrights can hardly be denied by anyone who has studied his output. His What Price Glory (1924), written in collaboration with Laurence Stallings, is still regarded by many as an important early landmark in stage realism. His friend the playwright Paul Green even considered this work to be the best in the entire corpus, but this is a view not shared by those who have thrilled at such verse dramas as Elizabeth the Queen (1930), Mary of Scotland (1933), Winterset (1935), and High Tor (1937)--the genre at which Anderson excelled and for which future generations are most likely to remember him. His heyday was no doubt the 1930's. But there was hardly a season from 1923 up to 1958, the year before his death, when he did not have one or more plays running on Broadway. His Both Your Houses (1933) brought him the Pulitzer Prize, and Winterset and High Tor two Drama Critics' Circle Awards. In 1954 the American Academy and the National Institute of Arts and Letters presented him with its Gold Medal for Drama. Two years later he was made a member of the American Academy of Arts and Letters.

The record shows that master's theses and doctoral dissertations continue to be written on Anderson's plays and that the plays continue to be studied in our universities, even though they do not get anthologized very much anymore, sad to say. Nor are his plays currently getting revived on the New York stage. But the years from 1957 up to the present date have seen six scholarly books published about him or his work, not counting William Klink's bi-author bibliographical study. Even though Anderson is no longer considered a popular American playwright, which is to say not quite in the same league with the recently deceased Tennessee Williams, he was once thought to rival the great Eugene O'Neill and is still taken seriously by many scholars and critics. After a famous writer dies, there usually follows a decline of interest in his or her work; however, if that work has true literary merit, and does not simply satisfy the passing whims of the public, interest in that work will usually revive, at least among the literati. Of course, some authors (such as Shakespeare, Dickens, and Twain) have been fortunate enough to suffer no decline in public interest at all. These are the glorious exceptions to the rule.

It may well be that Maxwell Anderson is due for an imminent revival on the stage again. But theatrical conditions in New York are so artificial, depending so much upon the craftiness of the businessman and the demands of labor unions, rather than the quality of the theatrical fare itself, that for the next several years we will have to look for the reemergence of Anderson in the regional theater and perhaps abroad. No matter what happens, there will always be readers who make their private study into a little theater of their own. Anderson is a much better playwright than Broadway or the current scholarship would lead one to think.

Anderson believed that unless the playwright was fortunate enough to get his plays onto the stage while he was still alive, they would never survive for future generations. Sometimes great novels, like Wuthering Heights, unappreciated in their day, get rediscovered and come into their own finally; and the same sometimes happens to collections of poetry, such as those by Keats and Shelley. But insofar as he could tell, this had never happened with any forgotten body of dramas by someone. It is comforting to report that all the outstanding Maxwell Anderson plays actually did reach the stage during his lifetime and, consequently, according to his way of thinking, now have their fair chance of survival.

Martha Cox's Maxwell Anderson Bibliography, published in 1958 and limited to whatever had reached print, was the first extended bibliography on the playwright. This 117-page work was a useful contribution for its day, even though it excluded several interesting categories of material and contained no annotations. Cox's book came out before the tremendous quantity of Andersonia, including unpublished poems and playscripts, had become available for scholarly study at the University of Texas, and of course before Laurence G. Avery's extensive Catalogue of that collection appeared. Back in 1958 Anderson was still alive and presumably still discouraging, as usual, anyone who attempted to write a book about him or his work. For this and no doubt for other reasons, the Cox bibliography is brief. Some comparisons are in order: The Cox book contains only nineteen entries about Anne of the Thousand Days, whereas the present book has ninety-nine; the Cox book contains only fifty-eight on Winterset, whereas the present book has one hundred and fifty-nine.

William Klink's Maxwell Anderson and S. N. Behrman: A Reference Guide (1977) came later, is annotated, but is much more limited even than Cox's. The section on Anderson runs to forty eight pages. It truly is a "reference guide" rather than a fullblown bibliography, one suited to the needs of hurried undergraduates looking mainly for the "best" sources, and as such it satisfies that need. An excerpt taken from the Introduction will suffice to show how severe this restriciton is: "... I have included some popular criticism with the annotated scholarly entries, to give a broader range of opinion on the key plays and also to demonstrate instances of fine perception by critics who are sometimes undervalued" [emphasis mine]. As a result, the section on Anne of the Thousand Days, for instance, contains only eight entries, presumably the crème de la crème. The organization is the book's chief drawback, for the entries are organized strictly according to the year of publication, not title or subject, and under that rubric listed in alphabetical sequence. Thus, if only the title is known, the user must refer to the index for further help.

In my book The Life of Maxwell Anderson I had occasion to point out a few of the personal faults of Mab Maynard, who was known until the time of her death as the second Mrs. Maxwell Anderson. No doubt she had admirable traits above and beyond those which I indicated--and I tried hard to show these. But I fear that the negative aspects stood out only too well. Nevertheless, it would be ungrateful of me not to acknowledge that I owe this ambitious and tortured woman a considerable debt for many of the play reviews and play notices found in this bibliography. During my research at the University of Texas, I culled hundreds of newspaper and magazine clippings from Mab's theater scrapbooks where she had carefully identified most of the items by penning in the source and date. From all this assiduously collected and filed material it became obvious to me that for many years, while her mind was still clear and before she had begun her affair with Jerry Stagg, she had shown a special kind of loyalty to her husband in identifying herself closely with and rejoicing in his career. No doubt this actress manqué found in his success some compensation for her own frustrated yearnings for the stage.

Of all the categories of information to include in a major bibliography, I have omitted only the incomplete plays. But these items are neither numerous nor important. Anyone interested in them can consult Avery's Catalogue (see later).

Wherever I mention the New York Public Library in this book, I refer to the division known as the Lincoln Center Library & Museum of the Performing Arts. The materials at Yale University are housed in The Beinecke Rare Book and Manuscript Library, materials at the University of North Dakota in the Chester Fritz Library, materials at Stephen F. Austin State University in the Ralph Steen Library, and materials at the University of Texas in the Humanities Research Center (the single largest repository of Andersonia in the world).

Wherever Yale University is cited herein as the repository of poems related to Josephine Herbst, it should be understood that this means that Josephine Herbst collection lodged in the Beinecke. These poems, the existence of which lately came as a surprise to Anderson's heirs, are in some instances unpublished. They were doubtlessly copied in ink by Josephine herself into her leatherbound diary, which she evidently kept locked. Elinor Langer writes in

Josephine Herbst (1984) that the poems are in Anderson's handwriting, but this is an error, as I convinced her shortly after her book was published, because the script differs sharply from the playwright's known script during that era (e.g., in the manuscript for White Desert). On the other hand, it matches closely what we see in Josephine's letter to her sister, Helen, around 1920. Langer claims persuasively that Anderson, who was still married to his first wife at the time, had an impassioned love affair with this unmarried novelist beginning late in February 1920 and ending the following summer. Moreover, that the woman became pregnant as a result and that he advised her to have an abortion. She had the abortion. Afterwards, she advised her pregnant (and married) sister, Helen, to get an abortion too, and her sister did. But Helen got infected from the bungled operation and died.

Unless otherwise indicated, the theaters named in this book are in New York City. One can always assume that there was an out-of-town tryout for each of the plays, also one or more tours following a successful Broadway run. The published version of the play almost invariably represents Anderson's intentions before the play went into production. He had no more confidence in the changes that stage directors required of him during tryouts than he had in the films that Hollywood sometimes made from his plays.

ACKNOWLEDGMENTS

I am indebted to Stephen F. Austin State University for the two faculty research grants that enabled me to do research and writing for this bibliography. I am also indebted to the board of regents and to officials and fellow staff members of the University, notably Drs. Roy E. Cain, Kirby L. Duncan, and Bobby H. Johnson for their generous letters of recommendation--and most of all to my two kind and enthusiastic sponsors, Dr. Patricia R. Russell and Mr. Lee W. Sullenger--for giving me the Regents Professor of Research award for 1984-85, which allowed released time to complete this book. I am grateful also because President William R. Johnson and other administrators, aware of how technology can come to the aid of the writer, wisely put aside the usual restrictions and allowed the award money to be used in this instance to help defray the cost of a TI Professional Computer. The latter proved to be a marvelous time-saver in this work.

Once again I must express my thanks to Lee. W. Sullenger, who happens to be not only a friend of mine but the head reference librarian at the Ralph Steen Library. In this project he went far out of his way to obtain interlibrary loan materials for me. Some of the Steen Library staff members who have helped me have retired or otherwise moved on, but I owe a debt of thanks to the following kind people for their encouragement and unstinting assistance over the years since I first started collecting bibliographical data:

Betty B. Bennett, Cleo B. Kelly, Elizabeth Jane Logan, Julia (Jewdi) Mach, Sara Mayfield, Carolyn Mallory, Ann H. Prasell, C. W. Romans, Jan C. Todd, and David Eugene Vancil.

To these librarians at the Chester Fritz Library, University of North Dakota, I am grateful for assistance in studying and identifying the Anderson holdings on file there: J. W. Bird (the former manuscript assistant) and Dan Rylance (coordinator of special collections). My thanks as well to the Anderson bibliographer Professor J. F. S. Smeall, of the Department of English.

I am indebted to Mary M. Hirth and her staff at the Humanities Research Center (University of Texas) for their cooperation and assistance during my several visits there. Likewise, the staff of The State Historical Society of Wisconsin (Madison, Wisconsin). Another note of thanks goes to Susan R. Rosenberg, archivist at The Stanford University Libraries (Stanford University).

On more than one occasion Mrs. Maxwell Anderson came to my aid with information about hitherto uncataloged items. Sometimes she sent me copies of these. For reasons too numerous to itemize here, I owe her a sizeable debt for the direct and indirect aid that she has furnished me over the years.

It was Elinor Langer who first told me about the existence of the Anderson poems in the Herbst diary at Yale University. My appreciation goes to her for this lead. In this connection, I want to express my gratitude to David E. Schoonover, curator at The Beinecke Rare Book and Manuscript Library, Yale University, for arranging to send me copies of the poems.

Last but far from least, I freely acknowledge my indebtedness to Laurence G. Avery's Catalogue of the Maxwell Anderson Collection at the University of Texas for enabling me to provide fuller and more accurate synopses of the unpublished poems and plays. My use of this book along with the bibliography by Martha Cox is a good example of how new scholarship depends so much upon that which has gone before. We each contribute a stone or two toward the great pyramid of knowledge.

Alfred S. Shivers
February 11, 1985
Nacogdoches, Texas

PART I:

PRIMARY WORKS

1. Three American Plays (in collaboration with Laurence Stallings). New York: Harcourt, Brace, 1926. This contains What Price Glory, First Flight, and The Buccaneer.

   a) What Price Glory was MA's first and Stallings' only stage success. MA completed the first draft in about a week; Stallings revised Act II to give the marine dialogue its salty authenticity, and shortly later talked Arthur Hopkins, the noted Broadway "manager" (as the producer was called then), into staging it. Hopkins gave the play a tryout in Stamford, Connecticut, and then its premiere performance at the Plymouth Theatre at 8:30 p.m. on Friday, September 5, 1924. The cast included Louis Wohlheim as Captain Flagg; William Boyd as Sergeant Quirt; Brian Donlevy as Corporal Gowdy; George Tobias as Corporal Lipinsky; and Leyla Georgie as Charmaine. What Price Glory had 299 stage performances in its first run.
   Captain Flagg and Sergeant Quirt, professional U.S. marines who have had much experience together, meet in France during WWI and wrangle over the favors of a French trollop. While Flagg is away, Quirt takes over the woman, but upon his return Flagg seeks revenge by trying to force his old rival to marry her. Quirt, however, refuses. The two men soon forget Charmaine when they get orders to pull out and head to the battle front.
   With its realistic portrayal of the language and behavior of front line troops, this play set a new standard in stage realism and influenced the course of subsequent American drama by making its dialogue more vernacular, sometimes more profane. Often reprinted in anthologies.
   Ms. of the complete first draft plus notes and outline are at the Univ. of Texas. The question mark usually seen at the end of the title does not appear in the first draft or in the first edition.

   b) First Flight, also produced and directed by Arthur Hopkins, turned out to be neither a critical nor a commercial success. After it was first presented at the Plymouth Theatre on September 17, 1925, it ran for only 12 performances. Rudolph Cameron enacted the role of the young Andrew Jackson; Helen Chandler portrayed Charity Clarkson.
   Captain "Andy" Jackson, on his trip to Nashville to settle

the affair of the free state of Franklin in 1788, stops over at
Peevey's Tavern. At the tavern several hotheads challenge
him to duels. He tries to defend a seventeen-year-old girl,
Charity Clarkson, who has fallen in love with him. Following
the duels, he kisses Charity farewell and rides off to Nashville. This is his first flight from his favorite weakness,
women.
   The location of the ms. is unknown.

   c) The Buccaneer had its first production, by Arthur Hopkins, at the Plymouth Theatre on Oct. 2, 1925. It was a
critical and commercial failure. There were only 20 performances. William Farnum played the role of the swashbuckling
Captain Henry Morgan; Estelle Winwood, the role of Dona
Lisa; Ferdinand Gottschalk, the role of Charles II.
   Capt. Henry Morgan, sailing on the Spanish main, deserts
the British navy and becomes a privateer. He captures a
port or two, sacking the towns in a gentlemanly manner. At
Panama City he meets and is prettily defied by (but only
briefly) one Dona Lisa, who, before she had married a Span-
iard, was known as Lady Elizabeth Neville. After successfully
wooing Dona Lisa he is abruptly separated from her by the
arrival of a British admiral, who places him under arrest.
Later, at Whitehall palace in England, King Charles II feels
so much respect for Morgan that he refuses to hang the man.
Instead, he dubs this erstwhile rascal a knight and even ap-
points him as governor of Jamaica. As the play closes, Morgan prepares to take Elizabeth to Jamaica as his new bride.
   The ms., incomplete and with corrections by Stallings, is
at the Univ. of Texas.

2. Gods of the Lightning and Outside Looking In. New York:
    Longmans, Green, 1928 (Gods written in collaboration with
    Harold Hickerson).

    a) Gods of the Lightning, based closely upon the famous
Sacco-Vanzetti trial earlier in the decade, was produced by
Hamilton MacFadden and Kellogg Gary at the Little Theatre
on Oct. 24, 1928. Like What Price Glory it incurred attempts
at censorship, e.g., at Boston, not because of its language
but because of its supposed inflammatory subject matter. It
died a quick and deserved death on the stage after only 29
performances. Charles Bickford played the role of Macready;
Horace Braham the role of Capraro.
   In this fiery, journalistic dramatization of the Sacco-
Vanzetti trial, Macready, a leader of the milltown strikers,
and Capraro, a passive but devoted anarchist, are arrested
for the murder of a payroll worker. The evidence against
them is purely circumstantial. At the trial the district attor-
ney, the judge, and the foreman of the jury are out to "burn"

the innocent defendants. In this crooked judicial system
there is no possibility of obtaining justice. Macready and
Capraro are found guilty and sentenced to die in the electric
chair.
The ms. is at the Univ. of Texas.

b) Outside Looking In, based on Jim Tully's novel Beggars
of Life, was produced by Messrs. O'Neill, Macgowan, and
Jones on September 7, 1925, at the Greenwich Village Theatre.
It had a moderate stage success, running to only 113 performances. The future screen actors James Cagney and
Charles A. Bickford took the roles of Little Red and Oklahoma
Red, respectively. Blyth Daly took the role of Edna.
In North Dakota, a hobo called Little Red meets and falls
in love with a young prostitute called Edna, who is on the
run from the law after having murdered her seducer, her own
stepfather. These two encounter a gang of hoboes led by
Oklahoma Red. The gang sets up a kangaroo court in a box
car to try Little Red on the charge that he is a "sissy," finds
him guilty, decrees that he is unworthy of their society, and
that his girlfriend become the judge's property. But Little
Red succeeds in defying the gang and wins the respect of
Oklahoma Red. The latter helps him and his girlfriend elude
the sheriff and his men.
The ms., 89 pp. plus notes, is at the Univ. of Texas.
Also a carbon copy.

3. Eleven Verse Plays, 1929-1939. New York: Harcourt, Brace,
1940. Contains Elizabeth the Queen, Night over Taos, Mary
of Scotland, Valley Forge, Winterset, The Wingless Victory,
High Tor, The Masque of Kings, The Feast of Ortolans, Second Overture, and Key Largo.

a) Elizabeth the Queen was produced by The Theatre
Guild on Nov. 3, 1930, at the Guild Theatre, where it ran
for 147 performances. The celebrated husband-and-wife team
of Alfred Lunt and Lynn Fontanne took the roles of Essex and
Elizabeth. MA's mistress at the time, Mab Anthony (née
Gertrude Higger), played the role of Mary, one of the queen's
ladies in waiting.
This is the first of MA's widely lauded plays about the English Renaissance (three of the four are about Elizabeth I) and
it is one of his plays that are most often reprinted and dis-
cussed. Even though Elizabeth the Queen does not fully embody his later enunciated theory of what a tragedy should be,
it represents a high-water mark in his dramaturgic art.
The setting is 1599-1601 in England during the reign of the
imperious and moody Elizabeth I. The queen is now approaching old age but is as passionate as a teenager in her love for
the young Essex. Raleigh and Cecil plot the downfall of Essex

because they envy his influence with the queen, and dupe
him into leading an army into Ireland. After Essex goes
abroad, his letters to and from Elizabeth are intercepted; as
a result, misunderstandings arise. But he finally discovers
the machinations against him, returns angrily to England,
storms the palace in a final bid for power, and makes the
queen his prisoner. By promising to share the throne with
him, Elizabeth tricks him into dismissing his guards and has
him thrown into the Tower. He is tried for treason, found
guilty, and sentenced to execution. At the end the queen
weakens and gives him the opportunity to sue for pardon but
he proudly refuses. Essex now realizes his own tragic fault:
he loves power too much; and though he still loves the queen
he would try to overthrow her again if he were released.
Result: he would bring England to ruin. He bitterly concludes that woman, being a natural coward, makes the best
ruler because she will preserve the peace.
A bound carbon copy is at the Univ. of Texas.

b) Night over Taos was produced by the Group Theatre
on March 9, 1932, at the 48th Street Theatre, where it ran
for only 13 performances. J. Edward Bromberg took the role
of the hero, Pablo Montoya; Franchot Tone, the role of his
treacherous son, Federico. Anderson's mistress and later
"wife," Gertrude Maynard (a.k.a. Mab Anthony and Gertrude
Higger) played the role of Conchita.
MA had gotten his inspiration for Night over Taos by reading Harvey Fergusson's series of six articles on the Rio
Grande Valley in American Mercury, published from May to
October 1931, particularly the last article, which is titled "The
Strange History of Padre Martinez of Taos." Though twice
published, the play lacks the conclusion that MA had intended,
namely a 12-line speech by Montoya. In Eleven Verse Plays
this speech is wrongly divided between the characters Montoya
and Diana.
In 1847 the American government in the north, representing
freedom and democracy, is encroaching against the feudal do-
main of Taos, whose leader is the noble Don Pablo Montoya.
But there are troubles within the Montoya family also. Pablo's
eldest son, Federico, tries to betray his father and is killed;
the youngest son, Felipe, would marry his father's fiancée.
Pablo fails in his revolt against the American settlers and takes
poison.
The ms. is in a ledger at the Univ. of Texas.

c) Mary of Scotland was produced by the Theatre Guild on
November 27, 1933, at the Alvin Theatre. It ran for 248 per-
formances. The cast consisted of Helen Hayes as Mary Stuart,
Philip Merivale as the Earl of Bothwell, and Helen Mencken as
Queen Elizabeth. Anderson's eldest son, Quentin, played the
role of a warder. Although Moroni Olsen enacted the part of

the bigoted Protestant preacher John Knox, MA is said to have told his little brother Lawrence that their father, the Reverend William Lincoln Anderson, would have been well suited on the basis of personality and narrow-mindedness to take on that role.

The plot structure of the play is interesting in that MA employs here for the first time in fully developed form his theory of tragedy (see his essay "The Essence of Tragedy").

In 1561 the beautiful Catholic Mary Stuart of Scotland returns to her homeland from France to assume the throne, and in so doing comes under the suspicion and envy of the unattractive Queen Elizabeth, who then plots her overthrow. Elizabeth arranges for Mary to marry the weakling Lord Darnley, by whom a male heir is born. The Scottish earls then have Darnley and David Rizzio, who is Mary's secretary, murdered. Elizabeth, still plotting, incites the fanatical John Knox to lead a rebellion against the Scottish queen, who has by now taken a new husband, her true love, the Earl of Bothwell. After a military defeat Mary flees to England and seeks refuge with her enemy, Elizabeth. The latter imprisons the woman in Carlisle Castle and will not release her except on condition that Mary abdicate in favor of her son. This act Mary proudly refuses. In a final confrontation scene (which never took place in history) the royal prisoner teaches Elizabeth the bitter truth, viz., that Elizabeth's life is in the main a failure, she being unloved and barren, whereas Mary's life has been fulfilled with love and motherhood. Hence, though victorious in force and guile, Elizabeth has lost out. Mary's son will become king of Scotland someday.

The ms. is filed at the Univ. of North Dakota. The last page of it contains the notation "Curtain / Santa Monica / July 14, 1933." Also on file at this library is a small record book that contains, in addition to some diary notes for the summer of 1933, the conclusion of Mary of Scotland. Moreover, this record book contains on its last page an alternate passage for the play. In the New York Public Library are two bound carbon copies, one of these being the stage manager's script used during production.

d) Valley Forge was produced by the Theatre Guild at the Guild Theatre, starting Dec. 10, 1934. It ran for only 58 performances. Philip Merivale portrayed the role of Washington, and Margalo Gilmore portrayed Mary Philipse.

MA was convinced, after the play was put on, that he had not sufficiently characterized the figure of Washington, and any reader can see that the drama does not build steadily in excitement to the end of the acts. The play is unusual in that it does not show Washington as a dominant, powerful leader using his iron will to hold together his half-frozen and half-starved army in the darkest hour of the American Revolutionary War. Instead, he is a beaten and discouraged gen-

eral who is ready to meet with the British Lord Howe to effect
a surrender. Washington has not received anywhere near the
support of the Congress and the private citizenry that he
should have. Fortunately for the American cause, the example of his own brave officers and soldiers stirs him to a new
resolve just as he is about to surrender. Also, news of the
hoped for French-American alliance arrives just in the nick of
time.
     The ms. in ledger form is at the Univ. of Texas; also, the
printer's typescript. In this collection can be found an incomplete carbon copy of a radio adaptation that was broadcast on
September 13, 1939, for propaganda purposes.

     e) Winterset, generally acknowledged to be MA's master-
piece, was produced by Guthrie McClintic at the Martin Beck
Theatre beginning September 25, 1935. During its first engagement it had 179 performances; during its second, 16.
Once again the author treats of the Sacco-Vanzetti case, but
this time with sufficient aesthetic distance and the use of
blank verse instead of prose. The cast of the first stage
presentation included Burgess Meredith in the role of Mio,
Margo as Miriamne, and Anatole Winogradoff as Esdras.
Winterset won the first Drama Critics' Circle Award ever presented.
     As in the case of What Price Glory, this play is a landmark
in the history of the theater. Winterset represents the first
(and thus far maybe the only) instance of a successful poetic
tragedy that uses a contemporary setting. All earlier tragedies had used the remote past.
     The story is about the teenage Mio, son of a radical, who
has been wandering about America in search of revenge.
Years before, his father had been judged guilty of and executed for a crime that he did not commit. In a waterfront
slum in Manhattan he chances to meet and fall in love with
the sister of a witness to the crime. The witness, Garth,
has been "lying low" out of fear of the gang leader, now new-
ly returned to the neighborhood. By the time Mio learns of
Garth's involvement, he is so fully in love with Miriamne that
out of respect for her he renounces all thoughts of vengeance.
Then, just after he reaches this noble state of mind, he and
Miriamne go out into the street where they are gunned down
by waiting thugs who, hired by Trock, do not want anyone
to reopen the murder case. Miriamne's father, the old rabbi
Esdras, delivers an inspired funeral oration over the bodies
of the young people--an oration generally misunderstood and
dismissed by published critics of this play.
     The corrected ms. is in a ledger at the Univ. of Texas.
On the last page there is this note: "begun March 21st 1935,
finished June 1st 1935, in the cabin in the woods." The fore-
mentioned cabin was located in the woods just behind MA's new
house on South Mountain Road in New City, N.Y. Also at the

Univ. of Texas is an extensively corrected and unbound carbon copy that was used by the stage manager for the first
New York production.

f) The Wingless Victory, produced by Katharine Cornell,
had its first performance in the National Theatre, Washington,
D.C., on November 24, 1936. After that, it moved to the
Empire Theatre in New York City, where it ran for 110 performances. The cast included Katharine Cornell in the role
of the heroine Oparre, Walter Abel as Nathaniel McQuestion,
and Kent Smith as the Reverend Phineas McQuestion.
As in Mary of Scotland and Sea-Wife, the author explores
here the motif of intolerance and bigotry in a Protestant community. The story, inspired by Euripides' Medea (the first
of many dramatic treatments down through history), uses the
locale of Salem, Massachusetts, in the winter of 1800. The
language is part poetry, part prose. Returning to Salem on
the Queen of the Celebes is the Yankee trader Nathaniel Mc-
Question. Many years ago he had left town as a vagabond
sailor determined not to return until he was rich enough to
"buy" the town, and now he has fulfilled the dream. The
hitch is that he has brought back with him into this nest of
hypocrites and bigots his beautiful Malay wife, Oparre, and
her two dusky children. McQuestion's relatives and fellow
townspeople are eager to share in his riches, but they cannot
stomach his alien family, especially Oparre, who, a converted
Christian, out-Christians the best of them. He imagines that
his wealth will overcome the town prejudice but, alas, he and
his wife and children do not receive a single social invitation.
Once the Salemites have milked him of most of his fortune they
confront him with information that his ship is actually a stolen
vessel once called The Wingless Victory. Then they blackmail
him into getting rid of his wife and children in exchange for
protecting him against the law and keeping him solvent. By
this time McQuestion has so absorbed the community's despica-
ble values that he goes along with the deal: choosing materialism over this remarkable woman and her children who love
him. Shamefully rejected, Oparre goes aboard ship and poisons
herself and the children because they have no place of refuge.
McQuestion, suddenly turned repentant, goes to them but it
is too late.
The ms. is in an unlabelled ledger at the Univ. of Texas.
At the end there is this notation: "begun August 7, finished
October 11th, 1935, in the cabin in the woods." The New
York Public Library owns a heavily corrected typed version
that was used as the prompt script during production; also, a
carbon copy that served as the stage manager's script; and,
finally, a slightly corrected carbon copy in library binding.

g) High Tor, a comic fantasy with touches of melodrama,
was produced by the Playwrights Producing Company at the

Martin Beck Theatre on Jan. 9, 1937. It ran for 171 performances, a critical and commercial success. Furthermore,
it received the Drama Critics' Circle Award for the 1936-37
season. Unquestionably this is one of MA's finest productions. The cast included Burgess Meredith in the role of
Van Van Dorn, the English actress Peggy Ashcroft as Lise,
and Mab Maynard (MA's live-in companion) as Judith.
   High Tor contains satirical hits at the U.S. Post Office,
F. D. R., and the kinds of rampant materialism that Thoreau
(something of a hero to Anderson) observed was overrunning
America even in the last century. The character Van Van
Dorn was based on an actual local resident in New City, one
Elmer Van Orden, who owned and lived on the mountain called
High Tor, which is part of the Palisades along the Hudson
River. It appears that the nearby Nanuet bank actually had
been robbed (as in the play). A neighbor of Anderson's, a
man named William A. Caldwell, wrote in an article for the
New Jersey Bergen County Evening Record that he could swear
he knew the names of the originals for the realtor and the
probate judge in the story.
   The young Van Van Dorn, a man of Dutch descent who
eschews conventional employment and fishes and shoots for a
living, finds himself beset with two crooks, Biggs and Skimmerhorn, who want to buy his beloved mountain High Tor for
a fraction of its worth and raze it for trap rock. He con-
temptuously rejects their offers. In addition to this main plot
there are four subplots: 1) Three amusing bank robbers have
narrowly escaped to the mountain with their loot, which then
falls into the greedy hands of Biggs and Skimmerhorn, who in
turn become lost on the mountain and get trapped in the
bucket of a steam shovel; 2) a crew of Dutch phantoms, ma-
rooned on the mountain since the seventeenth century, have
interactions with the live people there; 3) a philosophic old
Indian looks for a place in which to be buried; and 4) Judith,
the hero's girlfriend, tries to get him to take a regular job
or at least get some money before she will consent to marry
him. The plots about Van Dorn, the ghosts, and the Indian
are thematically united in that all three represent cultural
stages in history that are threatened with extinction. High
Tor induces in the reader or theatergoer a poetic nostalgia
for fair things dead and past, and a scorn for those greedy
hogs who would despoil natural beauty for the sake of material
gain.
   The corrected ms. is in a ledger filed at Yale University.
On the last page one reads this note: "Begun May 31, 1936.
Finished July 2, 1936. In the cabin in the woods." In the
New York Public Library rests the stage manager's script,
typed and bound in red vinyl; in this version the character
Judith does not appear in Act II.

   h) The Masque of Kings, produced by the Theatre Guild,

was staged at the Shubert Theatre on Feb. 8, 1937. Its run
of 89 performances showed that it was only a lukewarm popular success. This is one of MA's many plays about corruption
in power politics. Henry Hull played Crown Prince Rudolph;
Dudley Digges was the prince's father, Emperor Franz Joseph;
Margo enacted the prince's eighteen-year-old mistress, Baron-
ess Mary Vetsera; and Pauline Frederick portrayed the Em-
press Elizabeth.

On January 30, 1889, slightly over a month after Maxwell
Anderson was born, two mysterious deaths occurred in the
royal hunting lodge at Mayerling, Austria. Crown Prince
Rudolph, next in line for the throne of Austria Hungary, was
found shot to death with his mistress. Novels, plays, and
motion pictures have exploited this story. In The Masque of
Kings Anderson gives us his own plausible account of what
might have happened, colored as usual by his gloomy assess-
ment of the chances for idealism and young love making any
headway in the world of power politics.

The young Rudolph, wanting to bring freedom to his people,
engages in a plot to overthrow his aged father, the cruel
Emperor Franz Joseph. But Rudolph, like Shakespeare's
Hamlet, is sensitive about doing the brutal and ruthless acts
that are necessary to bring down the head of state, and he
grows disillusioned when he understands that he will have to
be just as oppressive as his father when he heads the new
regime, for freedom and power do not mix. Moreover, he
learns to his despair that the mistress he loves, and who is
now completely loyal to him, was originally employed as a spy
by his father. Aghast at the consequences of the revolt now
underway, Rudolph flees to the hunting lodge. Mary goes
there to join him, and the pair spend the night together.
The next morning Mary learns that he is still shocked at her
perfidy and knows that his father will never be reconciled
with him as long as she is around. Wanting to prove her
devotion, she kills herself. Now the Emperor arrives, ready
to forgive them and offer royal advancement to his son, but
the latter is fed up with the useless role of being crown
prince, and horrified that he will be required to walk someday in the bloody footsteps of his father. So, he takes his
own life. The Emperor hushes up the whole affair so that
history will be none the wiser.

The corrected ms. is in a ledger titled "Ultima Thule /
Masque of Kings" and on file at the Univ. of Texas. There
also is a carbon copy in library binding.

i) The Feast of Ortolans, a one-act play written especially
for radio, was aired over the Blue Network of the National
Broadcasting Company on September 20, 1937, from 9:30 to
10:00 p.m. The cast contained no notable figures from the
world of screen or stage, but the nature of the drama de-
emphasized the need for stars.

This was MA's first radio play, and as such it is decidedly experimental. He did not intend to have any individual protagonists in the action, with the result that during the early portion of the play the audience might not be able to tell for sure who is speaking. As he reportedly explained, "single individuals gradually emerge from the group less as individuals than as spokesmen for certain broad tendencies" ("Poetic Drama Spun for Air by Anderson," New York Herald Tribune, August 22, 1937).

In the year 1789 an assortment of artists, writers, intellectuals, and a few noblemen are seated about the dinner table of the Duke of Pompignan, some twenty miles from Paris. They await the serving of a feast of ortolans (a cooked bunting, prized as a delicacy, and in this case symbolic of the effete, aristocratic way of life that is about to end for most of those present). Among the guests are the playwright Beaumarchais; the friend of George Washington, the Marquis de Lafayette; and Phillipe of Orleans, an heir to the throne. The conversation turns to the current civil unrest. Lafayette tells the others that they have but played with the thought of revolution, they with their airy Rousseauistic doctrines, but there is a real social revolution afoot. Society will be radically altered. The figure called La Harpe goes further and prophesies that many of those present will soon die violent deaths at the hands of the militant proletariat. All who have had anything to do with the aristocracy will perish, save Lafayette, who will go into exile. The climax of the play comes when the chef enters, stabbed: the price for serving the nobility. The other servants flee. And the host, investigating in the kitchen, gets stabbed, too. This will be the last feast of ortolans for the Pompignan family and its friends. The horrors of the revolution have begun.

The ms. is bound in the same ledger with The Star-Wagon, at the Univ. of North Dakota, and runs from page 101 to 121.

j) Second Overture, a one-act play, was apparently written for presentation on radio but, insofar as this writer knows, has never been aired. Nor has it been acted professionally on the stage.

Like The Feast of Ortolans, this is a play about the terrors of a European revolution in which innocent people become victims of unreasoning violence. The scene is a village east of Moscow, Russia; the time, an evening in January 1918, when the Communist regime is completing its strangle hold upon the country. A group of fellow travelers who have been trying to flee the country by train have been captured by the revolutionary forces and taken to a cellar where a commissar is to decide their fate. Afterwards, a drunken captain will perform the executions. Charish, the commissar, assumes that all the prisoners in the room are guilty of capital offenses even though there has been no trial. Their running away from Russia is

sufficient proof of guilt; if allowed to escape, they might return and do the regime some mischief. They ought to be
proud to die in this great "cleansing" of the empire. One
of the condemned, Gregor, turns out to be a friend of the
commissar's; they had been fellow idealists during the abortive
1905 revolution. Gregor still retains those ideals for which
they had fought and is vastly disillusioned at how his friend
has changed to a policy of cruel expediency. Charish frees
Gregor, but the latter chooses to die with the others. He
overturns the table with its candles and makes it possible for
the prisoners to escape to a truck outside. Gregor, however,
remains behind, sacrificing himself for his fellow human be-
ings.

The incomplete ms. is at the Univ. of Texas.

k) Key Largo is one of many of MA's tragedies written
during his Golden Era of the 1930's. It consists of a prologue and two acts. The Playwrights Producing Company
staged the play at the Ethel Barrymore Theatre on Nov. 27,
1939, where it ran for 105 performances. It is one of the
author's most philosophical works. The cast included Paul
Muni in the role of King McCloud, Uta Hagen as Alegre d'Alcala, Harold Johnsrud as d'Alcala (the father), José Ferrer
as Victor d'Alcala, Frederic Tozere as Murillo, and Ralph
Theodore as Sheriff Gash.

The Prologue in Key Largo closely resembles MA's unpublished play The Bastion Saint Gervais (c.1938). In Key
Largo, as in so many of his other dramatic works, MA shows
his concern with the larger issues of life; and though the setting of the Prologue is the Spanish Civil War, the message is
universal in that it is about a man's need to redeem himself
after a failure in courage. The play also marks a turning
point in the author's attitude toward war: he is shifting
away from his stance of noninvolvement.

The story reminds one of Conrad's Lord Jim in that a young
man makes what appears to be a cowardly decision in a moment
of crisis, later becomes ashamed of what he did, and in a final
heroic deed wins back his lost honor. King McCloud had
signed up with the Loyalists in Spain in 1937 and became a
leader of a company of American fighters. Then, growing disillusioned, this idealist leaves his comrades to perish for what
he believes is a lost cause. The turncoat goes to Florida in
fulfillment of a promise to visit the families of his deceased
comrades, in this case the father and sister of Victor d'Alcala. At the d'Alcala hotel he falls in love with the sister,
Alegre, and hears from her father a confession of noble Ex-
istentialism that seems to come right out of the playwright's
heart. Soon an opportunity arises in which McCloud can
prove that he is courageous after all, for the gangster Murillo
and his hoodlums take over the hotel and threaten the occu-
pants. McCloud gets up enough courage to kill the gangster,

but in turn is killed by one of the gang.

Key Largo is prophetic about the rise of fascism that was then sweeping over Europe, and the need for freedom-loving people, especially disillusioned idealists, to take up courage and get involved in the great political and military issues of the day.

The ms. and a typescript copy are at the Univ. of Texas; also a ms. outline and 50 pages of revision.

4. Four Verse Plays. New York: Harcourt, Brace, 1959. Contains Elizabeth the Queen (no. 3-a), Mary of Scotland (no. 3-c), High Tor (no. 3-g), and Winterset (no. 3-e).

5. Saturday's Children. New York: Longmans, Green, 1927.
    Saturday's Children, a comedy, was produced by The Ac-
    tors' Theatre at the Booth Theatre on Jan. 26, 1927, where
    it ran for 310 performances. The cast included Ruth Gordon
    in the role of the heroine Bobby, Roger Pryor as Rims O'Neill,
    Ruth Hammond as Florrie Sands, Frederick Perry as Mr. Hal-
    evy, Lucia Moore as Mrs. Halevy, and Beulah Bondi as Mrs.
    Gorlic.
    On April 9, 1928, the play moved to the Forrest Theatre,
    where it ran for 16 more performances. Three changes were
    made in the cast: Humphrey Bogart took the role of Rims
    O'Neill, Grace Ruth Henderson took the role of Mrs. Halevy,
    and Anne Tonetti took the role of Mrs. Gorlic.
    Bobby, the young and very inexperienced heroine of this
    comedy of domestic life, learns that the old nursery jingle is
    true where it says that Saturday's child must work for a liv-
    ing. And she learns still more: that conventional marriage,
    with its endless debts and monotonous daily round of house-
    work, constantly threatens to destroy the love that newlyweds
    started out with. Her trouble begins when her meddlesome
    and smug married sister, Florrie, gets unnecessarily concerned
    that Bobby is all of 23 and still not married. She contrives a
    dishonest way for Bobby to trap her hesitant boyfriend into
    proposing. Rims, the husband-to-be, willingly foregoes a
    job in South America in order to get married. About six
    months later we find that Mr. and Mrs. Rims O'Neill are bur-
    dened not only with the problems of making a living but sim-
    ply in being happy together. Marriage has become a treadmill
    of economic woes and domestic arguments. Bobby tells him
    that she almost wishes she were married to some other man
    so that she might enjoy the excitement of having trysts with
    Rims at secret rendezvous. Her father supports this fantasy
    by declaring that she would have been happier having an af-
    fair, because marriage, if the truth must be known, consists
    of only a little romance mixed with no end of dishwashing and
    quarrels and bills. Soon their problems drive the newlyweds
    asunder, and Bobby ends up living alone and lonely in an
    apartment where a strict landlady stands guard over her ten-
    ant's virtue. At the end of the play Rims, lonely too, and
    desperate for affection, climbs the fire escape to Bobby's
    room. As the clandestine lover he would try to recapture
    some of the romance that marriage had destroyed.

This quiet, sentimental, unpretentious, and rather atypical
play of MA's has proved a favorite, going through three motion picture versions (1929, 1934, 1940) and three television
versions (1950, 1952, 1962).
The ms., corrected, is in a ledger filed at the Univ. of
Texas. The New York Public Library holds both an incomplete corrected carbon copy and a corrected typescript bound
in yellow vinyl (being the stage manager's script and bearing
the title Manhattan Marriage).

6. Elizabeth the Queen. New York: Longmans, Green, 1930; New
    York: Samuel French, 1934, acting ed. [See no. 3-a under
    Eleven Verse Plays.]

7. Night over Taos. New York: Samuel French, 1932. [See no.
    3-b under Eleven Verse Plays.]

8. Mary of Scotland. Washington, D.C.: Anderson House, 1933.
    This is the first of several of his books that MA published at
    Anderson House, a firm that he ran jointly with his brother
    Kenneth, who served as business manager. [See no. 3-c
    under Eleven Verse Plays.]

9. Both Your Houses. New York: Samuel French, 1933; acting
    ed., 1937. A slightly revised 1939 edition exists in ms. at
    the Univ. of Texas.
    Both Your Houses was produced by the Theatre Guild at
    the Royale Theatre on March 6, 1933, where it ran for 120
    performances. It received the Pulitzer Prize for the 1932-33
    season. The cast included Shepperd Strudwick in the role
    of the hero Alan McClean; Aleta Freel as his girlfriend, Mar-
    jorie Gray; Walter C. Kelly as Solomon Fitzmaurice; and
    Robert Strange as Simeon Gray.
    This play is a biting commentary on the crookedness of the
    American federal government. It is likewise one of many of
    MA's testaments of despair before the advent of WWII made
    him a champion of democracy and a supporter of the American
    cause. Both Your Houses was intended to be an attack on
    the Hoover administration, but MA had so much trouble get-
    ting the work produced that the old administration was out of
    office by the time this piece of satire reached the stage. An
    idealistic freshman congressman called Alan McClean discovers
    than an omnibus House appropriations bill is so laden with
    "pork barrel" as well as graft that it will cost the electorate
    many millions of dollars. One crafty congressman, Sol Fitz-
    maurice, has attached a rider that will cause the Atlantic
    Fleet to be anchored off his private resort area where he hopes

to profit considerably. The bill, however, even provides
money for a dam project in McClean's own district, but he
opposes the measure because he has learned that his political backer and campaign manager has made dishonest bids
on the project.

McClean encounters a moral dilemma. He learns that Con-
gressman Gray, the father of the woman that McClean is
courting, owns stock in an insolvent bank that stands to
gain from the appropriations bill. Now what should he do?
McClean follows his conscience. He loads onto the measure
such huge riders that the whole thing will, he hopes, fail
when it comes up for a vote in Congress. Amazingly, it
passes anyway. McClean, now disgusted with the whole rot-
ten system, resigns in the hope that in civil life he can effect reforms in government.

Corrected mss. of Acts II and III are at the Univ. of
Texas; also an incomplete, corrected ms. of Act III; an incomplete, corrected typescript of Act III; and a corrected
carbon copy of the whole play.

10. The Star-Wagon. Washington, D.C.: Anderson House, 1937.
This work was produced by Guthrie McClintic at the Em-
pire Theatre on Sept. 29, 1937, and ran for 223 perform-
ances--clearly a hit. The cast included the young actor
Burgess Meredith in the role of the hero Stephen Minch,
Russell Collins as Hanus Wicks, Lillian Gish as Martha Minch,
Kent Smith as Duffy, Edmund O'Brien as Paul Reiger, and
MA's middle son, Alan Anderson, in the role of Ripple.

The Star-Wagon, a sentimental fantasy, developed from
discussions that MA often had with his youngest brother,
Lawrence. They jointly conceived several mechanical inven-
tions, and speculated on what choices a man would make if
he were given the opportunity to go back in time and choose
his career or his spouse all over again. No play more fully
represents the sad, wistful, amusing, and nostalgic side of
the author than this one.

A poor, unassuming industrial scientist named Stephen
Minch develops with the aid of his quaint assistant, Hanus,
a time machine. They use the machine to travel back to a
town in eastern Ohio around the turn of the century--to a
town very much like Jefferson, Ohio, where MA had lived
as a boy--so that Stephen can discover whether he would
have been happier if he had wed the sexy and rich "other
girl" instead of his loyal and goodhearted Martha. The
scene in the choir loft, where Hanus pumps the organ, is
taken straight out of MA's childhood. The author's love of
music is apparent here too.

The Univ. of Texas holds a slightly corrected ms; also two
bound carbon copies, one of which was the script used by
the stage manager during the New York production. There
is still another ms. at the Univ. of North Dakota.

11. Knickerbocker Holiday (music by Kurt Weill). Washington,
    D.C.: Anderson House, 1938. Subtitle: A Musical Comedy
    in Two Acts.
        Based on Washington Irving's Knickerbocker History of
    New York, this is one of MA's two professional ventures into
    the musical play (the other one is Lost in the Stars). It was
    produced by the Playwrights Company at the Ethel Barrymore
    Theatre on Oct. 19, 1938. It ran for 168 performances.
    The cast included Ray Middleton in the role of the impres-
    sario Washington Irving, Richard Kollmar as the hero Brom
    Broeck, Jeanne Madden as Tina Tienhoven, and Walter Hus-
    ton as the dictator Peter Stuyvesant.
        Young Brom Broeck, an independent-minded and freedom-
    loving citizen of seventeenth-century New Netherland, gets
    into trouble by accusing Mynheer Tienhoven of selling brandy
    and arms to the Indians. Because it cannot tolerate such an
    accusation against one of its members, the state council con-
    demns the young rebel to be hung as a part of the holiday
    festivities honoring the governor. Stuyvesant arrives and
    frees him. However, when the governor learns that Brom
    is a defiant democrat infected with the new American disease
    of not being able to take orders, he jails him. Before the
    play is over, Brom proves himself a hero to the town of New
    Amsterdam and talks the council into reasserting its old pow-
    ers of democratic action (corrupt and clumsy though they
    were) and opposing the governor. The idea is to keep the
    government small and funny so that it won't become oppres-
    sive.
        There are mss. at the Univ. of Texas and the Univ. of
    North Dakota. One of the Texas mss. shows close corres-
    pondence to the version that was published.

12. Journey to Jerusalem. Washington, D.C.: Anderson House,
    1940.
        This play about the child Jesus was produced by the Play-
    wrights Company at the National Theatre on October 5, 1940.
    It ran for only 17 performances. Because of a New York
    State law that forbade the representation of the Deity on the
    stage, MA had altered the names of Jesus Christ and his
    mother. The cast included Sidney Lumet (later a well-known
    Broadway director) as Jeshua, Arlene Francis as Miriam,
    Horace Braham as Joseph, Arnold Moss as Ishmael, and
    Frederic Tozere as King Herod.
        Jeshua (Jesus), a fine and sensitive lad of 12, is taken by
    his parents, Miriam (Mary) and Joseph, to Jerusalem to cele-
    brate the Jewish festival of Passover. Jeshua is spiritually
    detached from his friends and relatives but is as yet unaware
    of that holy mission which will soon fall on him like a thun-
    derbolt and transform his life as well as the course of his-
    tory. On the road to Jerusalem the party is stopped by

Ishmael, a wild-looking outlaw from the mountains, who is carrying on a rebellion against the Romans. Drawn to the boy, Ishmael discovers him to be the promised Messiah who will reveal to mankind the kingdom of the spirit. Ishmael rescues the boy from the Roman soldiers at the city gate where, by order of Herod Antipas, all male children of 12 are to be stopped--and executed. Later, Jeshua encounters the wise men in the Temple and impresses them with his reasoning. Once again Ishmael protects the boy from the soldiers but is killed in doing so. Jeshua now believes in his mission and, despite the awful burden, responsibility, and danger that it entails for him, will carry on. A failure on the stage but remarkable as a play from a self-proclaimed atheist!

All the mss. and other MA papers related to the play are at the Univ. of Texas. See Avery's Catalogue for how the story in manuscript differs significantly from the one presented in the first edition.

13. The Miracle of the Danube. In The Free Company Presents.
     Compiled by James Boyd. New York: Dodd, Mead, 1941.
     Reprinted in The Best Short Plays, edited by Margaret Mayorga. Boston: Beacon Press, 1957.

     This is a 30-minute one-act radio play that was produced on The Free Company Series program of the National Broadcasting System on Apr. 27, 1941. Burgess Meredith was the narrator. Paul Muni played the role of Captain Cassell. The Miracle of the Danube is one of several pieces of propaganda that MA created during World War II to help the Allied war effort.

     The story is about a 30-year-old German officer, Captain Cassell, who is now the accused prisoner in a German military trial. He has a record of distinguished service and devotion to the army. But the court charges him with several offenses, in each instance involving the escape of one or more political prisoners facing execution. He denies he is guilty, and instead blames a mysterious figure who had appeared and disappeared in conjunction with the escapes. As he relates what happened, we learn that the figure has the face of the Giotto Christ, which painting hangs in his mother's room. Clearly he has become the victim of a divine madness: in spite of his murderous resolve to do his military duty, the spirit of Christ has come to dominate his life, haunting and tormenting him, and making him free his innocent captives. After he is sentenced to die by a firing squad, we see that Christ will save his soul.

     The corrected ms. and the typescript are at the Univ. of Texas. The Library of Congress has a corrected carbon copy.

14. <u>Candle in the Wind</u>. Washington, D.C.: Anderson House,
    1941.
        This play about the curse of Hitlerism in World War II was
    produced by the Theatre Guild and the Playwrights Company
    at the Shubert Theatre on Oct. 22, 1941. It ran for 95 per-
    formances. The cast included the tiny actress Helen Hayes
    in the role of the heroine Madeline Guest, Louis Borell as
    Raoul St. Cloud, John Wengraf as Colonel Erfurt, and Lotte
    Lenya (Kurt Weill's wife) as Cissie.
        In this kitsch-laden story the celebrated American actress
    Madeline Guest is in Paris just after the German invasion of
    France. She happens to be in love with a hero of the Re-
    sistance, the handsome and gallant Raoul St. Cloud. But
    Raoul is captured and goes to prison. She tries in vain to
    effect his release, but the subhuman Nazis, bent on the ruth-
    less domination of the country, are not moved by appeals of
    the heart. A year goes by. Finally Madeline succeeds in
    freeing her lover, but only at the price of losing her own
    liberty. Colonel Erfurt, the officer accountable for the loss
    of the French freedom-fighter, makes her give up her pass-
    port. He tells her that she is a virtual prisoner in occupied
    France, but he won't arrest her now. He will get her when
    the Germans take America. She replies with the patriotic
    speech: "We shall expect you and be ready.... In the his-
    tory of the world, there have been many wars between men
    and beasts. And the beasts have always lost...."
        The ms. is at the Univ. of North Dakota. The New York
    Public Library owns a typed copy dated Apr. 27, 1942.

15. <u>The Eve of St. Mark</u>. Washington, D.C.: Anderson House,
    1942.
        This two-acter was produced by the Playwrights Company
    at the Cort Theatre on Oct. 7, 1942, after it had been pro-
    duced successfully in many out-of-town places earlier that
    year. It ran for 307 performances. Along with <u>What Price</u>
    <u>Glory</u> it proved to be, for its time, one of the most popular
    works that MA ever wrote. The New York cast included
    William Prince in the role of the nominal hero Private Quizz
    West, Mary Rolfe as his girlfriend Janet Feller, James Monks
    as Private Francis Marion, Eddie O'Shea as Private Thomas
    Mulveroy, and David Pressman as Private Shevlin.
        The title of this war play derives from the legend that on
    the Eve of St. Mark a virgin, standing at the church door,
    will catch glimpses of all those people in the community who
    are going to die within the year. <u>The Eve of St. Mark</u> is
    also based on a visit that MA had made to Fort Bragg, North
    Carolina, in the spring of 1942; also, upon memories of a
    favorite nephew, Sergeant Lee D. Chambers, who had died
    in the crash of an army plane on Nov. 1, 1941. (The pub-
    lished play is dedicated to Chambers.)
        A virtuous but passionate American farm boy, Quizz West,

leaves his pleasant home and enters the army where he meets
some amusing soldiers at camp. One of the soldiers, Francis
Marion (modeled after the real-life soldier-writer Marion Hargrove), proves to be so witty and charming that he threatens
to steal audience interest away from the nominal hero, Quizz
West. Throughout the play, amusing military scenes alternate with tender domestic ones. While on leave, Quizz meets
a girl from his own district and falls in love with her, but
before these two have a chance to consummate their love or
to marry, Quizz is "shipped" off to an island in the Philip-
pines to fight a rear-guard action against the invading Japanese. He and his comrades have the option of retreating
honorably to live and fight another day, but all elect to remain and make a brave though hopeless stand against the
enemy. Back home, his loved ones adjust to the devastating
news that the enemy has captured the island. The boy's
mother and his girlfriend have already been informed in
dreams that he will sacrifice himself for his country.
  This sentimental play would have little interest today for
peace-time audiences, but it was quite otherwise in the dark
period immediately following the bombing of Pearl Harbor and
the Japanese victories in the Pacific when a proud nation of
over 130 million rose as one to battle the enemy. The Eve
of St. Mark seemed to embody the very spirit of idealism and
self-sacrifice that motivated our war effort.
  At the Univ. of Texas are a corrected ms. in ledger form;
a mimeographed script in library binding; a galley proof of
the revised edition; and the corrected galleys of the revised
edition.

16. Your Navy. In This Is War [:] A Collection of Plays About
     America on the March. Edited by Norman Corwin. Intro-
     duction by H. L. McClinton. New York: Dodd, Mead, 1942.
     Pp. 47-68.
       This half-hour radio play was broadcast on Feb. 11, 1942,
     on four major American radio networks. Music by Kurt Weill.
     First narrator: Fredric March; Second narrator: Douglas
     Fairbanks, Jr.
       Your Navy is a propaganda play about how the American
     navy was playing its part in World War II.
       The location of the ms. is unknown.

17. Letter to Jackie. In The Best One-Act Plays of 1943. Edited
     by Margaret G. Mayorga. New York: Dodd, Mead, 1944.
     Pp. 5-7.
       This bit of propaganda was acted in the Lunchtime Follies
     program, a branch of the famed Stage Door Canteen, during
     the noon-time recreation period of men and women on the fac-
     tory production lines. It was based on the letter penned by

Commander John J. Shea to his little son on the evening that
the father sailed to the South Pacific. Later the father sank
to his death on the aircraft carrier U.S.S. Wasp.
The five pages of ms. are at the Univ. of Texas.

18. Storm Operation. Washington, D.C.: Anderson House, 1944.
     This is a play in two acts and an epilogue that was pro-
duced by the Playwrights Company at the Belasco Theatre
on Jan. 11, 1944. It ran for only 25 performances. The
cast included Myron McCormick as the hero, 1st Sergeant
Peter Moldau; Gertrude Musgrove as his girlfriend, Lieutenant Thomasina Grey; Cy Howard as Technical Sergeant
Simeon; and Bramwell Fletcher as Captain Sutton.
     In order that MA could get permission to visit North Africa
during wartime and gather materials for his next forthcoming
play, he agreed to permit the War Department to censor Storm
Operation. The result: much of the forceful, realistic depiction of characters (e.g., the bed-hopping propensity of
nurse Grey) was toned down. For this and other reasons
the play was a brilliant failure.
     One of MA's goals was to convey to his audience an account
of the delicate relationships among the various Allied armies,
including their women, who participated in the vast amphibian
and aerial invasion of North Africa in the fall of 1942 that
was to lead to the defeat of Rommel's Afrika Korps.
     The Australian nurse Thomasina Grey and the American
Sergeant Peter Moldau, who had been lovers elsewhere, meet
this time in war-torn Tunisia and renew their romance. A
British officer, Captain Sutton, has been sleeping with the
nurse lately (in the published version of the play he is simply said to be in love with her). The all-too-experienced
Grey no longer believes in fidelity and marriage but Moldau
busily works to change her mind. A subplot is about the
funny technical and public relation achievements of Sergeant
Simeon with his "American know-how"; he is so clever that
he has even managed to buy himself an Arab girl. In the
final scene of the play, Sutton, who has grudgingly given
up his mistress to the "Yank," performs a marriage ceremony
for the pair in a tent while German planes strafe the camp.
But the fearless newlyweds ignore the attack and go on with
the ceremony.
     The ms. is at the Univ. of North Dakota.

19. Truckline Cafe. New York: Dodd, Mead, 1946. Martha Cox,
     in her Maxwell Anderson Bibliography, states that this play
was probably published but then withdrawn (the Cumulative
Book Index listed it). Neither she nor I have been able to
locate a copy other than the typescript owned by the New
York Public Library.

Truckline Cafe was produced by Elia Kazan and Harold
Clurman in conjunction with the Playwrights Company on
Feb. 27, 1946, at the Belasco Theatre. It ran for only 13
performances. Critics attacked it right and left, calling it
cheap melodrama. The cast included the outstanding young
actor Marlon Brando in the role of Sage McRae; Ann Shep-
herd as his wife, Tory McRae; Richard Waring as the hero,
Mort Carruth; and Virginia Gilmore as Anne Carruth.
     In this play MA is trying to expose one of the chief prob-
lems that he had discovered when he visited troops in America and overseas during the war: the moral decay that war
creates in servicemen and their women. The ex-serviceman
Mort, who had lived with a Polish girl after his escape from
a German prison, returns to California with his baby daughter (the mother had died at the hands of the Germans) and
finds his legal wife, Anne, working in a highway café.
Anne, believing that her husband was dead, had given herself up to drink and other men, but when she learned that
Mort was still alive, she submitted herself to an abortion and
tried to hide herself away in California. In the subplot,
which is likewise about sexual infidelity, a woman tries to
keep her husband ignorant of the fact that she had had as-
signations with his buddy in a cabin nearby. The husband,
Sage, learns about the infidelity and kills his wife. Meanwhile, Mort repents of his own adultery with the Polish girl
and brings his illegitimate child to the café in an all-too-
obvious bid to win back the affections of his wife. But Anne
will have none of this. Whereupon Sage, now remorseful
about the crime he has just committed, enters the café and
causes Anne to realize what a dreadful mistake she is making
in rejecting her loving husband. This object lesson is
enough to bring Anne and Mort together again.
     The Univ. of Texas owns the ms.

20. Joan of Lorraine. Washington, D.C.: Anderson House, 1946.
          This work was produced by the Playwrights Company at
     the Alvin Theatre on Nov. 18, 1946. It ran for 199 perform-
     ances--to packed houses--and would have run longer if its
     star had not had contractual engagements elsewhere. The
     cast included the internationally famous Ingrid Bergman as
     Mary Grey (Joan of Arc), Lewis Martin as the Bishop of
     Beauvais, Harry Irvine as the Archbishop of Rheims, Romney
     Brent as Les Ward (the Dauphin), and Sam Wanamaker as
     Jimmy Masters (the Inquisitor).
          Joan of Lorraine is the story of a New York rehearsal of a
     play dealing with the life of Joan of Arc. The actress Mary
     Grey, playing Joan, disagrees often with the director, Mas-
     ters, about the changes that the absentee author of the script
     has been inserting to show that Joan is deliberately compro-
     mising with evil people (e.g., the Dauphin) in order to carry

out the commandments of her angelic "voices." Masters differs from his leading lady in believing that an idealistic person like Joan would <u>have</u> to obtain the help of certain bad
people who are in power if she is to reach any of her goals.
And Masters illustrates his point by citing realistic problems
in getting the present production going. (Anyone acquainted
with MA would recognize that he has projected some of his
most deeply felt convictions into Masters.) At the end of
Act I, Mary is so irritated with the script that she walks out
to lunch, hinting that she might not come back. It is apparent that two strongly individualized stage heroines have
emerged thus far, she and Joan, and that each of them will
need to reexamine the basis of her faith before she can go
on with her idealistic course of action.

Back from her lunch break, Mary acts out the role of Joan
who recants her confession and reasserts her faith in her
"voices." Here the actress learns that she can go on with
the play as it is now written, for she realizes, like Masters,
that Joan herself would sometimes stoop to compromise on little things in order to fulfill her main objectives. But she
also learns that Joan would face death itself before she would
consent to compromise her soul.

The Univ. of Texas owns an extensively corrected ms.
(originally titled <u>Warrior's Return</u>) and three mimeographed
scripts.

21. <u>Anne of the Thousand Days</u>. New York: William Sloane, 1948.
This is MA's third Tudor tragedy, the other ones in this
group being <u>Elizabeth the Queen</u>, <u>Mary of Scotland</u>, and
<u>Masque of Queens</u> (unpublished and unacted). It was pro-
duced by the Playwrights Company at the Shubert Theatre
on Dec. 8, 1948. It ran for 286 performances. The cast included Joyce Redman in the role of the doomed Anne Boleyn;
Rex Harrison as King Henry VIII; John Merivale as Mark
Smeaton; Percy Waram as Cardinal Wolsey; and MA's youngest
son, Terence, as the Clerk.

The story is told in flashbacks: those of Anne Boleyn,
covering the "thousand days" of her relationship with Henry
VIII, and those of Henry as he waits to sign the final order
for execution. Henry is portrayed as a brutal, vain, lustful
ogre who cannot be satisfied with any one woman for very
long--a "Sexual Everyman," as the author calls him. We
learn that in the beginning he cruelly pressured Anne into
becoming his mistress. But she holds out for marriage and
gets it, though it is a "secret" marriage, for the groom is
still trying to get a divorce from Queen Katharine. Anne
becomes pregnant and insists on his getting a divorce immediately so that she can legitimize her child. Cromwell, the
evil genius in the story, convinces Henry that he can achieve
his new marriage and also tremendous wealth simply by making

himself head of the English church and looting the Catholic
monasteries. Henry follows this advice.
Anne is now married and queen at last. But she upsets
her husband's plans for a royal succession by bearing him
a female child, Elizabeth. As Queen she enmeshes herself in
crime by ordering the execution of Sir Thomas More, simply
because he had opposed the Act of Succession by which Elizabeth stood to become the next monarch. Meanwhile, Henry,
lusting after a new bedmate--especially one who can give him
a legitimate male heir--grows dissatisfied with her. Cromwell
plays on this dissatisfaciton by fabricating evidence that she
had committed adultery. As a result, she is brought to trial
and found guilty.
The ms. is at the Univ. of Texas.

22. Lost in the Stars (music by Kurt Weill). New York: William
    Sloane, 1949.
    This musical play, based on Alan Paton's novel Cry, the
Beloved Country, was produced by the Playwrights Producing Company at the Music Box Theatre on Oct. 30, 1949. It
ran for 273 performances. The cast included Todd Duncan
as Stephen Kumalo, Julian Mayfield as Absalom Kumalo, Warren Coleman as John Kumalo, Inez Matthews as Irina, and
Herbert Coleman as Alex.
    Alan Paton knew firsthand the kinds of social and racial
problems that he portrayed so movingly in Cry, the Beloved
Country because he had been for the last 12 years the prin-
cipal of the Diepkloos Reformatory for delinquent children in
Johannesburg. He had long written and lectured on African
race relations. Like the novel, Lost in the Stars is entirely
sympathetic to those blacks who have lost the important tribal
roots provided by village life when they moved to the big city
and got caught up in the whirlpool of temptation and crime.
The play uses not only individual singing parts but a chorus,
which unites the many separate scenes and comments on the
action.
    The Reverend Stephen Kumalo, a noble-minded resident of
a village near Ndotsheni, Natal, South Africa, receives a letter from Johannesburg telling that his sister is sick and
needs help. The kindly Stephen would indeed like to help
her, and also find his son Absalom as well, for the young
man has not been heard of since he left for the city many
months earlier. After scraping together some money from his
meagre savings, the poor black minister travels to the bustling
but sin-filled metropolis of Johannesburg, a place that has
proved to be the graveyard for the hopes of so many of his
people. In the city he learns from a fellow clergyman that the
sister has become a prostitute and a dealer in illegal liquor.
He manages to find the sister and persuade her to let him
take her tiny son, Alex, back to the village with him. Next

he visits his brother, John, a cynical merchant and small-
time politician, who lives a life of selfishness and grasping
opportunism. Stephen makes no headway with this man when
he advises him to return to the good life at Ndotsheni.
    Then commences a long search for Absalom, a trail that
leads to a reformatory and out again. The minister discovers
that his son has been living with a woman out of wedlock and
has made her pregnant. She waits patiently for the ne'er-
do-well to marry her. The worst discovery of all is that
Absalom is now in prison, charged with a murder he had
committed in the course of robbing a white man. One of the
trio of robbers was John's own son. And, irony of ironies,
the murdered man had gone out of his way to be kind to
blacks, including the Reverend Kumalo himself.
    The court sets John's son and the other young man free
but finds the minister's son guilty of murder. It sentences
Absalom to be hanged. In the last part of the story, the
murdered man's father, James Jarvis, is drawn to the minister because of their common grief in losing their sons--drawn
in spite of a lifelong prejudice against blacks. His grand-
child makes friends with Stephen Kumalo and sends badly
needed milk to help the poor black villagers. Thus, there
is some hope that kindness and love will create harmony between the races.
    The Univ. of Texas owns the ms. and a carbon copy.

23. Barefoot in Athens. New York: William Sloane, 1951.
    This historical tragedy was produced by the Playwrights
Producing Company at the Martin Beck Theatre on Oct. 31,
1951. It ran for only 30 performances. The cast included
Barry Jones as Socrates, Lotte Lenya as Xantippe, Bart
Burns as Satyros, and George Mathews as Pausanias.
    Written during the Senator Joseph McCarthy era of the
Communist "witch hunt" in America, Barefoot in Athens--
particularly the play's preface--represents the author's
strong espousal of the democratic way of life. Far cry from
the cynicism about government in Both Your Houses! In his
zeal to identify and defend democratic values, MA takes the
untenable position that ancient Athens was wholly democratic
with respect to its government (never mind the existence of
the slave population!), whereas its enemy, Sparta, was wholly communistic. The play, however, is not spoiled by the
extremist views made explicit in the preface. It is ironic
that one of the most likeable figures in the play turns out
to be a "communist," the Spartan king Pausanias.
    We learn that Socrates is a poor, loveable, unworldly phi-
losopher who refuses to take pay for his teachings, unlike
the sophists, and in so doing makes a shrew out of his long-
suffering wife. A trio of Athenian bigots has brought an in-
dictment against him charging impiety and the corruption of

the minds of young men. The truth is, however, that certain former students of his whom he is supposed to have
corrupted have strayed from his healthful teachings. He had
taught a relentless method of inquiry into every value held
under the sun, skeptical of every idea until it has been ex-
amined in the clear light of reason. But a few of his students, such as Alcibiades, had neglected to apply the test
of skepticism when they entered public life: they should
have questioned whether blood money, murder, and illegally
acquired office were morally defensible.

Before Socrates can be tried in court, Sparta defeats
Athens during the Peloponnesian War and installs the notori-
ous Thirty Oligarchs under the leadership of the unscrupu-
lous Critias, another of the philosopher's pupils gone astray.
Then a successful rebellion drives King Pausanias and his
army out of Athens.

Socrates is tried and found guilty by a prejudiced court
which, during his defense, he had managed to offend in
divers ways. He had even let himself be trapped into admit-
ting that he loves truth more than he does Athens--to the
jurors a clear sign of disloyalty. The play ends on a domestic rather than a heroic note--unlike in Plato--with the philosopher awaiting dawn in the company of his wife. He is
to drink hemlock at dawn.

The Univ. of Texas owns the ms. The collection there also
includes a mimeographed script that closely resembles the
first edition.

24. Bad Seed. New York: Dodd, Mead, 1955.

This thriller, based on William March's novel The Bad Seed,
was produced by the Playwrights Producing Company at the
Forty-Sixth Street Theatre on Dec. 8, 1954. It had a run of
332 performances. Patty McCormack played the role of Rhoda
Penmark, Nancy Kelly played Christine Penmark, John O'Hare
played Colonel Kenneth Penmark, Evelyn Varden played Monica
Breedlove, Henry Jones played Leroy, and Eileen Heckart
played Mrs. Daigle.

Bad Seed is a brilliant, sardonic commentary on the question of whether criminality can be inherited. Eight-year-old
Rhoda Penmark is a seemingly model child in pigtails, a real
charmer. But while her father is away in the military, she
murders a fellow student at a school picnic simply because
she coveted a medal of his. Back home, the simpering, sin-
ister building janitor, Leroy, pretends to know about her
guilt and teases her. Rhoda's teacher drops by and tells
the girl's mother, Christine, that an older student had seen
darling Rhoda grab at the medal and chase the boy toward
the wharf where he was later found drowned. Then the
boy's grieving mother arrives and announces that Rhoda
was the last person known to have seen her son alive, and

that the medal is missing from the boy's shirt. But Christine cannot believe that her own sweet daughter was guilty in any way. After these visitors have gone, Christine discovers that very medal in the girl's table drawer. Rhoda acts evasive. Christine reminds her about the case of old Mrs. Post, an acquaintance back in Baltimore, who had fallen down the stairs soon after she had promised the girl a certain crystal ball. After the woman died, Rhoda lost no time in asking for and receiving the promised trinket. Christine now has her doubts about her daughter's honesty.

Leroy makes the mistake of continuing to torment the girl with his insinuations. His habit of taking naps among the excelsior in the garage gives her an idea for revenge. Meanwhile, Christine is trying to come to grips with her own terrifying dreams and her growing suspicion that she was an adopted child. When her father arrives for a visit, she questions him repeatedly and at last learns that the dreams have a basis in fact: as a child she had narrowly escaped being murdered by her own mad mother, Bessie Denker; she was adopted, had her name changed, and was raised in a different household under the loving care of her new parents. Unlike Christine, her father is sure that criminality cannot be inherited and that Rhoda, far from being a "bad seed," is a perfectly sound daughter.

Later that night, Christine spies her "bad seed" carrying a suspicious-looking package to the incinerator, and the package turns out to contain Rhoda's cleated shoes which she had used to kill the schoolmate. Rhoda now turns her treacly charm on again and gushes that she has the prettiest, the nicest, the sweetest mother--one who would never inform on her darling. Thoroughly ashamed and horrified, Christine orders her to burn the shoes and keep quiet.

The next morning, Rhoda finds her chance to set fire to the excelsior in the garage, and does. Then she sneaks back to her apartment. While Leroy, screaming, is being burned to death, she calmly practices "Au Clair de la Lune" on the piano. Her mother, of course, catches on this time. She will have to put a stop to this string of murders. That evening, Christine administers an overdose of sleeping pills to her daughter, telling her that they are vitamins, and then shoots herself dead. But friends arrive in time to save the little girl's life. When the unsuspecting father comes home he is thoroughly mystified as to why his wife would kill herself and try to poison his wonderful little daughter. Rhoda, the very picture of sweet innocence, runs to him smilingly and lavishes on him her fatal, winning coquetry. All those who had known about her crimes are dead. And Colonel Penmark hasn't the least suspicion that the little beast he hugs to his bosom may murder again someday if the whim strikes her.

The ms. is at the Univ. of North Dakota.

25. The Masque of Pedagogues. In The North Dakota Quarterly,
     XXV (Spring, 1957), 33-48.
     MA wrote two senior class plays. The first one was Lost
     Labors Love, penned in collaboration with his fellow student
     R. H. Montgomery, and presented in 1909. The second was
     The Masque of Pedagogues, all his own work, and presented
     in his own senior year, 1911. The place was undoubtedly
     the opera house in Grand Forks, for the campus itself did
     not have a theater (even the 1911 graduation ceremony re-
     quired the use of the opera house).
          C. L. Roberts, who became a professor at Jamestown Col-
     lege, played the role of Dr. Libby in the Masque. Frederick
     J. Brockhoff wrote to me on May 6, 1978, that he had played
     a "minor role," but he could give me no more details.
          For anyone interested in MA's university life, this comedy
     is full of pleasant nostalgia. It is also a record of his abid-
     ing interest in certain famous authors. There are five ref-
     erences to Shakespeare and two to Keats (two of his top-
     most favorites). The plot itself is a take-off on the work of
     still another famous author, Marlowe. Along the way, MA
     gently satirizes various faculty members--by name, too.
          The time is evening during summer vacation. The place,
     Bemidji, Minnesota, the summer home of the University
     president, Frank L. McVey. McVey enters a forest and de-
     livers some blank verse monologue about the many vexations
     he has had to suffer back at the University. Tired, he lies
     down and has a dream.
          In the dream appear Professors Libby and LeDaum, who
     enter the forest and gleefully exchange with each other some
     of their fiendishly difficult classroom assignments. LeDaum,
     making believe that Libby is the class in French, asks wheth-
     er the students have memorized the 17 poems he had assigned
     for that morning. (None have.) Then he tells them the as-
     signment for tomorrow: draw a map of Australia and insert
     all the towns and cities that have any relation to French his-
     tory. And prepare separate colored maps of all the South
     American countries, including ranges of mountains, towns,
     homes of famous men, religious shrines, and big coffee planta-
     tions. And be sure to include a certain large banyan tree
     on the coast of Chile. This hellish assignment goes on and
     on. He ends by telling them to write out the French verb
     which means "to die." Another funny scene occurs when
     Professor Koch (one of MA's favorite teachers) enters with a
     claque of adoring, sentimental coeds, seats them about him in
     a circle, and rhapsodizes about the beauties of Shakespeare.
     He even cites his wife as an authority on the Bard. When
     the coeds applaud, he thanks them, for his artist's soul
     craves appreciation. He tells them that he will give them
     all an "A" for the day's work.
          The location of the ms. is unknown.

26. The Golden Six. New York: Dramatists Play Service, 1961.
     Posthumously published.
          This last published drama of MA's was produced by Warner
     LeRoy and Norman Twain at the off-Broadway theater known
     as the York Playhouse on Oct. 26, 1958. In spite of adver-
     tisements of seminudity in the cast--(a lovely slave girl bares
     her breasts several times), the play ran only 17 nights. Al-
     vin Epstein played Claudius, Viveca Lindfors played Livia,
     Paul Mann played Augustus, Thayer David played Tiberius,
     and Roger Evan Boxill played Caligula.
          As in Anne of the Thousand Days, this play about royal
     corruption is told by means of flashbacks in the mind of a
     disillusioned monarch who would have been happier if he had
     never risen to the purple. Emperor Claudius writes in his
     diary a record that, he hopes, will help those men of the
     future who try to bring back freedom. Perhaps such men
     will have armed themselves against kings and tyrants. But
     because there will always be some people who thirst to rule
     over others, and because absolute power is always pernicious,
     the future looks gloomy.
          Then follows the story of his life, from his boyhood in the
     palace of Augustus to his present embarrassing position as
     the latest emperor. Among the six young nephews of Augus-
     tus, all of them champions of freedom, the least promising
     of them is the shy, stammering Claudius. Augustus' wife,
     Livia, turns out to be a dangerous power behind the throne.
     Year after year she uses poison and other devices to insure
     that only her favorites, usually the degenerates, are in line
     of succession to the throne. One by one the nephews are
     mysteriously murdered at her behest, the last being the
     abominable Caligula, and of all the adult descendents of Au-
     gustus, only the seemingly ineffectual Claudius remains.
     The people clamor for him as the next emperor, but he re-
     sists with all his heart, convinced that he would be helpless
     in reforming the wretchedly cruel system of government. He
     won't become a part of the tyranny he has long been con-
     demning. But Livia knows otherwise. Frustrated at not be-
     ing able to select the latest emperor, she poisons herself,
     but not before sneering to Claudius that, regardless of his
     own desires, the public will force him to wear the crown.
     As she lies dying at his feet, he hears the crowd outside
     chant "Long live Claudius, long live the Emperor." Oh, bit-
     ter victory! The poor, miserable, stuttering idealist is
     trapped into a job he hates.
          The Univ. of Texas owns the ms., which bears the original
     title, The Stammering Prince; also, a carbon copy and a
     mimeographed copy. The Univ. of North Dakota owns a
     typed copy of the play, prepared by the Playwrights Produc-
     ing Company.

The plays are arranged alphabetically. The date in par-
entheses indicates the year or years written.

27. Adam, Lilith and Eve (1950). An unproduced comedy in three
     acts.
     A comic strip author, Adam Benedict (possibly based upon
     MA's friend and neighbor, cartoonist Milton Caniff) makes
     his second wife, Eve, jealous by having as their house guest
     his flamboyant first wife, Lilith, upon whom he has been
     patterning the most beguiling woman character in the strip.
     Together, Adam and Lilith arrange for their tax advisor to
     propose to Lilith and thus bring harmony back to Adam and
     Eve's marriage.
     The ms. is in an unlabeled ledger at the Univ. of North
     Dakota.

28. Bastion Saint-Gervais, The (1938). Unproduced one-act radio
     play.
     The story is much like that in the Prologue to Key Largo,
     except that the four Americans fighting for the loyalist cause
     on a hill outside Tervel during the Spanish Civil War choose
     to stay at their battle post, retain their ideals, and sacrifice
     their lives to hold back the fascist enemy.
     The Univ. of Texas owns a ms. and a carbon copy. The
     Library of Congress also owns a carbon copy.

29. Believe It or Not (c.1953). A two-page playlet in ms., un-
     published, apparently unstaged. No doubt written soon after
     MA had begun to live with Gilda Hazard and her children.
     The characters include Mr. Wrubel (probably Allie Wrubel,
     with whom MA was collaborating in California in 1953 on the
     never to be completed Devil's Hornpipe), Max, Mummy, Laurel,
     and Craig. A bagatelle apparently designed to teach the
     children good manners. Copy sent to me courtesy of Gilda
     Anderson.

30. Benvenuto (1922). Unproduced melodrama. MA's first full-
     length play.

Based on the early life of the exciting rogue Benvenuto
Cellini, the story follows his adventures at the Court of
King Francis I in Paris in 1540. The king's mistress, Madame
d'Etampes, plots revenge on Cellini. He narrowly escapes
death.
The Univ. of Texas owns an unbound typescript.

31. Cavalier King (1952). Unproduced melodrama.
Charles II of England, who had married Catherine so that
he would beget an heir, is disappointed that she is barren.
Accordingly, he turns his attentions to various mistresses,
of whom the beautiful Hortense is his favorite. When a political crisis develops, and Titus Oates threatens to lead a revolt against him unless he divorces the Catholic queen, she
proves her love for him by offering to leave the country.
But he won't hear of it because he loves her, too. As the
years pass, Charles' love and admiration for his wife in-
creases.
The Univ. of Texas owns a ms. and a typescript.

32. Chicot the King (1926). Unproduced melodrama.
In the French court of King Henri III, during the sixteenth
century, a handsome swordsman named Chico accidentally
happens upon a beautiful lady captive, and they immediately
fall in love with each other. He learns that her captors are
the wicked dukes of Mayenne and Guise, who plot to murder
the ineffectual Henri, place Guise on the throne, and make
Diana (the captive lady) marry the new king. But Chico
foils their plans by tricking the dukes into entering a mon-
astery to capture a man who they suppose is the king, but
who turns out to be none other than Chico in disguise,
ready with his supporters nearby in the disguise of monks.
The dukes are arrested. Henri learns from the courage of
this Cyrano-like hero that he can be a strong king after all.
Chico ends up happily reunited with his lady love.
The Library of Congress owns a bound carbon copy of the
play.

33. Christmas Carol, The (1954). A musical adaptation of Dickens'
famous story, perhaps the best ever done for TV. It starred
Fredric March in the role of Scrooge, and Basil Rathbone as
Marley. MA supplied some lyrics that were set to music by
Bernard Herrmann. On hand were the Roger Wagner Chorale
and a 40-piece orchestra. The one-hour production appeared
in color on the CBS "Shower of Stars" program, Dec. 23,
1954. It was rebroadcast in December 1957.

34. <u>Day the Money Stopped, The</u> (1957). This one-act melodrama
    is based closely on Brendan Gill's novel of the same name,
    except for the addition of two minor characters. Even most
    of the speeches are lifted verbatim from the novel. This
    play adaptation, directed by Harold Clurman, was produced
    at the Belasco Theatre on Feb. 20, 1958. It ran for only
    four performances. Richard Basehart played the role of
    Charles Morrow, Kevin McCarthy played Richard Morrow, and
    Collin Wilcox played Ellen Wells.
    The events in this contemporary story take place in a law
    office in a Connecticut town. After the old head of the firm
    dies, the business is taken over by the younger of two sons,
    Richard, who is a cold-hearted, stuffy Yale man bent on fol-
    lowing in the supposedly respectable footsteps of his father.
    Charles, the ne'er-do-well son, arrives, having run through
    a fortune since college days and now, at 40, is unemployed
    and broke. This wastrel, however, has the engaging ability
    to make people like him; his charm and wit soon captivate
    the pretty woman working in the office. Once Charles dis-
    covers that the old man had left him practically nothing in
    the will, he conceives of a plan to recoup his loss: he would
    blackmail his brother by means of a clever lie, viz. that El-
    len, the pretty woman working in the office, is actually the
    old man's illegitimate daughter, a bit of scandal that Richard
    and his sister, Kathie, would pay dearly to suppress. Final-
    ly, Charles has to admit that there is no real proof for the
    alleged illegitimacy.
    During their discussions, Charles and Kathie discover that
    their so-called sterling father had still another kind of shadow
    on his reputation. The old man had been responsible for
    hounding his wife into a madhouse where she then committed
    suicide. All three children are shocked at the news. But
    this discovery, combined with the new-found affection he has
    for Ellen, makes Charles give up his desire to blackmail his
    brother and sister. Moreover, the discovery enables him to
    wipe out the feelings of unworthiness and guilt that have been
    festering in him for years. He is now ready to stand on his
    own two feet as a responsible family member, without a penny
    of assistance from anyone. As the story ends, he and Ellen
    plan to meet again soon.
    The Univ. of North Dakota owns a corrected ms. The
    Univ. of Texas owns a mimeographed script along with the
    copy of Brendan Gill's novel that MA had used to prepare
    his dramatization. The book contains MA's notes and outline
    for the play. The New York Public Library owns still another
    mimeographed script.

35. <u>Feast of Cololaus, The</u>. Non-existent. This is a mistaken en-
    try on the inventory of papers held at the Univ. of North
    Dakota. MA's handwriting, being the crabbed thing it is,

led someone on the staff to misread The Feast of Ortolans
title.

36. Form Reveille to Breakfast (1942). Avery's Catalogue (p. 39)
    reads: "... a radio script, 'From Reveille to Breakfast,'
    in which he [MA] records, with 'nothing added, nothing
    dramatized,' his experiences in the barracks one morning [at
    Fort Bragg, North Carolina]," to which he had gone in the
    spring of 1942 in search of materials for writing The Eve of
    St. Mark. Apparently the work was never broadcast. The
    rumor that Marion Hargrove helped MA write the script is
    untrue, according to what Hargrove told me in person.
    The script is at the Univ. of Texas.

37. Get Together to Gather (c.1954). This is a five-page signed
    playlet in typescript. A photocopy of it was sent to me by
    Gilda Anderson in her letter dated Feb. 22, 1983. She said
    that this little work was written for the purpose of teaching
    MA's young stepchildren, Laurel and Craig, not to enter a
    room while talking. The playlet was acted out by the four
    of them.
        Two characters, Blinker and Dyou, hold an amusingly non-
    sensical dialogue on a platform set on an elephant's back.
    To add to the confusion, it is dark and a big storm blows
    up.
        Gilda Anderson and I own copies. Not listed in Avery's
    Catalogue.

38. Greeks Remember Marathon, The (c.1944). Radio play. Ap-
    parently this piece of war propaganda was never broadcast.
        The crew of an American bomber, flying over Crete during
    WWII, bail out when the plane runs out of gasoline. The
    Germans capture two members, but the others escape through
    the help of Mitsos, a nine-year-old boy, and his mother.
    The Americans join a Greek guerilla band and help them de-
    stroy a German patrol. But Mitsos is killed in action. His
    dying mother makes an impassioned appeal for aid to Greece
    in its fight for freedom.
        The whereabouts of the ms. is unknown. Not listed in
    Avery's Catalogue.

39. Gypsy (1927). This melodrama about the effects of bad heredi-
    ty and bad upbringing was produced by Richard Herndon at
    the Klaw Theatre on Sept. 7, 1927, at which time it had a
    short run. Then on Jan. 14, 1929, it was revived at the
    Klaw and ran for 64 performances, during which time Ellen
    (Gypsy) was played by Claiborne Foster, David by Lester

Vail, Marilyn (Ellen's mother) by Mary Young, and Cleve by Louis Calhern.

There are two versions of Gypsy, both of them represented by playscripts at the Univ. of Texas: the ms., apparently being the original, shows Ellen turning off the gas at the end and going to the telephone to receive the call of her latest lover; the carbon copy shows her suicide at the end. However, both versions, contrary to what Avery implies in his Catalogue, wound up on the stage at the Klaw Theatre. Audiences were not enthusiastic about Ellen resuscitating herself. Accordingly, after the telephone scene had been used a few times, Ellen went through with the suicide, and it was this version that was used most of the time.

Ellen, who is the daughter of a wanton mother, "loves" her violinist husband and acknowledges that he is handsome and passionate and unselfish. Nevertheless, she is unable to control her itch to bed down with random men. She undergoes a rapid deterioration and finally decides that she deserves to die. In the play version where Ellen resuscitates herself and answers the telephone, one gets the feeling that she is only postponing her death a little while--until she tires of her newest lover and sinks into remorse again. Students of MA's life almost inevitably draw a parallel between Gypsy and the playwright's second "wife," Mab Maynard, who also had an unstable, promiscuous mother and was herself neurotic and unfaithful to Anderson, ending up killing herself with gas.

The Univ. of Texas owns a corrected ms. of Act III plus a carbon copy of the whole text as it was ready for production in 1927.

40. Hell on Wheels (c.1928). This unproduced musical comedy, done in collaboration with Jack Niles (who composed the music) and Douglas Moore, bears the copyright date of 1928 on the title page of the manuscript. The ridiculous admiral in the play was possibly inspired by Rear Admiral Charles P. Plunkett, a man known in the AEF for his foul tongue. During WWI, Plunkett disobeyed orders and transported his 16-inch naval guns up to the battlefront on oversized railroad cars. Upon arriving there, he discovered that the guns faced in the wrong direction and that there wasn't a turntable in Flanders big enough to turn them around. MA almost unquestionably knew about Plunkett and his foolhardy exploit because the admiral became a public figure later in trying to censor What Price Glory on the New York stage--until a letter exposing the Flanders fiasco appeared in Heywood Broun's column in the World (on which MA had recently worked).

Hell on Wheels, the nickname given to an overly zealous American admiral, has become frustrated because none of the

fighting is being done at sea--his natural element--and he
believes that the Allied armies are inept. Therefore, he
contrives just the secret weapon needed to turn the tide of
battle: one of his ship's huge cannon mounted on a flatcar.
He sends the cannon ahead on a rail line, but the cannon is
so unwieldy that it knocks down houses and train stations
along the route. In a village behind the front, a stationmaster's daughter so gladdens the heart of an American
courier that he is inspired to stop the flatcar before the
station there is destroyed. And he does. The steaming
admiral arrives, rages at the delay, and orders the courier
to be shot by a firing squad. The stationmaster arrives in
the nick of time to announce that the war is over! The play
ends with the admiral in retreat and the condemned hero set
free. In the celebration by the villagers, the stationmaster's
daughter and the courier dance joyously together.
  The Univ. of Texas owns a ms. and a carbon copy.

41. John Keats and America (c.1941). This is a 30-minute radio
     play that was broadcast on NBC on Apr. 7, 1941. Keats
     was, along with Shakespeare, one of MA's favorite poets.
        Not having been able to locate any copy of this play--which
     is mentioned in Avery's Letters (p. liii)--I am unable to pro-
     vide a synopsis.

42. Madonna and Child (1956). This three-act play has never been
     staged. Written near the end of MA's life, Madonna and
     Child illustrates the increasing importance that physical love
     played in his works. The subject, however, is treated real-
     istically rather than sentimentally, and in this respect the
     heroine, Molly, will remind some readers of Shaw's Candida.
     For a detailed discussion of Madonna and Child, see Laurence
     Avery's "Maxwell Anderson: A Changing Attitude Toward
     Love," Modern Drama, X (Dec., 1967), 241-48.
        In this comedy Freya, an archaeological field worker, takes
     to Professor John Clayman what appears to be an ancient
     Egyptian tablet for translation. They decide that it was
     written by the famous pharaoh Akhenaton. The translation
     reinforces Clayman's theory that Akhenaton got his inspira-
     tion for creating the world's first recorded monotheistic re-
     ligion because of his love for his queen, Nefertiti. In the
     course of their working together, Freya and Clayman become
     infected with that consuming passion for each other that
     Akhenaton supposedly had for Nefertiti, and they imagine
     themselves ranking among the great lovers of history. Since
     the professor is married, this glorious love that they share
     is forbidden, like that of Tristan for Iseult, like that of
     Paolo for Francesca. Meanwhile, Clayman's wife, Molly, who
     is more mature and sensible than he, resists the temptation

to have an affair of her own.

When she discovers her husband's amour she goes through a period of uncertainty about what to do, but finally takes the chance of making it possible for the pair to go off together and perhaps learn how ridiculous their grand passion is. And, true enough, when these ecstatic lovers do climb into bed together, Clayman learns that he, the marvelous lover, is impotent and that his hot little inamorata has become frigid from contemplating the ideal too much. As if to complete their disaster, they learn that the tablet that had inspired their romance is actually a forgery. The repentant Clayman returns home to the wise Molly who, after treating him to a well-deserved verbal lashing, forgives him.

The ms. and a mimeographed script are on file at the Univ. of Texas.

43. Marriage Recipe, The (c.1929). There are no known professional performances of this one-act drama, which seems to be a preliminary draft of Act I of Saturday's Children.

Bobby and Florrie are roommates--not sisters as in Saturday's Children. Florrie, who had been married before, gives her roommate some unwanted advice on how to trap a husband for herself. Bobby, however, has her own method which she now uses on her boyfriend, Rims, who is about to go down to Buenos Aires on a new job. Failing this way, she uses Florrie's method and succeeds in winning a marriage proposal. But her conscience bothers her and she confesses the plot to him. He admires her so much for being honest that he forgoes the trip abroad and wants to marry her anyway.

The Library of Congress owns a carbon copy.

44. Masque of Queens, The (1954). There are no known professional performances for this two-act drama, which is written partly in verse. This is MA's fourth and final tragedy about the Tudor era.

It appears that Mary of Scotland's son, James, will inherit the English throne, but the aging Queen Elizabeth vows to block this by touting what she falsely alleges are the stronger claims of a certain young earl, whom she happens to be in love with. The earl reminds her of Essex, her former lover. Elizabeth is irritated that Essex's beautiful young widow has been having the luxury of mourning her husband in solitude whereas she, Elizabeth, has had to conceal her sorrow behind a public mask, and she orders the widow to give up her solitude and live at the court. Soon, however, the widow falls in love with the earl. This proves to be more than the jealous queen can bear and she stops supporting the earl in his bid for the succession. She learns to her

sorrow that the responsibility of holding great political power
makes it impossible for her to have close human attachments.
At the end she suffers a stroke.

The word "masque" in the title takes on some of the meaning that it has in the plays Masque of Pedagogues and
Masque of Kings, namely, that continuous power over the
lives of others in the public arena eventually takes on the
aspect of a spectacle or theatrical performance but without
assuring the holder any degree of personal happiness.

The corrected ms. is at the Univ. of Texas.

45. Meeting in Africa (c.1943). As far as is known, this one-act
     piece of WWII propaganda has never been staged.

The story illuminates one of the prime difficulties that the
Allies had faced when they invaded Algeria in November of
1942 and found that they had to win over the Vichy-controlled
French forces to their side before they could fight Rommel's
Afrika Korps successfully.

An American naval lieutenant, bearing supplies, arrives at
a French command unit on the coast of North Africa and finds
that the unit is too weak to resist an expected German attack.
The French captain there, who is loyal to Marshal Petain,
will not cooperate with the French general, who is loyal to
General de Gaulle and his free forces. Since they each sus-
pect that the American is too friendly with the other, they
won't cooperate with him either. Obviously, in light of the
clichés of propaganda literature in that day, the problem
calls for some good old American public relations know-how.
Accordingly, the lieutenant convinces them to put aside their
rivalry for the sake of their common mother, La France.
They unite just in time, too, for the Germans begin to attack.

The corrected ms. is at the Univ. of Texas.

46. Princess Renegade, The (1932). As far as is known, this
     three-act work has never been staged.

In this most implausible melodrama, a Russian princess,
engaged to be married, is on a train fleeing from the Red
army in 1917. When she disembarks to get some food, some
townspeople assault her. Luckily, in her case, there is
present a Siberian trapper who is also being chased by the
Reds, and he takes it upon himself to rescue Her Highness.
Together they journey cross-country to catch up with the
train that they had missed. And they succeed. By the time
she is safely in Austria the princess has fallen in love with
her trapper. When she meets the British diplomat to whom
she is engaged, she turns him down in favor of the commoner
who has saved her life and won her heart.

A bound typescript is at the Library of Congress.

47. Raft on the River [also called River Chanty] (1950). This is
     a two-act musical adaptation of Twain's The Adventures of
     Huckleberry Finn, Kurt Weill providing the musical score.
     Weill died in April of 1950 before he could complete the mu-
     sic. Later, Irving Berlin worked on the music, and Joshua
     Logan on a revision of the text, but somehow Raft on the
     River never quite satisfied MA enough for it to reach the
     stage.
        The story deals with the episode in the novel where Huck
     rescues Mary Jane from the machinations of the Duke and the
     Dauphin, Jim gets captured, and Huck makes his momentous
     moral decision to go to hell rather than betray his friend to
     slavery once again.
        The Univ. of Texas owns an extensively corrected ms. and
     a typescript of Act I.

48. Richard and Anne (1955). This two-act drama, written partly
     in verse, went unstaged during MA's lifetime. But a group
     of professionals and amateurs staged it at the annual general
     meeting of the Richard III Society, Inc., on Oct. 3, 1981,
     at the Explorers Club, 46 East 70th Street, New York City.
     Stefan Rudnicki, chairman of the Department of Theatre &
     Film at Long Island University, directed the performance.
     The cast included Stephen Bonnell, Judith Ann Cummings,
     Gene Choquette, Nina Ciancio, Russ Fast, Susan Greenhill,
     Richard Mover, Eileen O'Connor, Kevin O'Leary, Gene Orne-
     las, Portia Patterson, and David Petrarca.
        This is a modern dress rehearsal of Shakespeare's Richard
     III which is invaded by the ghosts of the original characters.
     Richard's jester, Dag, has become infuriated at this continu-
     ing calumny of his master, and summons the shades of Rich-
     ard himself and various people connected with the monarch,
     including Anne (his wife), as well as the evil Henry VII,
     and allows them to relive certain key episodes in their lives
     so that everyone can see what actually happened. In this
     reenactment of history one can see that the character of
     Richard, contrary to the version given to us in books, is al-
     most as white as the driven snow. Henry VII, his successor,
     had falsified the record in order to keep the Plantagenet line
     from succeeding to the throne again. Shakespeare, having
     inherited these lies about the noble Richard, then used his
     glorious imagination and made them into a stage version that
     is more satisfyingly real to audiences now than the actual
     one would be. By means of this reenactment of history, the
     ghost of Richard manages to make his fellow ghost, Anne,
     realize that he had not been unfaithful to her--contrary to
     what she had come to believe after his death--and so they
     are able to ignore the world's misjudgment of them and go
     back to their graves and rest in peace.
        The Univ. of Texas owns a corrected ms. and two bound
     carbon copies.

49. Sea-Wife (1924). This three-act verse fantasy never reached
     the professional stage, but it was produced twice by amateur
     groups: in 1932 at the Univ. of Minnesota, and in 1936 at
     Syracuse University. Professor Sawyer Falk, at the latter
     school, wrote to V. M. Gilbert that the drama was "'excep-
     tionally well received' there" (Vedder Morris Gilbert, "Max-
     well Anderson, His Interpretation of Tragedy in Six Poetical
     Dramas," unpublished master's thesis, Cornell Univ., 1938,
     pp. 19-20). The acknowledged source is Matthew Arnold's
     "Forsaken Merman." Unlike Arnold, MA focuses the interest
     on the wife rather than on the husband.
          In an early nineteenth-century fishing village on an island
     off the coast of Maine, Margaret has just returned to her
     fisherman husband, Dan, following a mysterious three-year
     absence. During that time, she says, she has lived with a
     sea king and borne him two children, but now she has re-
     turned to the land so that she can enjoy once more the warmth
     of human love and also save her soul. (Clearly the story is
     open to symbolic interpretation.) Her husband, despite being
     a kind and patient man, does not believe this account of her
     absence, nor do the bigoted villagers, who would like to see
     her hanged as a witch. Margaret wants to stay with Dan in
     spite of the intolerant community, and in spite of the fact that
     her other husband, the cruel sea king, has allowed her only
     three days to visit before he will destroy their children.
     Just as in High Tor, the protagonist here has the misfortune
     to dwell simultaneously in what are to her two very real
     worlds, the natural and the supernatural, and has problems
     in adjusting to both. When a fisherman reports that he has
     seen two strange children lying dead on the beach, Margaret
     realizes that the sea king has taken his vengeance. Life
     then becomes meaningless to her and she kills herself.
          The Univ. of Texas owns a corrected ms. and a bound
     reproduction of a typescript. The New York Public Library
     owns a reproduction of the typescript; and copies of this
     reproduction are on deposit with Stephen F. Austin State
     University, Gilda Anderson, and myself.

50. Ulysses Africanus (1945). This is a two-act musical comedy
     with a score by Kurt Weill. Based on the novel Aeneas Afri-
     canus, by Harry Stillwell Edwards. Never staged.
          In the South during the Civil War, a wealthy plantation
     owner entrusts his black slave with the responsibility of tak-
     ing care of the family silver by heading south with it and
     staying clear of the Yankees until the war is over. Ulysses
     pledges his word of honor to take care of the silver and to
     return it. He also promises his wife, Pennie, that he will be
     faithful to her. After the war is over, Ulysses tries to re-
     turn but is pursued by the Ku Klux Klan, tempted by a
     woman, and tricked into becoming a member of a minstrel

show. In time he becomes owner of the business and gets
rich and has beautiful women at his beck and call. Along
the way he disposes of the silver.
Ten years have passed since he left the plantation. His
wife, Pennie, accidentally learns of his whereabouts, visits
him at the show, and informs him of dire troubles back home,
where carpetbaggers have taken over the mansion and put
the master's son-in-law into jail. Ulysses is now confronted
with the choice of keeping his wealth or fulfilling his long
ago pledged obligation to the white "massa." He decides that
he wouldn't be able to like himself if he didn't do the right
thing. So, loyal Ulysses sells the minstrel show, buys back
the silver, and returns to the plantation just in the nick of
time. By means of the largesse that this former slave provides, the planter is able to buy back the house and ransom
his son-in-law. Pennie forgives Ulysses for his inconstancy.
The Univ. of Texas owns a corrected ms.

51. White Desert (1923). This verse tragedy in four acts and a
    prologue was the first MA play to reach the professional
    stage. Brock Pemberton produced it at the Princess Theatre
    on Oct. 18, 1923, where it ran for only 12 performances.
    The cast included Frank Shannon in the role of Michael
    Kane, Beth Merrill as Mary Kane, George Abbott as Sverre
    Peterson, and Ethel Wright as Annie Peterson.
       The setting for White Desert is the bleak and frigid North
    Dakota landscape. Michael and Mary Kane have moved to a
    homestead there in the middle of winter. Their nearest
    neighbors are Sverre and Annie Peterson, both of whom wel-
    come the newlyweds by paying them a call. Sverre is a ban-
    tering romantic who appreciates the company of the beautiful
    Mary, a woman much more attractive than his own wife. His
    show of pleasure is such as to arouse Michael's jealousy.
       Michael, who suffers from a rigidly repressed sexuality,
    cannot tolerate the presence of sexuality in his vivacious
    wife, and he remembers only too well that she had come to
    him and yielded herself before they were married. Owing to
    the shortage of chairs in the cabin, Mary thinks nothing of
    sitting on the bed with Sverre as they chat, but this innocent
    gesture Michael interprets as an erotic blunder. Very sus-
    picious. After the Petersons leave he accuses her of being
    morally loose. That night he cannot sleep for worry. The
    next day, when he questions her again on the topic of sex,
    she dumbfounds the puritan by admitting that she derives
    pleasure from having sexual intercourse with him. This re-
    sponse fills him with disgust. He calls her wicked names.
    At first Mary believes that all of this is a cruel joke, but
    when he continues to abuse her she openly threatens to pay
    him back. Michael, angry now, goes away to town for two
    days to get supplies.

A blizzard blows in. Sverre chances to get lost on his
way home, turns up at the Kane cabin, and Mary invites
him in. He volunteers to sleep in the barn. But this is her
opportunity to seduce him and get revenge on her husband.
He ends up staying in the house and sharing the bed with
her.

Michael comes back as planned. He feels guilty now about
his intolerant attitude and says that he ought to have seen
that she was only being natural and human. This leads her
to confess the infidelity. However, he realizes that it was
his unhealthy attitude that had driven her into sin in the
first place, and the two of them patch up their differences.
Just when it seems that all will go well for them, Sverre
makes another appearance on the scene, and the sight of him
is more than Michael can stand. He knows now that he can't
forgive Mary in spite of himself. And Mary realizes that her
act is irrevocable, that her marriage can never be the same
again. She leaves for town in the company of her fellow
sinner. This makes Michael boil with rage. He hurries inside, snatches up a rifle, and goes out and shoots his wife
dead.

The Univ. of Texas owns two corrected typescripts plus
various fragments, some handwritten, some typed.

■ BOOKS OF POETRY

52. A Stanford Book of Verse 1912-1916. The English Club of
    Stanford University, 1916.
    Contains these poems, along with some by his former class
    mates:

    "Youth's Song"
    "The Instrument"
    "End-All"
    "Shakespeare Went to Italy"
    "Kings"
    "Youth"

53. Notes on a Dream. Introduction by Laurence G. Avery. Aus-
    tin: Univ. of Texas Press, 1971. [Limited edition of 750
    copies.]
        The poems are about his new wife, Gilda. All dates and
    all Roman numerals added by Avery:

    "For Gilda: I (August 1952)"
    "Triton (August 1952)"
    "Evadne (September 1952)"
    "Written, as You Will Notice, on a Day When There Was to
        Be No Phone Call (September 1952)"
    "For Gilda: II (October 1952)"
    "Here in the East (1952)"
    "For Gilda III (1952)"
    "Dear Gilda (1952)"
    "Night-Thought (1953)"
    "Sometimes I See You (1953)"
    "For Gilda: IV (February 1954)"
    "Emotion Recollected in Tranquility (1954)"
    "Darling (1954)"
    "In Dream (1954)"
    "For Gilda: V (February 1956)"
    "Notes on a Dream (1957)"
    "For Gilda: VI (February 1958)"
    "Valentine for Gilda (February 1959)"

54. You Who Have Dreams. New York: Simon & Schuster, 1925.
    [Of the 1000 copies that were printed, the first 25 were auto-
    graphed by MA.]

["She said, though you should weave and freeze"] dedication
"'The Time When I Was Plowing'"
"'You Who Have Dreams'"
"Prayer After Youth"
"Judith of Minnewaukan"
"Telemachus Muses"
"Sea-Challenge"
"Rain-Fugue"
"Prayer from the Cliff"
"End-All"
"Beatrice Dead"
"Dust Remembering" [MA's sister Lela claims that this poem
    is about his maternal Aunt Emma or his maternal grand-
    mother, Charlotte Shepard, at whose Atlantic, Pa., farm
    he had often stayed as a child. The two women were dear
    to him.]
"In Winter"
"St. Agnes' Morning"
"Variation on an Old Theme"
"'Lady Titania' (Queen Mab to Some)"
"Toll the Bell for Damon"
"'Don Juanita, Day-Dreaming at Night'"
"Full-Circle"
"'The Fire Is Out in Acheron'"
"Earth Evanescent"
"'When We Have Heard That Time Is Only Seeming'"
"Lucifer"
"The Beggar God"
"Storm Flower"
"Epilogue"
"Winter Song"

     Also, in You Who Have Dreams, MA includes a final section
called "Epigrams." All but the last item are in prose:

"Evolution"
"Compost"
"Prohibition"
"Alone"
"Graybeard Days"
"Shadow of Youth"
"Erinne"
"The Bayonet"
"Civilization"
"A Voice from the Loom"
"Winter Song"

     [The Univ. of Texas is said to have the ms. for 21 of the
poems in this volume.]

■ INDIVIDUAL PUBLISHED POEMS

55- "Again," The Dacotah 1910, IV [a classbook] (Grand Forks:
7. Univ. of North Dakota, May 27, 1909), n.d. [signed: "M.
A."] The Dacotah was technically not a school annual in the
old-fashioned sense. Rather, it was issued biennially from
1904 to 1923, with a gap between 1916 and 1921. The Dacotah 1910 was actually issued in 1909, and was labeled Vol.
IV. The Dacotah 1912, on which MA worked as editor-in-
chief during his senior year, was issued in 1911, and was
labeled Vol. V. MA had items published in both volumes of
this classbook.

58. "Autumn Again," The Midland, V (Mar.-Apr., 1919), 74. This
is one of a pair called "Two Poems" in this issue.

59. "Bald The' at the Play," The Measure: A Journal of Poetry,
no. 9 (Nov., 1921), 12-13. MA helped found and edit this
journal.

60. "The Ballad of Magna Carta," published with musical score
(date unknown) by Chappell & Company, music publishers.
In a Sept. 10, 1940, letter from MA to the company, he refers to the work as complete and published. Chappell &
Company planned to distribute the work among choral groups
and colleges [from MA letter on file at the Univ. of Texas].

61. "The Beggar God," The Measure: A Journal of Poetry, no.
10 (Dec., 1921), 3-5.

62. "Bird and the Thunderstorm," The New Yorker, XXIII (Apr.
26, 1947), 34.

63. "Blue Pencil," New Republic, XVII (Dec. 14, 1918), 192-94.

64. "Carissima." The Shaft: A Literary Magazine, IV (The Quill
Club at the Univ. of North Dakota) (Spring, 1938), 17. Although Thomas McGrath and Marian Points, who were students
at the Univ. of North Dakota in 1937-38, date the poem as
having been published in "the spring of 1909," Joseph F. S.
Smeall (a later faculty member there) reports that he was unable to locate it in either The Student or The Dacotah, which
were the only two student publications at the university in
1909.

65. "Certainly," The Student, XXIV (student newspaper at the
    Univ. of North Dakota), Jan. 20, 1910, p. 4. Signed:
    "J. M. A." After his youth, MA dropped the "James" from
    his name.

66. "Dark Oracles," The Chapbook, no. 19 (Jan., 1921), 5-8. A
    London publication.

67. "Despair," The Midland, V (Mar.-Apr., 1919), 73.

68. "Earth Evanescent," New Republic, XIII (Dec. 22, 1917), 217.
    Collected in You Who Have Dreams.

69. "Emptying Ashes," New Republic, XXV (Jan. 19, 1921), 231.
    Written c.1920.

70. "Epigrams," The Nation, CXI (Dec. 15, 1920), 689.

71. "Epilogue," The Measure: A Journal of Poetry, no. 45 (Nov.,
    1924), 14.

72. "Epitaphs for All Who Died in Wars," The Freeman, V (Aug.
    9, 1922), 519.

73. "Evening," in Josephine Herbst, by Elinor Langer. New York:
    Little, Brown, 1984, p. 62. This is the first publication of
    the poem, which in Herbst's diary at Yale is titled "Evening
    (after a certain day)." According to Langer (p. 62), Jo-
    sephine Herbst enclosed a copy of the poem in a letter to
    her sister, Helen. MA reportedly had sent the poem to Jo-
    sephine to commemorate an evening that they had shared to-
    gether, probably sometime in September 1920. Incidentally,
    the fact that MA had sent the poem reinforces my conviction
    that the copy of it in script on the pages of Herbst's diary
    was placed there by Herbst herself and not by MA, as Langer
    once contended. Langer claims in her book that MA and Jo-
    sephine had a sexual affair which began early in 1920 and
    ended later that year. Herbst wrote such novels as Nothing
    Is Sacred, Money for Love, Pity Is Not Enough, etc.

74. "Feb. 14, '11," The Dacotah 1912, V [a classbook] (Grand
    Forks: Univ. of North Dakota, May, 1911), n.p. Signed:
    "J. M. A." Republished in Thomas McGrath and Marian
    Points' "Maxwell Anderson: Portrait in Pencil," The Shaft:
    A Literary Magazine, IV (The Quill Club at the Univ. of
    North Dakota) (Spring, 1938), 16. The impulse to reprint
    a work by their most famous alumni, Anderson, must have
    seemed natural to the university students there in the 1930's,
    for this was MA's golden era in the theater.

75. "The Fire Is Out in Acheron," The Smart Set Anthology, edited

by Burton Rascoe and Groff Conklin (New York: Reynal &
Hitchcock, 1934).   Written c.1920.   Collected in You Who
Have Dreams.

76.   "The Fisherman," The Dacotah 1912, V [a classbook] (Grand
Forks: Univ. of North Dakota, June 14, 1911), n.p. Signed:
"J. M. A." Reprinted in North Dakota Quarterly, XXXVIII
(Winter, 1970), 32.

77.   "Flame from Ashes," New Republic, XIII (Dec. 22, 1917), 217.

78.   "Full-Circle," New Republic, XXIII (June 23, 1920), 110. Josephine Herbst copied this poem into her diary and followed
it with a note that the poem was the first one that MA had
written after Mar. 1, 1920. See my comments about the poem
"Evening." "Full-Circle" was reprinted in Current Opinion,
LXIX (Aug., 1920), 265-66; also, in Halford E. Luccock and
Frances Brentano's The Questing Spirit [:]   Religion in the
Literature of Our Time (New York: Coward-McCann, 1947),
279-80. Collected in You Who Have Dreams.

79.   "The Grail," The Student, XXIV (student newspaper at the
Univ. of North Dakota), Mar. 31, 1910, p. 4. Reprinted in
The Dacotah 1912 [a classbook] (Grand Forks: Univ. of
North Dakota, June 14, 1911), n.p.

80.   "Grief Castle," in Josephine Herbst, by Elinor Langer. New
York: Little, Brown, 1984, pp. 65-66. Herbst herself had
copied this, her lover's poem, into her leather diary under
the heading of "Grief." It had been sent to her just "the
other day," as she wrote in a letter to her sister, Helen,
on October 20, 1920 (Helen was already dead from a fouled-
up abortion). The subject matter of the poem relates to the
breakup between Herbst and MA.

81.   "Here Below (Ici-bas)," The Student, XXIII (student newspaper at the Univ. of North Dakota), Mar. 4, 1909, p. 4.
Signed: "--Translated from the French of Sully Prudhomme
by J. Maxwell Anderson." Prudhomme is fictional, of course.

82.   "Her Heart Was Curiously Wrought," Smart Set, LXIX (Sept.,
1922), 97.

83.   "Hi-yo, Hi-yo, Discernible Today," The New Yorker, XXIV
(May 1, 1948), 26.

84.   "Ho Logos," The Student, XXIV (student newspaper at the
Univ. of North Dakota), Nov. 4, 1909, p. 4. Signed:
"J. M. A."

85.   "Hylas," Contemporary Verse, IX (Apr., 1920), 57.

86.   "Immortality," Smart Set, LIV (Feb., 1918), 128.

87.   "In an Afternoon," Smart Set, LIV (Jan., 1918), 28.

88.   "In Vishnu-land What Avatar?" The Dial, CXVII (Nov. 29,
      1919), 477-78.

89.   "Is It?" The Dacotah 1912, IV [a classbook] (Grand Forks:
      Univ. of North Dakota, May 27, 1909), n.p. Signed:
      "J. M. A."

90.   "Judith of Minnewaukan," The Measure: A Journal of Poetry,
      no. 7 (Sept., 1921), 7-11. Written during the period 1911
      to 1920. MA's sister Lela says that the poem was inspired
      by a nearly dried up lake that existed at Minnewaukan,
      N.D., when he taught school there (1911-13). In 1920,
      when she was having an affair with MA, Josephine Herbst
      copied this poem into her diary. Collected in You Who Have
      Dreams.

91.   "Lucifer," The Measure: A Journal of Poetry, no. 11 (Jan.,
      1922), 7. Collected in You Who Have Dreams.

92.   "Mazurka (to Anna)," Chapbook (London), no. 30 (Oct., 1922),
      23-24. Occurs in Herbst's diary but without the "(to Anna)."

93.   "Morning and Night," Literary Digest, LXXI (Oct. 15, 1921),
      32.

94.   "Mr. Fish Crosses the River," The New Yorker, XX (May 13,
      1944), 28. This is a satiric attack on Hamilton Fish, a long-
      time U.S. congressman from New York. In the years prior
      to World War II, Fish had sided with Germany and opposed
      Selective Service, Lend Lease, and other preparations for the
      war. He had even visited Germany as a guest of such Nazi
      bigwigs as Hermann Goering.

95.   "Mye Bllondye Deare," The Student, XXIII (student newspaper
      at the Univ. of North Dakota), May 27, 1909, p. 7. [Attri-
      buted to MA.] A notice in this school paper reads: "Ex-
      temporaneous speeches by the following: Wiley, De Noyer,
      R. White and Max Anderson. The following poem which was
      recited by Mr. Anderson during his speech caused numerous
      colors to flash upon the face of a certain member." Perhaps
      the person who blushed was Blondie Holt, who was to become
      an associate editor for MA when he managed The Dacotah
      1912 classbook.

95a. "A New Year," The Student, XXIV (student newspaper at the
      Univ. of North Dakota), Jan. 13, 1910, p. 4. Signed
      "J. M. A."

96. "1908-1935 (For F. H. Koch)," Grand Forks, N.D. Herald,
    June 11, 1935. This is a nostalgic tribute to Professor Fred-
    erick H. Koch, a favorite teacher at the Univ. of North Da-
    kota; to Professor Gottfried Hult, another such teacher; and
    to Margaret Haskett, MA's future wife, who was a student
    there when MA was. The poem was reprinted in the Carolina
    Play Book (Univ. of North Carolina), VIII (Sept., 1935),
    85-86, a work which Koch edited.

97. "Noon in a Wood," The Measure: A Journal of Poetry, no.
    15 (May, 1922), 12.

98. "No Thing of Lasting Worth We Gain," The Student, XXIII
    (student newspaper at the Univ. of North Dakota), Mar. 11,
    1909, p. 1. [Attributed to MA.] The newspaper item reads:
    "M. R. White read the following Ad Altiora [student forensic
    society] poem written by one of its members, Maxwell Ander-
    son."

99. "Now Could I Trace the Passages Through Air," New Republic,
    LV (June 13, 1928), 89.

100. "Parallax," The New Yorker, XX (July 8, 1944), 24.

101. "Prayer After Youth," New Republic, XXXXI (Dec. 3, 1924),
     39. Collected in You Who Have Dreams.

102. "Prometheus Bound," The Nation, CXI (Aug. 14, 1920), 187.

103. "The Raven-ing Budge-ites," The Student, XXIII (student
     newspaper at the Univ. of North Dakota), Apr. 22, 1909,
     p. 3. Budge Hall was a campus dormitory in which MA re-
     sided after leaving Sayre Hall. After the end of his first
     school year MA moved out of Budge and into his parents'
     house on University Avenue in Grand Forks.

104. "Robert E. Sherwood," Variety, June 6, 1956, p. 56. MA
     read this poem at an annual meeting of the American Acad-
     emy of Arts and Sciences, following the death of his friend
     and fellow-playwright Sherwood on Nov. 14, 1955. Reprinted
     in John F. Wharton's Life Among the Playwrights (New York:
     Quadrangle, 1974), pp. 232-33, 235.

105. "St. Agnes' Morning," New Republic, XXVI (Mar. 12, 1921),
     74. In the Josephine Herbst diary, where Josephine had
     copied it, the poem carries a dedication to "Helen." The
     "Helen" may be Josephine's younger sister by that name,
     who died from an abortion in October of 1920.

106. "Salute (To the author of 'Sunset Gun')," clipping from an
     unidentified newspaper. Undated. Clipping on file at the
     Univ. of Texas.

107. "Sea-challenge," New Republic, XXV (Dec. 8, 1920), 48.
     Collected in You Who Have Dreams. Also found in Herbst
     diary.

108. "She Said, Though You Should Weave," Bookman, LVI (Oct.,
     1922), 184; also, New Republic, XXXI (July 5, 1922), 161.
     This is a tribute to the beauty of the author's first wife,
     Margaret, as she stands under the waterfall back of the old
     farmhouse at 170 S. Mountain Road, in New City, N.Y.

109. "Sic Semper," New Republic, XII (Sept. 8, 1917), 159. Here
     MA celebrates the Russian Revolution as symbolic of the fall
     of kings and tyrants everywhere. This poem so deeply im-
     pressed Alvin Johnson, an editor on the New Republic, that
     he arranged to get a position for MA on that journal. This
     new job required that the aspiring writer move to New York
     City. Here he would, in time, gain access to the Broadway
     stage.

109a. "A Slave Prays to the Wind," Contemporary Verse, VI (Sept.,
     1918), 35-36.

110. "So Long Ago," The Dacotah 1910, IV [a classbook] (Grand
     Forks: Univ. of North Dakota, May 27, 1909), n.p.

111. "Spirit Legion," The Nation, CVI (May 25, 1918), 623.

112. "Telemachus Muses," Literary Digest, LXVII (Nov. 6, 1920),
     38.

113. "There Comes a Time," The Dacotah 1910, IV [a classbook]
     (Grand Forks: Univ. of North Dakota, May 27, 1909), n.p.

114. "Threnos," New York Herald Tribune (in F. P. Adams' "Con-
     ning Tower" column), Nov. 28, 1933. Newspaper clipping
     at Univ. of Texas.

115. "Time When I Was Plowing," New Republic, XXXI (June 21,
     1922), 104. The poem expresses his deep and lifelong dis-
     taste for agricultural labor.

116. "To Certain Several Poets," clipping from some unidentified
     newspaper, n.d. Three stanzas. Clipping at Univ. of
     Texas.

117. "Toll the Bell for Damon" in Innocent Merriment: An Anthol-
     ogy of Light Verse. Compiled by Franklin P. Adams. New
     York: McGraw-Hill, 1942, p. 322. Collected in You Who
     Have Dreams.

118. "Tragedy for Humphrey," New Republic, LXXIII (Nov. 30,
     1932), 65-67.

119. "Transient," in Franklin P. Adams' column "The Conning
     Tower" in the New York Tribune, n.d., n.p. Four stan-
     zas. Clipping at Univ. of Texas.

120. "View South from 50th Street," The New Yorker, XXVI (Jan.
     27, 1951), 33.

121. "Welcome to Earth," Contemporary Verse, VIII (Oct., 1919),
     52.

122. "What Answer Shall We Make Him?" (from the Cavalcade of
     America Radio Program), printed in "The Star Spangled
     Ball Souvenir Program" brochure. Undated. Copy of bro-
     chure at Univ. of Texas.

123. "What Were You Seeking, Sailor?" printed in "The Star
     Spangled Ball Souvenir Program" brochure. Copyright 1940
     by MA. Copy of brochure at Univ. of Texas.

124. "When We Have Heard That Time Is Only Seeming," New Re-
     public, XXXXIII (June 24, 1925), 126. Collected in You
     Who Have Dreams.

125. "Whether the Dark Had Ushered in the Rain," New Republic,
     XXXVIII (May 31, 1924), 331. Reprinted in Thomas Mc-
     Grath and Marian Points' "Maxwell Anderson: Portrait in
     Pencil," The Shaft: A Literary Magazine, IV (The Quill
     Club at the Univ. of North Dakota) (Spring, 1938). The
     foregoing article was itself reprinted in The North Dakota
     Quarterly, XXXIII (Winter, 1965), 10-13.

126. "'Who Has Burned His Wings,'" The Measure: A Journal of
     Poetry, no. 19 (Sept., 1922), 5.

127. "Words for Sir Basil Zharoff," Scholastic, XXXI (Nov. 6,
     1937), 23-E.

128. "The World of Mathematics," The New Yorker, XXXII (Dec.
     22, 1956), 70.

129. "Yellow-Breasted Chat," Ladies' Home Journal, LXX (Jan.,
     1953), 160.

130. "Your Love Is Like a Quicksand Where Men Build," New Re-
     public, LV (May 23, 1928), 19. Served as lyrical introduc-
     tion to Gypsy.

131. "You Who Have Dreams Born in the Bones," New Republic,
     XXXVIII (Mar. 26, 1924), 124.

132. "According to All Report, My Dear." [A boy tells a girl that, since winter nights are long, winter is the best season in which to get married.] Two 6-line stanzas. Ms. at the Univ. of Texas.

133. "After the Cows," c. 1899-1900, signed "J. M. A." [The author, as a little boy, tells about rounding up the cows at his Grandmother Charlotte Shepard's farm at Atlantic, Pa.] This and the mistitled "Mama" are the earliest known MA poems. They are said to have been written at his maternal grandmother's farm and mailed to his mother while he was there during the winter and the following spring. Fourteen lines. Photocopy of ms. sent to me by Gilda Anderson (Mrs. Maxwell Anderson).

134. "All These Remain," c.1920. [Nature remains essentially unchanged but man with all his aims and errors eventually perishes.] Four stanzes of 4 lines each. Ms. at Yale University. Two typescripts and a carbon copy at the Univ. of Texas.

135. "Along Comes November." [The harvest season is praised.] Three stanzas of 4 lines each. Ms. at the Univ. of Texas.

136. "Along the River." [The poet's uneventful life is contrasted with his dreams of adventure.] Four stanzas of 8 lines each. Ms. at the Univ. of Texas.

137. "Archie at the Pomona Tower," c.1942. [This is a stream-of-consciousness letter about Archie, who went to the Civil Defense Tower at Pomona, N.Y., to see the actress Paulette Goddard, but failed to see her and got absorbed in looking for enemy planes.] The item draws upon MA's own wartime experience as an airplane spotter at Pomona Tower. Fifty-nine lines. Ms. at the Univ. of Texas.

138. "Arthur and Roland, 1914-18," c.1920. [Death during wartime cuts off possibilities for happiness.] Five stanzas of 4 lines each. Typescript and carbon copy at Univ. of Texas.

139. "As for the Government," c.1927. [This is a bitter statement about evil at the root of all government.] Petrarchan sonnet. Ms. at the Univ. of Texas.

140. ["As Franklin says"]. [This poem makes a sardonic statement about crookedness in public places.] Forty-one lines, apparently incomplete. Photocopy of ms. sent to me by Gilda Anderson.

141. "As One New-Blind Waking." [An elegy about the death of one's beloved.] Three stanzas of 4 lines each. Ms. and typescript at the Univ. of Texas.

142. "At the Corner of Four Fields." [This is a nostalgic poem about the author's early days living in the old farmhouse on South Mountain Road at New City, N.Y.] MA's own property there was first called Seven Fields, because stone walls divided the acreage into seven sections. Three quatrains. Ms. at the Univ. of Texas. Written in pencil.

143. "Bacchanal." [It is better to sing even in despair than to be quietly bitter.] Three stanzas, the first two containing 4 lines each; the last stanza is unrhymed. Typescript at the Univ. of Texas.

144. "Bearing in Mind How Sunlight Ends in Rain." [In the midst of love the poet recalls that death will cut him off from his beloved someday.] Petrarchan sonnet. Two mss. at the Univ. of Texas.

145. ["The children were hard to care for"]. [The poet recalls the early days of marriage, almost certainly with his first wife, Margaret, and some incidents foreshadowing their breakup. Sorrowful.] Twenty-four lines. Ms. on back of an envelope stamped "May 13, 1958." Envelope at Univ. of Texas.

146. "Churchill," c.WWII period. [This is a tribute to Winston Churchill, who offered Britain hope in her dark hours of the war.] Two stanzas; the first one containing 11 lines, the second one containing 7 lines. Photocopy of typescript sent to me by Gilda Anderson.

147. "Clair De La Lune." [A man asks a good looking woman for directions in the city while he is pretending to be lost.] Eight lines. Ms. at the Univ. of Texas.

148. "Cold Night After Night." [A pessimistic poem about death.] Five stanzas of 4 lines each. Ms. at the Univ. of Texas.

149. "The Darkness Coiled About These Streets." [A night scene in the city street.] Eight lines. Ms. at the Univ. of Texas.

150. "Dear Bruce." [A political letter to a friend.] Three stanzas of 4 lines each. Ms. and typescript at the Univ. of Texas.

151. "Dear Helen, Well, the Play Is Bound," 1934. [The writer
      praises the actress Helen Hayes for her performance in
      Mary of Scotland. In the light of her fine acting, however,
      the recently published version of the play will seem lame.]
      Twenty-two lines in couplets. Ms. at the Univ. of Texas.

152. "Death's Mazurka," c.1920. [Disillusionment with war.]
      Thirty-eight lines. Typescript at the Univ. of Texas.

153. "Dedication." [Love poem to a lady.] Eight lines. Three
      carbon copies at the Univ. of Texas.

154. "Earth in Dust Goes Down to Dust." [Spiritually hopeless
      man will go back to the dust from which he came.] Five
      lines. Ms. at the Univ. of Texas.

155. ["Fainter than faltering"], c.1920. [A bitter love poem.]
      This work, copied by Josephine Herbst into her diary at
      about the time of her affair with MA, probably relates to
      them. Eight lines. Ms. at Yale University.

156. "Farewell to the Dance." [A cynical, 30-year-old man says
      farewell to youth.] Twenty-four lines. Ms. at the Univ.
      of Texas.

157. "Footnote (To the Earth We Live On)." [About the poet's
      good fortune to have a beachfront for clams and gulls.]
      Thirty lines in couplets. Typescript at the Univ. of Texas.

158. "For a Box." [The love that lovers share is all they have of
      consequence before death finds them.] Possibly relates to
      MA's affair with Josephine Herbst. Two stanzas; the first
      one containing 8 lines, the second 6 lines. Ms. at Yale
      University.

159. "For Anna Huntington's Diana." [Death of a child.] The
      Anna here is the sculptress Anna Hyatt Huntington, wife
      of MA's millionaire neighbor and friend Archer Milton Hunt-
      ington. Petrarchan sonnet. Ms. at the Univ. of Texas.

160. "For Craig (with apologies to John Keats)." [MA gives a
      childlike account of his stepson's experiences in traveling
      to California.] Lawrence Craig Anderson (b. 1945) is one
      of two children by Gilda Romano's marriage to the script-
      writer and dramatist Lawrence Hazard. The other child is
      Laurel (b. 1942). Gilda became the third Mrs. Maxwell
      Anderson in 1954. Forty-nine lines. Photocopy sent to
      me by Gilda Anderson.

161. "For Gilda," Feb. 1957. [The poet recounts what little he
      and his wife, Gilda, need to make them happy. He con-

cludes that he needs only food, a bed, and her--as long as
she needs only him.] Gilda, the third Mrs. Maxwell Anderson, was born Gilda Romano on July 17, 1913, in Providence,
Rhode Island, one of three children of a Swedish mother
and an Italian father. Sixteen lines. Photocopy of ms.
sent to me by Gilda Anderson.

162. "For Helen." [A tribute to the actress Helen Hayes, who in-
      spired life into his dramas.] Helen Hayes, a neighbor and
      friend in New City, N.Y., acted in his <u>Mary of Scotland</u>
      and <u>Candle in the Wind</u>. Ten lines. Ms. at the Univ. of
      Texas.

163. "For Mab," Feb. 14, 1936. [Valentine note to Mab Maynard,
      his companion.] She was known to everyone as Mrs. Max-
      well Anderson, from 1933 to 1953, when she killed herself.
      Mab was born Gertrude Higger on Sept. 27, 1904, in Mon-
      treal, Canada, the eldest of two daughters of Russian immi-
      grants. Four lines in couplets. Ms. at the Univ. of Texas.

164. "Gawayne Sings." [A lover petitions his beloved to linger
      with him, else he will do mischief with his powers of en-
      chantment.] Three stanzas of 4 lines each. Ms. at Yale
      University.

165. "Grief Passes." [The passage of time assuages one's grief fol-
      lowing the death of a loved one.] The poem might refer to
      the death of Josephine Herbst's sister, Helen, who died
      from a bungled abortion in the summer of 1920. This poem,
      along with several others by MA, was found in the diary of
      Josephine Herbst, a novelist with whom he was having an
      affair in 1920. Petrarchan sonnet. Ms. at Yale University;
      also, at the Univ. of Texas.

166. "Habanera." [About fickle love.] Thirty-two lines. Carbon
      copy at the Univ. of Texas.

167. "Harper's Grace." [A minstrel sings a sad song to his lover
      because he knows that they will both die and no one will
      remember them.] A typically pessimistic poem from MA's
      early period--despair and death were common topics of his
      poetry then. Four stanzas of 4 lines each. A ms. and a
      carbon copy are at the Univ. of Texas.

168. "Having No Answer." [Apparent meaninglessness of the deaths
      of those who perished by war.] Three stanzas of 4, 9, and
      6 lines. A ms., a typescript, and a carbon copy are at the
      Univ. of Texas.

169. "Heaven Is Only Hell Seen in the Dawn." [About the death of
      a loved one.] Shakespearean sonnet. Ms. and carbon copy
      at the Univ. of Texas.

170. "Henry David (Walden Pond) Thoreau." [A tribute to Thoreau's independence from a materialistic society.] From his high school days onward MA seems to have been greatly impressed with Thoreau's way of life. He did much of his writing in a simply furnished cabin in the woods behind his new house at New City, N.Y., and his hero Van Van Dorn shows many resemblances to Thoreau (see pp. 119-20 of my Maxwell Anderson). Thirty-one lines. Ms. at the Univ. of Texas.

171. "Her Ears Strained Outward Toward the Noisy Street." [A devoted invalid wife strains to hear the feet of her returning husband on the stairs even though he had mistreated her.] Shakespearean sonnet. Ms. at the Univ. of Texas.

172. "Hobo," c.1920. [The hobo is the only free man.] Petrarchan sonnet. Typescript at the Univ. of Texas.

173. "Home." [Celebration of home life.] Thirteen lines. Carbon copy at the Univ. of Texas.

174. "I'd Walk Home from There," c.1950-1953. [A soldier voices his discontent with the way the Korean War is going.] Four stanzas of 8 lines each. Ms. at the Univ. of Texas.

175. ["I envy you the sea"], c.1920. [The poet envies the person who goes to sea, who has freedom, even if that person is lonely, because it is better to be wild and wounded than to be tame and well fed.] Seven lines. Ms. at Yale University.

176. "I Have Outlived All Poets Who Died Young." [The author laments his failure to write great poetry, comparable to that of certain famous poets who died young, but he rejoices in the pleasure that poetic composition gives him.] Petrarchan sonnet. Carbon copy at the Univ. of Texas.

177. "In After Times How Many a Man and Maid." [Love poem.] Petrarchan sonnet. Typescript at the Univ. of Texas.

178. "In a Thronged Street." [The poet has empathy with people he meets even though he realizes that all human life is ultimately meaningless.] Seven stanzas of 4 lines each. Two mss. at the Univ. of Texas.

179. "In Scribbled Levin over the Midnight Scroll." [About the ravages of World War I and how man will finally make himself a better world.] Two stanzas of 15 and 16 lines, respectively. Typescript at the Univ. of Texas.

180. ["In the rainy dark I touch my hand to your cheek"], c.1920.

[A prose poem about a lonely man's love for a woman.]
Very possibly this work is about MA's love for Josephine
Herbst, because she copied it into her diary during the
time she was having an affair with him. Twelve lines (87
words). Ms. at Yale University.

181. "Irish Tune for Country Derry." [The Irish rebellion brings
      death to young men.] Thirty-four lines. Ms. at the Univ.
      of Texas.

182. "It Has Been Autumn Often." [Praise for the autumn season.]
      Three stanzas of 5 lines each. Ms. at the Univ. of Texas.

183. "I Was Wrong to Think We Could Live by the Light of Reason."
      [Only the heart, not the reason, can give us meaningful
      guidance.] Prose poem in six lines. Ms. at the Univ. of
      Texas.

184. "John Barleycorn," c.1956. [Be kind to drunks; cast your
      blame on alcohol instead. Amusing slant.] This work was
      used in the CBS television musical version of High Tor that
      was presented on Mar. 10, 1956. Music supplied by Arthur
      Schwartz. Three stanzas of 4 lines each. Carbon copy at
      the Univ. of Texas.

185. "Johnny Was Not the Lad to Stay Home." [Johnny roams
      around a good deal because he fights with his wife.] Seven-
      teen lines; incomplete. Ms. at the Univ. of Texas.

186- "The King's Chamber." [A sleeping king is peacefully unaware
7.   of whether the approaching footsteps of a man bode death
      to the king or trouble to the kingdom.] Fourteen lines.
      Typescript at the Univ. of Texas.

188. "Lady of Dust." [A variation on Andrew Marvell's "To His
      Coy Mistress," this poem about love and death possibly re-
      fers to MA's first wife, Margaret, whose burial urn he kept
      in his successive houses and later in his cabin, over a
      period of 23 years.] Five stanzas of 4 lines each. Type-
      script at the Univ. of Texas.

189. "Lady of Melita." [Portrait of a heartless woman.] Six lines.
      Two carbon copies at the Univ. of Texas.

190. "Lament." [A woman sorrows over her dead lover.] Three
      stanzas of 4 lines each. Ms. at the Univ. of Texas.

191. "Lancelot and Sandryn." [A narrative account of Lancelot's
      rape of Sandryn and what happens to her after that.] Con-
      tains 577 lines in couplets. Ms. at the Univ. of Texas.

192. "A Little Love, A Little While," c.1956. [The poet regrets
      that love won't last always.] This work was used in the
      CBS television musical version of High Tor that was pre-
      sented on Mar. 10, 1956. Music supplied by Arthur
      Schwartz. Twenty-three lines. Carbon copy at the Univ.
      of Texas.

193. "The Little Tin God." [In the absence of religious faith, the
      only justification for living is the desire for self-respect.]
      Two stanzas of 4 lines each. Ms. at the Univ. of Texas.

194. "Living One Day at a Time," c.1956. [It is enough to live
      for the present moment.] This work was used in the CBS
      television version of High Tor that was presented on Mar.
      10, 1956. Music supplied by Arthur Schwartz. Two stanzas
      of 6 and 8 lines, respectively. Carbon copy at the Univ.
      of Texas.

195. "Lo, Father, I Have Come with a New Thing." [Symbolic
      story of man's discovery of fire.] Three stanzas, the first
      two having 8 lines; the last stanza having 6 lines. Ms. at
      the Univ. of Texas.

195a. "Lord, If You Would Keep Your Sweetheart." [A girl laments
      the death of a lover killed in the war.] Four stanzas of 4
      lines each. Ms. at the Univ. of Texas.

196. "The Lord Made Adam." [Arrested spirituality is the price
      for lusting after women.] Fourteen lines. Ms. at the
      Univ. of Texas.

197. "Lovers Are Always Parting by the Sea." [When two lovers
      part, their sorrowful situation is quite common, but the
      parting will live on in their memory because of the intensity
      of their emotion.] Nine lines. Ms. at the Univ. of Texas.

198. "Love Was Mine." [Now that fame, prosperity, and love have
      failed us, nothing can sustain us in the end.] Seven lines.
      Typescript and two carbon copies at the Univ. of Texas.

199. "Mama," c.1899-1900, signed "J. M. Anderson." [The au-
      thor, as a little boy, tells about a chipmunk that bit him on
      his finger at his Grandmother Charlotte Shepard's farm, At-
      lantic, Pa.] This and "After the Cows" are the earliest
      known poems by MA. They are said to have been written
      on his grandmother's farm and mailed to his mother during
      his stay there. Thirty-six lines. Photocopy of ms. sent to
      me by Gilda Anderson.

200. "Mermaiden." [Evocation of a mood in which the narrator pic-
      tures a Mermaiden alone in a rainy sea amid the cresting

waves.] MA's play <u>Sea-Wife</u> contains a merman and his mor-
tal wife who live in the ocean with their children. Four
stanzas, each consisting of 8 lines. Ms. at Yale University.

201. "Mid-May." [The poet voices his feeling of loneliness and
emptiness, and states that because of him his erstwhile
lover (?) is in a worse frame of mind than he is.] Twelve
lines. Ms. at Yale University.

202. "Mother Earth." [The poet questions life's meaning.] Four
stanzas of 4 lines each. Ms. and typescript at the Univ.
of Texas.

203. "Night in the Queen's Garden." [This is a severe picture of
a queen, incapable of giving love, now alone and sitting on
a moonless terrace. The poem ends with the suggestion
that it would have been better if she had simply pitied the
men in her life rather than tried to love them.] The subject matter invites comparison with what we find in the por-
traits of Queen Elizabeth in <u>Elizabeth the Queen</u>, <u>Mary of
Scotland</u>, and <u>The Masque of Queens</u>. Four stanzas of 5,
5, 10, and 9 lines, respectively. Ms. at Yale University;
also at the Univ. of Texas.

204. "Noon in a Wood." [A cavalier talks himself out of wanting
revenge.] Three stanzas of 6 lines each. Carbon copy at
the Univ. of Texas.

205. "Octave and Sestet." [Love and the uncertainty of life.]
Petrarchan sonnet. Two mss. at the Univ. of Texas.

206. "Oh, Beat the Drum Slowly and Play the Fife Lowly." [A
dying cowboy regrets his wasted life.] Four stanzas of 4
lines each. Ms. at the Univ. of Texas.

207. ["Oh how I was a young lad"], Jan. 6, 1934. This art ballad
starts off,

> Oh how I was a young lad
> When I was twenty-two,
> I married and got a child
> And sang the winter through.

Consists of five stanzas of 4 lines each. The ms. is located
in Vol. 2 of the Anderson papers at the Univ. of North
Dakota. This volume contains, also, the beginning of a
diary and the conclusion of <u>Mary of Scotland</u>.

208. "Oh, Love, I Cannot Say That in a Song." [Death of a wife.]
Five stanzas of 8 and 6 lines alternating. Ms. at the Univ.
of Texas.

209. "Oh, You Will Put Me Easily Out of Mind." [Passionate love
      vanishes and leaves a few memories.] Petrarchan sonnet.
      Ms. at the Univ. of Texas.

210. "Old Tales Hang Round Old Woods; How a Man Fell." [The
      poet remembers the people who had lived and died in a cer-
      tain wood, then takes refuge in the idea that lovers ought
      to look into each other's eyes and find there the gift that
      will keep them from being lonely.] Petrarchan sonnet.
      Carbon copy at the Univ. of Texas.

211. "On Getting a New Pair of Glasses." [Amusing account of
      how vivid life looks now that the author has new glasses.
      But the beautiful girls are gone.] Twenty-seven lines.
      Ms. at the Univ. of Texas.

212. "Our Fathers Brimmed a Cup of Night." [Past generations
      are responsible for the current mood of disillusionment.]
      Four lines. Ms. at the Univ. of Texas.

213. "Over the Laggard Evening." [The poet describes how he
      feels after a day of writing in his cabin in the woods.]
      Three stanzas of 3, 4, and 7 lines, respectively. Ms. at
      Yale University; typescript at the Univ. of Texas.

214. "The Painter Speaks." [A painter speculates whether he is
      faithful in his work to his own perception of life, or is
      simply drawing his ideas from older paintings that them-
      selves were not true to experience.] Nine lines. Ms. at
      the Univ. of Texas.

215. "Palinode," c.1942. [The poet tries to goad the home town
      people into more actively supporting the war effort.] 112
      lines in couplets. Ms. at the Univ. of Texas.

216. "Place Names and Rue." [The poet barely recalls a Paris girl
      he had known; this makes him aware of how swiftly time
      flies.] Seven stanzas of 4 lines each. Carbon copy at the
      Univ. of Texas.

217. "Pocahontas' Body." [Speculates whether Pocahontas, being
      dead, can now remember.] Five lines. Ms. at Yale Univer-
      sity.

218. "Poem," on back of an envelope dated May 13, 1958. [The
      poet expresses his anguish about his breakup with his wife,
      Margaret, many years before.] Apparently this is a genuine
      and accurate account of what happened. Three stanzas con-
      taining a total of 24 lines. Ms. at the Univ. of Texas.

219. "The Poets Have Called Him Dark Death." [The poet awaits

death stoically because he has already suffered deeply the
loss of his friend.] Nine lines. Ms. at the Univ. of Texas.

220. "Prairie Mood." [The wild weather of the prairie is matched
by the tempestuous youth of the poet.] Six stanzas of 4
lines each. Typescript at the Univ. of Texas.

221. "The Prayer." [Sometimes ironic and sometimes straightfor-
ward salutation to the Virgin Mary.] Five stanzas; the
third and fifth containing 9 lines; the other stanzas containing 6. Typescript at the Univ. of Texas.

222. "Red Riding Hood and the Wolf." [Nursery story retold except that Red Riding Hood and the wolf go to bed together
and get married; also, there is a moral at the end.] Eleven
stanzas of 4 lines each. Ms. at the Univ. of Texas.

223. "Reform in Cloud-Cuckooland," c.1930. [Satiric fantasy.]
Eleven stanzas of 9 lines each. Typescript at the Univ. of
Texas.

224. "Robert E. Sherwood," 1955. [Elegy for Sherwood, his
friend.] One hundred and eleven lines. Mimeographed
copy at the Univ. of Texas.

225. "Sample of the Work Done on This Machine," c.1943. [A
three-line quotation consisting of a parody of Franklin P.
Adams satirizing MA's poetry, followed by two stanzas of 8
lines each.] Carbon copy at the Univ. of Texas.

226. "The Sea Is Gray," accompanied by the musical score. [A
lover parts from his beloved on a rainy day at the beach,
but he prophesies that his partner will remember their time
together and suffer heartache.] Because this piece by MA
was copied by Josephine Herbst into her diary at about the
time of her affair with him in the spring of 1920, the situation in the poem probably relates to her. Six rhymed quatrains. Ms. at Yale University.

227- "Sky-Trail." [The poet, not finding any gods that he can
8.   pray to, is content to be an atheist.] Three stanzas: the
first stanza contains 3 lines, the second stanza 8, and the
third 9. Ms. at Yale University.

229- ["Stay your golden head upon my arm"]. [About a father's
31. fears for his child's future when the child grows up.]
Petrarchan sonnet. Typescript at the Univ. of Texas.

232. "Testament." [When two lovers cease to be in love, they
should be candid about it to each other.] Petrarchan sonnet. Typescript at the Univ. of Texas.

233. "Third Reich," c.1940. [Verbal assault on Adolf Hitler.]
      Four stanzas of 4 lines each. Typescript at the Univ. of
      Texas.

234. "This Is Your Hour, Americans!" c.1940. [The poet tells
      Americans to defend their liberty against Nazi Germany.]
      Three stanzas of 5, 4, and 5 lines, respectively. Type-
      script at the Univ. of Texas.

235. "Thou of Macedon." [The poet contrasts unfavorably the life
      he sees about him with what he finds represented in Greek
      literature.] Five lines. Two carbon copies at the Univ. of
      Texas.

236. "The Time of the Cherries." [Celebration of spring and
      young love.] Two stanzas of 13 lines each. Typescript at
      the Univ. of Texas.

237. "To a Critic Who Gives Me Nothing." [The poet speaks of his
      dissatisfaciton in trying to capture his "vision" on paper.]
      Petrarchan sonnet. Ms. at the Univ. of Texas.

238. "To a Love Disavowed." [The poet, after his beloved had
      died, disavowed for her sake the joy he was experiencing
      in living; after a brief resurgence of cheer he despairs
      again.] Eighteen lines. Carbon copy and typescript at the
      Univ. of Texas.

239. "To Archer Huntington on His Attaining to Something Biblical
      in the Number of Days." [Using the metaphor of time as a
      potter turning out vessels and then destroying them (the
      vessels being people), the poet trusts that time will spare
      an especially good vessel (Huntington) so that it will remain
      around to encourage human progress.] Huntington, the son
      of the builder of the Central Pacific Railroad, was a multi-
      millionaire scholar, poet, and philanthropist who lived near
      MA on South Mountain Road in New City, N.Y. In 1897 he
      published the manuscript text of Poema del Cid; in 1907 a
      translation of this famous work; and in 1908 some textual
      notes. He died in 1955 at the ripe age of 85. MA's poem
      about him is a Petrarchan sonnet. Two mss. at the Univ.
      of Texas.

240. "Tomorrow There Is Work to Do," c.1920. [On the futility of
      dying in a war.] Four stanzas, the first 3 containing 5
      lines each; the last one containing 10 lines. Ms. at the
      Univ. of Texas.

241. "To My Valentine," Feb. 14, 1935. [Addressed to his com-
      panion, Mab.] Three stanzas of 4 lines each. Ms. at the
      Univ. of Texas.

242. "Transient." [The poet's house, where he had lived with his beloved, is being torn down; the house will exist now only in his memory; and when he is dead even the memory of the house will be gone.] Four stanzas of 4 lines each. Two mss. and a typescript at the Univ. of Texas.

243. "Under the Walls of Sevilla." [Carmen seduces Don Jose.] Eighty-one lines. Typescript at the Univ. of Texas.

244. "Vista." [Another of MA's frequent expresisons of despair in his writings--before he made his mark on the New York stage and began to enjoy commercial and critical success.] Seven lines. Ms. and typescript at the Univ. of Texas.

245. "We Always Get Together Again." [Lovers always get reconciled with each other after a fight.] Two stanzas of 4 lines each; two refrains of 4 and 5 lines. Ms. at the Univ. of Texas.

245a. ["We are forever like two parallels"]. [Even lovers, despite their closeness to each other, retain their individual identities.] Italian sonnet. Typescript at Univ. of Texas. This poem is part of a group of six sonnets that Laurence Avery in his Catalogue of the Maxwell Anderson Collection labels as a "Sonnet Sequence."
    However, I exclude from my list these two that appear in Avery's Catalogue:
    ["I know you do not mean to wound my heart"]. [A woman is unhappy that her husband divides his thoughts between her and a woman who is dead.] Italian sonnet. Typescript at the Univ. of Texas. The unhappy woman is probably Mab Maynard, MA's second "wife," who had to put up with MA's fond memories of his first wife, Margaret. The latter died of a stroke in 1930.
    ["This room she had defiled must be swept clean"]. [A woman, in the process of cleaning a room she had defiled by making illicit love in it during the preceding night, learns too late that she has disgraced herself because she still loves the man she broke herself away from and then betrayed.] The woman here is probably Mab Maynard, castigating herself for having had an affair with Jerry Stagg. MA discovered the affair and moved out of the house, but Mab continued to see Stagg. See my Life of Maxwell Anderson, pp. 240-49.
    I exclude these two poems from the canon because MA's son Terence, along with his wife, Lulu, has convinced me that the authorship lies elsewhere. Back in 1978 Terence told me that two of the poems listed in Avery's Catalogue were actually written by Mab. But, not having a copy of the Catalogue on hand, he could not identify the poems by title or description. In 1984 I sent to Mr. and Mrs. Terence

Anderson photocopies of pages from the Catalogue where
the unpublished poems are listed and asked these people to
identify all apocryphal items. In her letter to me dated
Sept. 15, 1984, Lulu returned to me a photocopied page on
which the Mab Maynard items were circled. She explained
in the letter that she and her husband were certain that the
two circled items referred to poems done by Mab. Mab was,
of course, Terence's stepmother and neighbor for many
years in New City, N.Y.

245b. ["We are two stars reflected in a lake"]. [A celebration of
       ecstatic lovemaking; the moment of physical joy is brief but
       the memory lasts forever.] Petrarchan sonnet. Typescript
       at the Univ. of Texas.

246. "We Have Come Down to This Mile's End." [The poet yearns
       to escape to the open sea and leave the unpleasant land be-
       hind.] Petrarchan sonnet. Ms. and carbon copy at the
       Univ. of Texas.

247. "A Westering Mars." [A fantasy in which a crazy leader ex-
       horts men to die in the latest war, then he is informed that
       he himself is already dead.] Thirteen lines. Ms. and type-
       script at the Univ. of Texas.

248. "What Is the Place of the Minister's Wife," 1945. [A descrip-
       tion of a minister's wife who lets superficialities form the
       basis of her spiritual welfare.] Thirteen lines. Ms. at the
       Univ. of Texas.

249. "What Shall Be Said of Us When We Are Dead," Aug. 27, 1933.
       [The poet voices no apprehension about what the books will
       say about him after he dies, but he hopes that they will not
       be dull.] It was about this time that MA first announced to
       his relatives that he had remarried, this time to Mab May-
       nard, whereas no actual wedding ceremony had taken place
       or would take place between them. Perhaps this poem de-
       rived from some uneasiness he felt because of this irregular
       union. Petrarchan sonnet. Typescript at the Univ. of Texas.

250. "When Poetry Pays Dividends." [The poet, addressing this
       piece to his wife, tells her that when people pay him for his
       verse, and pay him fairly for his plays, he will buy her as
       many flowers as she wants. He assumes that both of these
       conditions are impossible.] Eight lines. Carbon copy at the
       Univ. of Texas.

251. ["When you're away"]. [The poet describes his feeling of loss
       when his loved one is gone.] Eight lines. Photocopy of ms.
       furnished to me by Gilda Anderson.

252. "The White Moon." [A celebration of night.] Three stanzas
     of 6 lines each. Ms. at the Univ. of Texas.

253. "You and I, En Passant." [About the rapid passage of years.]
     Thirty-five lines. Typescript and carbon copy at the Univ.
     of Texas.

253a. ["You ask for truth, I answer you with lies"]. [A man rec-
     ognizes that neither he nor his lover can face the unvar-
     nished truth; therefore, he will continue to speak to her in
     conventional terms that will spare them disillusionment.]
     Petrarchan sonnet. Typescript at the Univ. of Texas.

■ FICTION

NOVEL

254. Morning Winter and Night (published under the pseudonym of
     John Nairne Michaelson). New York: William Sloane Asso-
     ciates, 1952. Simultaneously published by George J. McLeod
     at Toronto, Canada. It was also reprinted in paperbound
     form in New York by Berkley Books. In the late 1970's it
     was reissued in a limited and unauthorized paperbound edi-
     tion--this time under the name of Maxwell Anderson--by
     Xanadu Productions, a motion picture firm that was once
     producing a film based on the novel.
         Ross Berria and David Peters, the producers of the film,
     had hired the famous actor Cliff Robertson to direct and to
     act in the role of Fowler. The beautiful child-star Brooke
     Shields was to play the sensual Hallie Haviland. The child-
     actor Mark McLaughlin was to play Jaimie. The producers
     hired MA's daughter Hesper to write the film script, which
     was duly completed and ran to 144 pages. But the script
     proved to be unsatisfactory. Worse still, the producers
     failed to complete the financing--for a budget of $1,011,101.
     Preliminary winter scenes were "shot" in Greenfield, Mass.,
     in order to spur on investors, but the production languished
     after that and was finally abandoned.
         In my book The Life of Maxwell Anderson, I devote sev-
     eral pages to exploring the autobiographical versus fictional
     basis of the novel's story.

SHORT STORIES

255. "The Battle of Gibraltar," Collier's, LXXXV (May 10, 1930),
     26, 31, 36, 38.

256. "La Belle Dame SANS MERCI," The Student, XXIV (student
     newspaper at the Univ. of North Dakota), Nov. 11, 1909,
     p. 4. [Signed "M. A."]

257. "West Coast, Night." Written in 1947. Ms. at the Univ. of
     Texas.

258. Incomplete, untitled, unpublished short story or novel in

holograph form about the character Shepan Illylch Miklasoff.
A prologue in verse is attached. Photocopy sent to me by
Gilda Anderson. Twenty-two pages including prologue.

■ BOOKS OF CRITICISM

259. The Essence of Tragedy and Other Footnotes and Papers.
     Washington, D.C.: Anderson House, 1939.

260- Off Broadway: Essays About the Theatre. New York: Wil-
4.   liam Sloane Associates, 1947.

■ SHORTER PROSE WRITINGS

265. "About the Playwrights Company," Stage, XVI (Dec., 1938), 17.

266. "An Age of Hired Men," The Freeman, II (Sept. 22, 1920), 31-32.

267. "An American Observer in Greece," New York Herald Tribune, Nov. 28, 1947, p. 26.

268. "An American Playwright Looks at Greece," New York Herald Tribune, Jan. 18, 1948, II, 7. Reprinted in Avery's Letters, pp. 218-20.

269. "Ancient Struggle to Uphold Democracy, The," New York Herald Tribune, Aug. 12, 1951. This article is taken from the Preface to Barefoot in Athens.

270- "Anderson Calls Drama Critics 'Jukes Family,'" New York
2.   Herald Tribune, Mar. 4, 1946.

273. "The Arts as Motive Power[:] Certain Reflections on the State of the World and upon the Position of the Arts in It." Text of an address delivered at the Founders Day exercises at the Carnegie Institute, Pittsburgh, Pa., on Oct. 14, 1937. Published in The New York Times, Oct. 17, 1937, XI, 1, 2. Included as "Whatever Hope We Have" in The Essence of Tragedy and Other Footnotes and Papers (1939). Also, in Essays Annual, edited by Erich A. Walter. New York: Appleton-Century, 1939, pp. 212-19.

274. "Assembling the Parts of a Musical Play," New York Herald Tribune, Oct. 30, 1949, V, 13.

275. "Author Looks Back on Ten Years and Concludes That the Hopes of His Company Have Been Fulfilled," The New York Times, Oct. 10, 1948, II, 3.

276. "Basis of Artistic Creation, The," in The Bases of Artistic Creation. New Brunswick, N.J.: Rutgers Univ. Press, 1942. Essays by MA, Roy Harris, Rhys Carpenter et al.

277. "Blue Pencil," New Republic, XVII (Dec. 14, 1918), 192-94.

278. "By Way of Preface: The Theatre as Religion," The New
      York Times, Oct. 26, 1941, drama section, p. 1. A con-
      densation of "Off Broadway." The address "By Way of
      Preface" was delivered at Rutgers Univ. in October 1941.

278a. "A Confession," The New York Times, Dec. 5, 1954, II, 7.

279. "Conflict in Greece, The," New York Herald Tribune (Paris
      edition), Nov. 27, 1947.

280. "Critical Mr. New York," New York World, Mar. 9, 1934, 6E.

281. "Curtains--Iron and Asbestos," The New York Times, Feb. 16,
      1958, II, 3.

282. "Day Dreams," speech reported in The Student (Univ. of
      North Dakota student newspaper), XXIX, Nov. 18, 1909,
      p. 4. "The Ad Altiora meeting last Monday night [Nov.
      15th].... The following speeches were given: ... 'Day
      Dreams'--Mr. Anderson."

283. "Decapitation." Letter to the editor of The Student (Univ.
      of North Dakota student newspaper), XXIV, Apr. 19, 1911,
      p. 2. Signed: "--Maxwell Anderson."

284. "Democracy's Temple," Saturday Review of Literature, XXXII
      (Aug. 6, 1949), 135.

284a. "A Dramatist's Playbill," New York Herald Tribune, Sept. 19,
      1943, V, 1, 4.

285. "Epigrams" [11 in prose], The Nation, III (Dec. 15, 1920),
      689.

286. Flag Day Pageant. Educational Radio Script and Transcription
      Exchange. U.S. Office of Education [c.1944]. Written for
      the Writer's War Board. Library of Congress.

287. "Foreword," See Here, Private Hargrove, by Marion Hargrove.
      New York: Henry Holt, 1942, pp. ix-xi. MA tells in a
      greatly simplified but dramatically heightened way how and
      where he first met the inimitable Hargrove. He interested
      the Henry Holt company in Hargrove's book, which subse-
      quently became a best seller. Furthermore, he was Har-
      grove's friend and neighbor for several years in New City,
      N.Y.

287a. "A Foreword by the Playwright," Maxwell Anderson Festival.
      Pamphlet dated Sept. 29, 1958, and issued by the Dakota
      Playmakers of the Univ. of North Dakota in announcing the
      presentation of two MA plays in October of that year.

288. "Freedom in Greece," New York Herald Tribune (Paris edition), Nov. 25, 1947.

289. "Friendly Advice," The Freeman, I (Mar. 17, 1920), II [letter].

290. "Further Prejudiced Words on Amy Lowell," The Measure: A Journal of Poetry, No. 8 (Oct., 1921), 18.

291. "Get Mad, America!" The New York Times, Feb. 22, 1942, I, 8.

292. Guaranteed Life, The. Irvington-on-the-Hudson, N.Y.: Foundation for Economic Education [c.1950], pp. 10. Library of Congress.

293. "How a Play Gets Written: Diary Retraces the Steps," New York Herald Tribune, Aug. 21, 1949, V, 1-2. MA explains, without mentioning Francis Hackett's charge of plagiarism, how the play Anne of the Thousand Days developed in his mind independent of any particular published source of information.

294. "How Storm Operation Grew," National Theatre Conference Bulletin, VI (Jan., 1944), 21-26.

295. "How Will It Be Done Again?" The Freeman, II (Sept. 15, 1920), 9-10.

296. "Immortality in the Plays and Sonnets of Shakespeare." Master's thesis, Leland Stanford University, 1914.

297. "Incommunicable Literature," The Dial, LXVI (Nov. 2, 1918), 370.

298. "Inside Story of a Musical from Book to Broadway," Toledo Blade, Oct. [30], 1949. Taken from New York Herald Tribune.

299. "In Which the Author of Winterset Sets Forth His Reasons for Attempting a Modern Theme in Verse," The New York Times, Oct. 6, 1935, XI, 6.

300. "Journey to Jerusalem," The New York Times, Sept. 29, 1940, IX, 1, 2.

301. "Kurt Weill," Theatre Arts Monthly, XXXIV (Dec., 1950), 58.

302. [Letter] in Heywood Broun's column "It Seems to Me," The World, Oct. 23, 1923.

303. "Looking Back at Synge," The Measure: A Journal of Poetry, No. 4 (June, 1921), 20-21.

304. "Lost in the Stars; From the Idea to the Production," San Francisco Chronicle, Aug. 6, 1950.

305. "Love Letter to a University," The North Dakota Quarterly, XXXVIII (Winter, 1970), 89-90. Reprinted from Univ. of North Dakota Alumni Review, Dec. 5, 1958. Letter written Nov. 3, 1958. A copy can also be found in Avery's Letters.

306. "Maxwell Anderson Interview." Transcribed from a tape recorded interview conducted by Louis M. Starr, May 10, 1956, at MA's home. Oral History Research Office, Columbia University. Typescript is 34 pages. Edited version in Avery's Letters.

307. "Menace of World War III," The New York Times, Mar. 8, 1948.

308. "Mighty Critics, The," The New York Times, Feb. 16, 1947, II, 1-2.

309. "Modern Casuists," The Freeman, I (Aug. 25, 1920), 565.

310. "More Thoughts About Dramatic Critics," New York Herald Tribune, Oct. 10, 1948.

311. "New Theater, The." An MA talk mentioned in The Student (Univ. of North Dakota student newspaper), Apr. 28, 1910, p. 1. "During the rest of the week several lectures and talks of special interest will be given at the University.... At the Sock and Buskin meeting Friday night Max Anderson will give a talk on 'The New Theater.'"

312. "New York's Theatre" [editorial], The Measure: A Journal of Poetry, No. 34 (Dec., 1923), 17-19.

312a. "A Note on Modern Poetry," New Republic, XXVII (June 22, 1921), 112-13.

313. "Notes for a New Play," PM (New York City), Jan. 9, 1944, IV, n.p.

314. "Notes for Barefoot in Athens." Box #22, papers of the Playwrights Producing Company, Wisconsin State Historical Society, Madison, Wisc. Unpublished.

315. "Notes on Socrates," The New York Times, Oct. 28, 1951, II, 1-3.

316. "One Future for American Poetry," The Dial, LXVI (May 31, 1919), 568-69.

317. "On Government, Being a Brief Preface to the Politics of
      'Knickerbocker Holiday,'" The New York Times, Nov. 13,
      1938, IX, 1.

317a. "An Open Letter to Writers of Verse," The Measure: A Jour-
      nal of Poetry, No. 2 (Apr., 1921), 17-19.

318. "Playwright Tells Why He Wrote 'Joan' and How He Signed His
      Star," The New York Times, Dec. 1, 1946, II, 3.

319. "Plight of the Greek People, The," New York Herald Tribune,
      Dec. 1, 1947, p. 22.

320. "Preface," Four Verse Plays. New York: Harcourt, Brace &
      World, 1959, pp. v-viii.

321. "Preface," November Hereabout, by Amy Murray. New York:
      Henry Holt, 1940, pp. xiii-xv. Murray was an impoverished
      musician, singer, and poet who was MA's neighbor on South
      Mountain Road. November Hereabout is a collection of her
      poems.

322. "Prelude to Dramatic Poetry," The New York Times, Oct. 6,
      1935, XI, 1, 3.

323- "Prelude to Poetry in the Theatre," Preface to Winterset.
4.   Washington, D.C.: Anderson House, 1935, pp. v-xi; also
      Players Magazine, XII (Jan., 1936), 12-13, 31.

325- Review. The Blood Red Dawn, by Charles Caldwell Dobie.
6.   The Freeman, I (Aug. 11, 1920), 525-26.

327. Review. Dramatic Legends and Other Poems, by Padraic Col-
      um. The Measure: A Journal of Poetry. No. 22 (Dec.,
      1922), 17-18. Colum was one of those nine poets who, in-
      cluding MA, founded The Measure in 1921.

328. Review. European Theories of the Drama, by Barrett H.
      Clark. New Republic, XVIII (Mar. 29, 1919), 283-84.

329. Review. For Eager Lovers, by Genevieve Taggard. New Re-
      public, XXXIV (May 2, 1923), 276-78. Taggard was one of
      those nine poets, including MA, who founded The Measure
      in 1921.

330. Review. "Further Prejudiced Words on Amy Lowell"--MA's
      editorial reply to a reader, S. Foster Damon, who had com-
      mented on MA's review of Amy Lowell's Legends (see the
      Aug., 1921, issue). The Measure: A Journal of Poetry,
      No. 8 (Oct., 1921), 18.

331. Review. Hymen, by H[ilda] D[oolittle]. The Measure: A
     Journal of Poetry, No. 14 (Apr., 1922), 18.

332. Review. "Irish History in Little." The Measure: A Journal
     of Poetry, No. 15 (May, 1922), 17-18.

333. Review. The Keats Memorial Volume, published in New York
     and London by John Lane (no editor listed). The Measure:
     A Journal of Poetry, No. 10 (Dec., 1921), 17.

333a. Review. Legends, by Amy Lowell. The Measure: A Journal
     of Poetry, No. 6 (Aug., 1921), 17-18.

334. Review. The Moon and Sixpence, by W. Somerset Maugham.
     The Dial, LXVII (Nov. 29, 1919), 477-78.

335. Review. Nets to Catch the Wind, by Elinor Wylie. The Meas-
     ure: A Journal of Poetry, No. 11 (Jan., 1922), 18.

335a. Review. Priapus at the Pool, by Conrad Aiken. The Meas-
     ure: A Journal of Poetry, No. 18 (Aug., 1922), 16.

335b. Review. Punch: The Immortal Liar, by Conrad Aiken. The
     Measure: A Journal of Poetry, No. 3 (May, 1921), 25-26.
     Aiken was MA's favorite of all the contemporary poets.

336. Review. Rio Grande, by Harvey Ferguson. The Nation,
     CXXXVII (Aug. 16, 1933), 190-91. It was the reading of
     this book that inspired MA's Night over Taos.

337. Review. Salvo One: A Few Figs from Thistles, Poems and
     Four Sonnets, by Edna St. Vincent Millay. The Measure:
     A Journal of Poetry, No. 1 (Mar., 1921), 25-26.

338. Review. Second April, by Edna St. Vincent Millay. The
     Measure: A Journal of Poetry, No. 7 (Sept., 1921), 17.

339- Review. Slabs of the Sunburnt West, by Carl Sandburg.
40. The Measure: A Journal of Poetry, No. 17 (July, 1922),
     15-16.

341. "Revolution and the Drama, The," The Freeman, I (July 14,
     1920), 425-26.

342. "Robert E. Sherwood," The New York Times, Nov. 17, 1955,
     p. 35. Reprinted in Theatre Arts Magazine, XL (Feb.,
     1956), 26-27, 87; and in Time, LXVI (Nov. 28, 1955), 26.

343. "Scholar Too Late, The," The Dial, LXVII (Sept. 20, 1919),
     239-41.

344. "Socrates and His Gospel." Preface to Barefoot in Athens.
      New York: William Sloane, 1951, pp. vii-xvi.

345. "Stage Money," Colliers, LXXIX (May 28, 1927), 24, 30.

346. "Summons form Valley Forge," The New York Times Magazine,
      Feb. 22, 1942, p. 8.

347. "Temple of Democracy, The," Ladies' Home Journal, LXIV
      (Feb., 1947), 34-35.

348. "Thunder in the Index," The Measure: A Journal of Poetry,
      No. 1 (Mar., 1921), 23-25. This is the editorial for the
      first issue.

349. "To the Theatre Public," The New York Times, Mar. 4, 1946.

350. "Tribute to G. B. Shaw at 90," The New York Times, July
      26, 1946, p. 23. MA finally came to believe that Shaw was
      the greatest playwright of the age.

351. "What America Means to Me," America's Future [a magazine]
      (Jan., 1939), p. 23.

352. "Working with Kurt Weill," Theatre Arts Monthly, XXXIV
      (Dec., 1950), 58.

■ AUTOBIOGRAPHICAL SKETCHES

353. "Love Letter to a University." Dated Nov. 3, 1958, at his
home in Stamford, Connecticut. The University of North
Dakota, from which he graduated in 1911, was scheduled to
hold its Seventy-Fifth Anniversary Convocation and Faculty
Conference on November 6, 7, and 8, 1958. It invited the
University's most famous graduate to speak about "The Cultural Influence of the University" during the first day's
program and to receive an honorary doctorate degree. Unable to travel there because of sickness, he sent the present letter, which was duly read to the assembled alumni
and then published in the University of North Dakota Alumni Review, Dec. 5, 1958. The letter was reprinted in the
North Dakota Quarterly, XXXVIII (Winter, 1970), 89-90;
also in Letters, pp. 288-90. In this most affecting letter
MA points out not only some interesting biographical facts
about his life but what the chief value the university experience has for students in the creative arts.

354. "Maxwell Anderson Interview." This is a 34-page, typed
transcript of a tape recorded interview done at MA's home
at Stamford, Connecticut, on May 10, 1956, by Louis M.
Starr of the Oral History Research Office of Columbia University. Copyrighted in 1972 by The Trustees of Columbia
University. Transcript not corrected by MA. Published in
microform by Columbia University. Appears in Letters, pp.
301-18. This is certainly the most detailed account of his
life that he ever gave to an interviewer, and in doing so
committed a complete turnaround from his stance in 1930
when Burns Mantle, preparing his book American Playwrights
of Today, asked him for personal details about his life:
"When a man starts peddling personal stuff about himself
they should send a squad of strong-arm worms after him,
because he is dead" (facing p. 68).

■ LETTERS

355. Dramatist in America[:] Letters of Maxwell Anderson, 1912–
1958. Edited by Laurence G. Avery. Chapel Hill, N.C.:
Univ. of North Carolina Press, 1977. This is the only published collection thus far and it consists of 212 letters,
liberally annotated, on a wide variety of topics. Avery
acknowledges that MA "wrote at least several thousand letters" altogether. In Appendix IV he lists all of the omitted
letters known to him, identifying them by date, recipient,
place of composition, and type and location of the original.
Avery mentions four groups of letters that were not available to him for consideration, namely those to 1) Josephine
Herbst, at the Beinecke Rare Book and Manuscript Library,
Yale University (a collection subsequently opened to re-
searchers); 2) MA's sister Ethel Chambers and her family,
which letters are now controlled by her heirs, notably her
son Ralph R. Chambers; 3) MA's brother John Kenneth
Anderson, 827 King St., Olean, N.Y.; and 4) various other
Anderson family members, particularly MA's daughter Hesper,
which letters were deposited by his widow in 1973 at the
Humanities Research Center at the Univ. of Texas. Although Avery does not mention this, at least two other important gorups were also omitted, namely those to MA's
middle son, Alan H. Anderson, 170 S. Mountain Rd., New
City, N.Y.; and the widow, Mrs. Maxwell Anderson (referred to as Gilda Anderson in this bibliography), 141
Downes Ave., Stamford, Connecticut.
    Extremely few letters are available from the early period
of his life, such as up to and including his brief teaching
career at Polytechnic High School in San Francisco. The
restricted letters filed at the University of Texas deal with
the mental breakdown and suicide of his second "wife,"
Mab Maynard--Avery calls her by her natal name "Gertrude"
--and with the troubled love life of MA's daughter Hesper
and with her groundless accusations that he was in some
way responsible for Mab's death.

PART II:

SECONDARY WORKS

■ BOOK-LENGTH STUDIES OF ANDERSON

356. Bailey, Mabel Driscoll. Maxwell Anderson[:] The Playwright
as Prophet. New York: Abelard-Schuman, 1957. A short
book of dramatic criticism based on the author's Ph.D. dissertation. Brilliantly written. Many perceptive comments,
especially on Barefoot in Athens. Completed before MA had
quite finished his writing career. No biography.

357. Clark, Barrett H. Maxwell Anderson, the Man and His Plays.
New York: Samuel French, 1933. A pioneer study covering
some of the early plays. The biographical part consists of
six tiny pages--testimony to the playwright's polite refusal
to volunteer vita about himself. Clark was one of the earliest critics to recognize MA's unusual talent.

358. Shivers, Alfred S. Maxwell Anderson. Boston: Twayne,
1976. Based not only on a study of the dramatic works
themselves and on the published "secondary sources," but
on the archival materials at the Univ. of Texas and a cor-
respondence with knowledgeable Anderson relatives and
friends who volunteered a lot of fresh information about
the playwright and his art. As a result, the first chapter
offers much more biography than had yet appeared in print.
The remaining chapters consist of critical studies of the
major plays and some of the minor ones.

359. _____. The Life of Maxwell Anderson. Briarcliff Manor,
N.Y.: Stein and Day, 1983. This is the first full-length
biography, the fruit of 11 years of research and writing.
A passage in the Acknowledgements section reads: "This
biography is based on miscellaneous items published in
periodicals and books; on many letters included in Dr.
Laurence G. Avery's volume of the Anderson correspon-
dence ... as well as on many not included there; on diaries;
on business papers, such as those of The Playwrights Producing Company; on notes; on legal documents; on important
oral and unpublished written reminiscences from Anderson's
relatives and friends (most such accounts generated especially for this book); on a memoir that Anderson left with
... Columbia University; on family genealogical records; and
on hitherto unpublished photographs owned by the family."
The book includes photographs, a family genealogy, a

lengthy bibliography, a list of the Playwrights Company
productions, a list of Anderson's addresses, and a full index.

■ SHORTER ITEMS OF A GENERAL NATURE
ABOUT ANDERSON OR HIS WORK

360. Abbott, George. "Mister Abbot." New York: Random House,
      1963. Abbott, a friend of MA's, had acted in the role of
      Sverre Peterson in White Desert and then collaborated with
      MA in writing an early version of the melodrama called A
      Holy Terror.

361. Adams, Val. "Playwright Doing a Musical for TV," The New
      York Times, Jan. 6, 1955, p. 34. The article is about a
      90-minute version of Raft on the River, a musical based on
      Huckleberry Finn. MA's collaborator, Kurt Weill, had writ-
      ten five songs for it, but he died in 1950 before seeing the
      work to completion. Now MA was trying to get the assist-
      ance of other collaborators.

362. Albright, H. D.; William P. Halstead; and Lee Mitchell (eds.).
      Principles of Theatre Art. 2nd ed. Boston: Houghton
      Mifflin, 1968, pp. 334, 414, 428, 430.

363. Allison, Gordon. "New $1,000,000 Combine Enters New York
      Theater Field," New York Herald Tribune, July 21, 1953.

364. _____. "Television: Doing Dreams by Our Great Play-
      wrights," New York Herald Tribune, Oct. 28, 1951. This
      article is about the Celanese Theatre, a twice-weekly TV
      series of one-hour shows featuring adaptations of former
      Broadway plays, including some of MA's. Mab Maynard and
      Jerry Stagg (from the William Morris agency) had organized
      this program, which went far to raise the standards of tele-
      vision, even winning the Peabody Prize. On Oct. 31, 1951,
      Celanese presented Winterset. (Although the article doesn't
      say it, MA's future wife, Gilda Hazard, was working on the
      program as a production assistant when Anderson paid a
      visit during the rehearsals for Winterset; the two took an
      immediate interest in each other.)

365. Allison, Temple E. "The Pasadena Summer Festival," Players
      Magazine, XVI (Oct., 1939), 9-10, 20. The Fifth Annual
      Midsummer Drama Festival, held in the Pasadena Playhouse
      at Pasadena, Calif., devoted its entire program to MA's
      plays, a fact that should be of interest now when this play-
      wright is being ignored on Broadway and when it is fashion-

able for scholars to damn him with faint praise. Eight were
presented: Elizabeth the Queen, Valley Forge, The Wingless Victory, The Masque of Kings, Both Your Houses, Gods
of the Lightning, Winterset, and The Star-Wagon.

366. Anderson, Gilda. "Make Your Dreams Come True," National
      Sunday Magazine in Buffalo Evening News, Oct. 24, 1959,
      p. 5. The last Mrs. Maxwell Anderson recounts a sentimen-
      tal incident that occurred during MA's last days, viz., his
      long desired but long-put-off purchase of a copy of Shake-
      speare's famous First Folio. (A sad postscript: after An-
      derson's death she had to sell the book in order to help
      pay off a huge federal income tax debt that the playwright
      had incurred during his lifetime.)

367. Anderson, Hesper. "Someone Else," Part I. Unpublished.
      77 pp. Typescript written c.1973. Copies owned by Alfred
      S. Shivers, Hesper Anderson, and possibly one or two oth-
      er members of Maxwell Anderson's family.
           As of the date of this writing, Hesper's document is the
      closest thing to a biography of her father that has yet
      emerged from the family circle, and yet she herself explicit-
      ly discounts it as objective biography, preferring to con-
      sider it as a freely embellished "literary" portrait of herself
      as a young girl and teenager. Without exception, members
      of the Anderson family that I interviewed considered "Some-
      one Else" as shocking and, in some instances, unfairly
      slanted if not downright erroneous. The serious biographer
      should use it with caution. Weaving back and forth in time
      Hesper gives an agonizingly frank, melodramatic, myopic
      appraisal of her mother (Mab Maynard), her playwright
      father, plus some of Anderson's friends and neighbors in
      the artist's colony at New City, N.Y. Much of the document
      is given over to her long-drawn-out infatuation with a neigh-
      bor on South Mountain Road, one Marion Hargrove (See
      Here, Private Hargrove), who was a protegé of her father's.
      As for faults in "Someone Else," the statements are rarely
      qualified, there is no documentation, and the author shows
      no interest in being objective or in introducing supporting
      material from letters, diaries, legal documents, notes, etc.
      Part I takes the reader up to Hesper's sexual affair with
      Hargrove and her subsequent nervous breakdown. The au-
      thor promises to complete the book someday. Copy furnished
      to me courtesy of Dave Peters (Cambridge, Mass.).

368. Anderson, Jane McDill. Rocklandia[:] A Collection of Facts
      and Fancies, Legends and Ghost Stories of Rockland County
      Life. Nyack, N.Y.: Jane McDill Anderson, 1977. This is
      the book to consult for learning about the legends that form
      the background of MA's long residence in New City.

369. Anderson, John. The American Theatre (bound in one volume
with Rene Fulop-Miller's The Motion Picture in America).
New York: Dial Press, 1938, pp. 82-83, 92-95.

370. _____. "Dramatic Serenade to Success Tires Mr. Anderson,"
New York Journal, Dec. 28, 1935.

371. _____. "Playwright Declares Practical Men Always Find
Poets Ahead of Them," New York Evening Journal, May 5,
1937.

372. "Anderson, Maxwell." Academic American Encyclopedia, Vol.
I. Danbury, Conn.: Grolier Educ. Corp., 1982, p. 402.

373. "Anderson, Maxwell." Crowell's Handbook of Contemporary
Drama. Edited by Michael Anderson et al. New York:
Thomas Y. Crowell, 1971, pp. 12-13.

374. "Anderson, Maxwell." The Oxford Companion to American
Literature, 4th ed. Edited by James D. Hart. New York:
Oxford University Press, 1965, pp. 31-32.

375. "Anderson, Maxwell." Oxford Companion to the Theatre, 3rd
ed. Edited by Phyllis Hartnoll. London: Oxford University Press, 1950.

376. "Anderson, Maxwell." Reader's Encyclopedia of American Literature. Edited by Max J. Herzberg. New York: Thomas
Y. Crowell, 1962, pp. 32-34.

377. Anderson, Quentin. Unpublished funeral address delivered
by Quentin (MA's eldest son) at the time the father's ashes
were interred in the old Anderson cemetery near Geneva,
Pa., on Oct. 19, 1963. Three typed pages. Copy given
to me by the playwright's sister Lela Chambers.

378. Anderson, Robert Woodruff. Funeral address on Maxwell
Anderson delivered by Robert Anderson (no relation) at
Columbia University, Mar. 4, 1959. Printed in John F.
Wharton's Life Among the Playwrights (New York: Quad-
rangle, 1974), pp. 257-59, 261; also in my book The Life
of Maxwell Anderson (Briarcliff Manor, N.Y.: Stein and
Day, 1983), pp. 268-69. The ellipses found in these print-
ings do not represent omissions; they are the author's own.

379. Atkinson, Brooks. Broadway Scrapbook. Westport, Conn.:
Greenwood Press, 1970 [first published in 1947], pp. 43,
82, 145, 251-54.

380. _____. "Exercising the King's English," The New York
Times, Feb. 21, 1937, X, 1.

381. _____. "Ruminations of Anderson," The New York Times,
       June 4, 1939.

382. _____, and Albert Hirschfeld. The Lively Years 1920-1973.
       New York: Association Press, 1973, pp. 30-33, 80-84, 103-
       06, 213-15.

383. Avery, Laurence G. "Maxwell Anderson," Twentieth Century
       Dramatists, Part I. Detroit: Gale Research Co., 1981,
       pp. 23-35.

384. _____. "Maxwell Anderson: A Changing Attitude Toward
       Love," Modern Drama, X (Dec., 1967), 241-48.

385. _____. "The Maxwell Anderson Papers," The Library
       Chronicle of the University of Texas, VIII (Spring, 1965),
       21-33. This is a description of the Maxwell Anderson hold-
       ings in the Humanities Research Center at the Univ. of
       Texas, where one can find the largest such collection in
       the world. Three years later, Avery was to bring out his
       detailed and valuable book A Catalogue of the Maxwell An-
       derson Collection at the University of Texas.

386. Bailey, Mabel Driscoll. "Anderson, Maxwell," Dictionary of
       American Biography, Supplement Six 1956-1960. Edited by
       John A. Garraty. New York: Charles Scribner's Sons,
       1980, pp. 14-16. Contrary to what Bailey says here, both
       Sea-Wife and Gypsy were produced on the stage, the first
       one in amateur theaters (in 1932 at the University of Minne-
       sota, and in 1936 at Syracuse University), and the second
       one in the professional theater in New York City in 1927.
       Also, contrary to what Bailey says, MA had worked on the
       Herald newspaper in Grand Forks, N.D., during his under-
       graduate days there before he went to Stanford. Once he
       went to Stanford, he never worked on that paper again.
       Furthermore, he did not (as Bailey and a host of other
       writers affirm) actually marry Gertrude (Mab) Maynard.
       Instead, he simply lived with her as her husband, starting
       at sometime before his first wife died, in 1930, and extend-
       ing up into the summer of 1952, when he learned that Mab
       was being unfaithful to him. Nor did he share a common-
       law marriage with her, for this condition of grace was denied
       him by Chapter 606 of the New York State laws of 1933
       whereby, effective on Apr. 29, 1933, there could be no more
       common-law marriages entered into in New York State. (It
       was in the fall of 1933 that he first announced to his rela-
       tives, none of whom had attended his "wedding" or had any
       forewarning that it would take place, that he was now a
       married man and that Mab was his wife.) Many years later,
       MA told his third wife, Gilda, that he had never legally mar-
       ried Mab Maynard. I myself found no record of such a mar-

riage despite exhaustive inquiries among the bureaus of
vital statistics in those states where he was known to have
lived in 1932-33. Dr. Laurence Avery confessed to me that
he had found no such record either. The real domestic
situation was known to several members of the Anderson
family, but was kept secret from the public.

387. _____. Maxwell Anderson[:] The Playwright as Prophet.
New York: Abelard-Schuman, 1957. Originally a Ph.D.
dissertation, this book offers many sensitive insights into
some of the major dramas. No biography.

388. Behrman, S. N. People in a Diary: A Memoir. Boston:
Little, Brown, 1972, pp. 213, 217, 220-21, 224. (Published
in England as Tribulations and Laughter.) This book is of
special interest because the playwright-author was a friend
of Anderson's as well as a member of the Playwrights Producing Company with him for many years. He says that he
once turned down an offer of $30,000 from a reputable pub-
lisher to do a book on Anderson.

389. Beiswanger, George. "The Playwrights' Company[:] Promise
and Fulfillment," Theatre Arts, XXVII (May, 1943), 299-306.
Covers the history of the Company from its founding on
Apr. 12, 1938, up to 1943. The founding playwrights were
Anderson, Elmer Rice, Robert E. Sherwood, S. N. Behrman,
and Sidney Howard. All of them were desirous of avoiding
some of the restrictions and interference common in the
Broadway production circles by producing their own plays,
and this they did, profitably and harmoniously, much to
the surprise of many theater aficionados.

390. _____. "Politicians in American Plays," Theatre Arts,
XXVII (Dec., 1943), 741-50.

391. Bennett, Florence Mary. "A Contemporary Renaissance,"
Poet Lore, XXXVI (Mar., 1925), 126-35.

392. Bentley, Eric. In Search of Theater. New York: Alfred A.
Knopf, 1953, pp. 7-9, 267. Bentley was a Broadway theater
critic.

393. Bergin, Edward. "Poets and Players at Cuffs," Catholic
World, CXVIII (Dec., 1923), 347-54.

394. Bergman, Ingrid, and Alan Burgess. Ingrid Bergman[:]
My Story. New York: Delacorte Press, 1980, pp. 162-63,
167, 169-71, 173, 175, 178-79, 188, 270. She acted to
packed houses in Joan of Lorraine. However, she omits
mentioning her interference in the film script that Anderson
was doing later for Joan of Arc. Encouraged by her acting

coach, she insisted upon changes in the dialogue, e.g.,
literal translation of the Old French transcript of the trial
scene. She was all for historical accuracy. The result was
a dull, dull film.

395. Bird, Carol. "The Men Who Write the Hits," Theatre, XXXIX
     (Dec., 1924), 28, 50.

396. Blake, Ben. The Awakening of the American Theatre. New
     York: Tomorrow Publishers, 1935, p. 46.

397. Bliven, Bruce Ormsby. Five Million Words Later: An Auto-
     biography. New York: John Day, 1970, pp. 11-13, 15, 21,
     27-28, 30, 35. Anderson's friend and fellow student at
     Stanford University. Later they worked on the Globe news-
     paper together in New York City.

398. Block, Anita (Cahor). The Changing World in Plays and
     Theatre. Boston: Little, Brown, 1939. Block shares the
     left-wing slant common to literary and dramatic criticism in
     the 1930's. For instance she prefers the inartistic Gods of
     the Lightning to Anderson's so-called "confused escape
     plays," of which she says High Tor is a sample. The book
     is mainly of historical interest by giving us insight into the
     changing world of Marxist social criticism.

399. Blum, Daniel (ed.). A Pictorial History of the American
     Theatre[:] 100 Years 1860-1960. New York: Bonanza
     Books, 1956, pp. 210-11, 242, 247, et passim.

400. Bonin, Jane F. Major Themes in Prize-Winning American
     Drama. Metuchen, N.J.: Scarecrow Press, 1975, pp. 42,
     65, 102-05, 145-46.

401. Bottomley, Gordon. "Poetry Seeks a New Home," Theatre
     Arts Monthly, XIII (Dec., 1929), 920-26.

402. Breuer, Bessie. Take Care of My Roses. New York: Athen-
     eum, 1961. Bessie Breuer, wife of the painter and architect
     Henry Varnum Poor, and a neighbor of Anderson's on South
     Mountain Road in New City, N.Y., was a magazine writer
     who turned her hand to doing experimental short stories
     and novels that often were but thinly disguised accounts of
     people and events in her life. But the reviewers of Take
     Care of My Roses evidently had no inkling that it was a
     roman à clef involving one of America's most famous drama-
     tists and his successive wives. Several of Anderson's
     neighbors and relatives assured me that the character por-
     traits and events in the story are surprisingly like the
     originals, and these people readily made identifications. Nor
     did Breuer try much to hide this aspect of her art. In a

letter to Maxwell Anderson's son and wife, Mr. and Mrs.
Alan Anderson, written soon after the book appeared, she
clearly associates this book (which she could not "evade"
writing; it "rose up and blocked every exit") with the "torment" they had just experienced (the death of the playwright). Breuer told them she felt gratified that they found
so much "validity" in reading the "many incidents" she had
"invented," but she made no attempt to deny the real-life
basis of these and other incidents.

Despite the melodramatic material the story shows little
forward motion and often gets bogged down in stream-of-
consciousness narration. The author evidently assumes that
the people and events in the story are as fascinating to the
reader as they are to her and yet she will not budge an
inch to make them so.

Take Care of My Roses is about Mrs. Alma Salter, who
tries without success to mend her marriage with her novelist husband, 25 years her senior, and at last ends her life
by jumping off a cliff by the river.

The time in the story is the recent past, the locale a
riverside community rather like New City. Long years
ago, the grasping and ambitious Alma, who does stenogra-
phy to pay for her husband's voice lessons, deliberately
wrecks the idyllic marriage that Harvie has with his first
wife, the sweet and innocent Ellen. Although Ellen permits
him to have unlimited freedom to "experience life," i.e.,
to bed down with any woman who strikes his fancy, and he
is true to his promise in keeping her informed of his con-
quests, there comes a point where she cannot suffer this
disgraceful treatment any longer and she dies of a broken
heart.

In his second marriage, to Alma, Harvie finds out to his
disgust that she is being unfaithful to him and he leaves
home. A case of wounded male egotism, Breuer seems to
indicate; moreover, this cold, selfish, withdrawn man ought
to remember his own sins and take Alma back. But Salter
does not. Now he is in hot pursuit of the next feminine
prey in his life, Beryl. Alma kills herself.

The portrait of Gertrude (Mab) Maynard as Alma is strik-
ingly accurate and detailed, as Mab's daughter, Hesper,
and some other Anderson relatives told me. No doubt the
cold, unsympathetic depiction of Anderson under the name
of Harvie Salter owes something to Breuer's envy of the
playwright for his commercial success. Ida is a greatly
whitewashed version of Martha Stamper, the nosey and gos-
sipy housekeeper in the Anderson family. Other identifica-
tions include Morgan (Marion Hargrove), Dolly Engisch
(Lotte Lenya), Josepha (the Ukrainian Catholic washerwoman
Teppi), Beryl (Gilda Hazard), Via (composite of Quentin and
Hesper Anderson), and George Mills (the cuckolding Jerry
Stagg).

403. Bricker, Herschel L. Our Theatre Today. New York: Sam-
      uel French, 1953, pp. 173, 175, 350.

404. Brockett, Oscar G. Century of Innovation[:] A History of
      European and American Theatre and Drama Since 1870.
      Englewood Cliffs, N.J.: Prentice-Hall, 1973, pp. 485, 496-
      97, et passim.

405. _____. History of the Theatre. 3rd ed. Boston: Alleyn
      and Bacon, 1977, pp. 537, 539-41, 558.

406. _____. Modern Theatre[:] Realism and Naturalism to the
      Present. Boston: Allyn and Bacon, 1982, pp. 93, 97-99,
      119.

407. _____. The Theatre[:] An Introduction, 3rd ed. New
      York: Holt, Rinehart & Winston, 1974, pp. 361, 478.

408. Broussard, Louis. American Drama[:] Contemporary Allegory
      from Eugene O'Neill to Tennessee Williams. Norman, Okla.:
      Univ. of Oklahoma Press, 1962, pp. 4, 50, 117.

409. Brown, Harold. "Queen 'Mab' Rules Roost in Adapting Plays
      for 'Celanese Theater,'" New York Herald Tribune, Mar. 9,
      1952. This article is of special value because it is one of
      the extremely few that give us a glimpse of what the second
      Mrs. Maxwell Anderson was doing during her last few months
      alive. The job with Celanese meant a great deal to her; she
      was an ambitious woman and, besides that, she wanted to
      help relieve the tremendous federal income tax burden that
      lay on the family's shoulders ever since Anderson mishan-
      dled the money he had earned on the sale of the movie
      rights to Eve of St. Mark. By all accounts, Mab was an
      important figure in his life. She had been associated with
      him since around 1927, which period includes his most pro-
      ductive years and all his masterpieces. And although they
      did not actually marry, contrary to the claim they made,
      the world at large considered them husband and wife.
          This five-foot Gertrude (Mab) Maynard worked as a super-
      vising script writer on the twice-weekly TV program called
      Celanese Theatre of the Air. Her role was to read and re-
      read the past Broadway plays that they wanted to adapt
      and then assign the appropriate script writers; sometimes
      she made major changes in the adaptations turned in to her.
      Celanese had already presented her husband's Winterset,
      Elmer Rice's Counselor at Law, Rachel Crothers' Susan and
      God, and S. N. Behrman's No Time for Comedy. They were
      scheduling Saturday's Children for presentation on March
      19, using a script written by Alan Anderson and starring
      Mickey Rooney.
          Mab is quoted as saying that she tries hard to preserve

the emotional impact of the original plays. Although admittedly not a creative person, she is supposed to have developed a "rare, intuitive knowledge of the theater" owing to her intimate association with her husband during their "nineteen years of married life." Anderson never interferes with the adaptation of his plays, and rarely gives suggestions (actually they were barely on speaking terms, such was the disharmony of their personal relationsip). Not one of the playwrights has ever complained about the adaptations done thus far. Alex Segal does all the directing. Jerry Stagg chooses the stars for each show.

Not reported in this article is the emotional upheaval going on behind the scenes in the lives of Anderson, his companion, and her associate Jerry Stagg. Mab and Stagg were having an affair which Anderson would accidentally discover in July that year, an affair that would drive Anderson into the arms of another woman; split up Stagg's marriage and throw his wife, Maxine, into morbid seclusion; and, after bouts of depression at losing Anderson, send Mab to her death by suicide.

410. Brown, John Mason. The Ordeal of a Playwright: Robert E. Sherwood and the Challenge of War. New York: Harper & Row, 1970, pp. 35, 65, 71, 81. Sherwood, Anderson's friend and fellow playwright, practically abandoned his career in the theater when he went to Washington during World War II to give his services in the Office of War Information and to write some of F. D. R.'s speeches for him. He won his last Pulitzer Prize for writing the biography Roosevelt and Hopkins.

411. _____. "Two on the Aisle" column, New York Evening Post, Feb. 17, 1954.

412. _____. "What a Dramatist Must Be in Order to Survive," New York Evening Post, Apr. 3, 1937, p. 8.

413. _____. The Worlds of Robert E. Sherwood[:] Mirror to His Times 1896-1939. New York: Harper & Row, 1965, pp. xiv, 163, 237, 273, 306, 341, 372-80. Sherwood got his inspiration for becoming a playwright when he saw a production of What Price Glory. Not long after that he and Anderson became good friends and eventually became charter members of the Playwrights Producing Company. Although pacifists starting with World War I (during which Sherwood was grievously wounded) and extending up through much of the 1930's, by the end of the decade they were taking a militant stance in favor of America's involvement in World War II and the defense of democracy. Whereas Sherwood regarded Roosevelt as a hero, Anderson viewed the president's New Deal program with increasing suspicion wherever it led

to the enlargement of federal powers and the suppression of
individual liberties.

414. Buck, Philo M., Jr.; John Gassner; and H. S. Alberson
      (eds.). A Treasury of the Theatre[:] An Anthology of
      Great Plays from Ibsen to Odets. New York: Simon and
      Schuster, 1940, pp. 133-34.

415. Burdick, Jacques. Theatre. New York: Newsweek Books,
      1974, pp. 143-44.

416. Calverton, V. F. "Maxwell Anderson," Modern Monthly, X
      (May, 1937), 3-5.

417. Cameron, Kenneth M., and Patti P. Gillespie. The Enjoyment
      of Theatre. New York: Macmillan, 1980, p. 158.

418. Carmer, Carl. "Maxwell Anderson[:] Poet and Champion,"
      Theatre Arts Monthly, XVII (June, 1933), 437-446. Writing
      when MA had entered his golden decade of the 1930's and
      had published his first important verse play (Elizabeth the
      Queen), Carmer gives a sensitive and knowledgeable survey
      of MA's career. He points out correctly the man's "inten-
      sity of attack on things he believes to be unjust, poetic
      feeling, and greatness of ambition...." However, he insists
      that the man has talents which have not yet been developed
      in dramaturgy. MA early showed a remarkable persistence,
      even though by the end of 1925 only one of the six (actual-
      ly seven) plays he had worked on--and that one a collabo-
      ration--had been a commercial and artistic success.

419. Chambers, Ethel Mae. "Out of Dark and Bright," an 18-page,
      typed, incomplete, and unpubished autobiography containing
      only two short chapters, is the work of MA's older sister.
      The title is taken from MA's poem "Dust Remembering."
      This only known copy (Ethel is said to have destroyed the
      original) gives a touchingly sentimental and highly detailed
      description of the visits that Ethel made, at age six, with
      her family to Grandmother Charlotte Shepard's farm at At-
      lantic, Pa., and to grandfather James Anderson's farm at
      nearby Geneva. After completing these two richly detailed
      chapters she sent them to her brother Max for comment, and
      he replied in a handwritten, undated, three-page letter
      which he titled, "Footnote by Max." The sketch and the
      letter were probably written about 1956, when both writers
      were in their old age. No biographer of MA's would want to
      ignore these documents. The mss. are at the Univ. of
      Texas.

420. Chambers, Lela Blanch. ["Lela Chambers' Biographical Notes."]
      This document is typed, unpublished, and runs to 11 pages.

It was prepared by Lela Chambers for my use and mailed
to me in her letter of Apr. 26, 1972. Furnishes a chronol-
ogy of birthdates and family movements. Lela, the third
child in the family (b. 1891), is considered to be the "un-
official family historian." Of all the children, she and the
latest-born, Lawrence, were probably the most intimate with
the playwright. Other copy lodged with Lela Chambers.

421. _____"Life." This 178-page unpublished typescript was
written during the period 1960-1975. The emphasis is on the
lives in the close-knit Anderson family that began with the
marriage of William Lincoln Anderson to Charlotte Perrimela
Stephenson. Eight children came from this union, in this
order of birth: Ethel Mae, James Maxwell, Lela Blanch,
Harold Alfred, Ruth Virginia, the twins John Kenneth and
Dorothy Elizabeth, and Lawrence. The father, who early
became an itinerant Baptist preacher at Andover, Ohio,
moved his ever-enlarging family from one small community
to the next in Pennsylvania, Ohio, Iowa, and North Dakota.
It was practically an annual migration. Items that stand out
in Lela's account are the numerous hardships that all the
Andersons endured year after year. Max made gifts of
money to his parents and to the families of his brothers and
sisters (he gave considerable support to Lela and Ethel's
families during the Depression). Genteel in approach; significant omissions with respect to the lives of Max, Ruth
Virginia, and the parson father. Copy sent to me by Lela
Chambers.

422. Cheney, Sheldon. The Theatre[:] Three Thousand Years of
Drama, Acting and Stagecraft. New York: David McKay,
1958, pp. 463, 522, 569.

423. Childs, Herbert Ellsworth. "Playgoer's Playwright: Maxwell
Anderson," English Journal, XXVII (June, 1938), 475-85.
The defects in MA the dramatist are 1) his failure to com-
pose great dramatic poetry, and 2) his lack of a philosophy
that would give one courage to act rather than simply suc-
cumb to pessimism and despair. The first failure, Childs
tells us, is "probably caused by the inescapable comparison
of his historical plays with the blank verse of Shakespeare."
As for the second failure, MA should try to show us the
"fun and dignity" in struggling to win at least the minor
battles of life, even though the sophisticated intellect knows
that the war against hostile circumstances is lost even before we are born; that is, we need to be able to "hope for
a temporary delusion of victory before we die." The author
is confident that MA will continue to be read and staged after he dies.

424. Chinoy, Helen K., and Linda W. Jenkins. Women in American
Theatre. New York: Crown, 1981, pp. 219, 247, 250.

425. Churchill, Allen. The Theatrical Twenties. New York:
     McGraw-Hill, 1975, pp. 111, 113-14, 127, 191, 242, 301.

426. Clark, Barrett H. Maxwell Anderson, the Man and His Plays.
     New York: Samuel French, 1933, pp. 3-32. Pioneer study
     on MA. The remarkable shortness of the biography is ow-
     ing to the fact that the dramatist was unwilling to supply
     Clark with any vita. "This modern craze for biographical
     information leaves me cold for many reasons," he wrote to
     Clark. Nevertheless, a sympathetic study.

427. _____. "Stallings and Anderson," An Hour of American
     Drama. Philadelphia: J. P. Lippincott, 1930, pp. 89-95.

428. Clark, Norman. "Five Playwrights After Prosperous Year
     Look Ahead," The Baltimore News-Post, Aug. 2, 1939.

429. Clemens, Cyril. "James Branch Cabell, Robert W. Service
     and Maxwell Anderson," Hobbies[:]   The Magazine for Col-
     lectors, LXIV (Jan., 1960), 107-08.

430. Clurman, Harold. All People Are Famous. New York: Har-
     court Brace Jovanovich, 1974, p. 245. Clurman was a
     Broadway director.

431. _____. The Divine Pastime[:]   Theatre Essays. New York:
     Macmillan, 1974, pp. 79, 157, 175, 194.

432. _____. The Fervent Years[:]   The Story of the Group
     Theatre and the Thirties. New York: Alfred A. Knopf,
     1945 (revised 1957).

433. _____. "Maxwell Anderson," Lies LIke Truth. New York:
     Macmillan, 1958, pp. 33-35, 255.

434. _____. "Theatre: Maxwell Anderson," New Republic,
     CXIX (Dec. 27, 1948), 29.

435. _____. "The Theatre of the Thirties," Tulane Drama Re-
     view, IV (Dec., 1959), 3-11. Surveys the theatrical era
     during which MA wrote his greatest plays. Clurman gives
     some attention to MA's colleagues in the Playwrights Produc-
     ing Company.

436. Collijn, Gustaf. "Maxwell Anderson," Bonniers Litterara Maga-
     sin, IX (Nov., 1940), 689-93.

437. Cooper, Charles W. Whittier[:]   Independent College in Cali-
     fornia. Los Angeles: Ward Ritchie Press, 1967, pp. 127-
     28, 130-32, 219, 261. Gives a picture of Whittier and its
     faculty at the time when MA taught English there. It in-

cludes details about the Arthur Camp episode in which the
future playwright defended a draft dodger's right to free
speech and then fell under the pressure of the administra-
tion and the community to moderate his libertarian ways
(the madness of pro-war sentiment and star-spangled patri-
otism was then at its height). MA left the school under
pressure, never again to return to teaching.

438. Curley, Dorothy Nyren, and Maurice Kramer. Library of
Literary Criticism[:] Modern American Literature, Vol. I.
New York: Frederick Ungar, 1969, pp. 32-35.

439. Davidson, David. "Playwright Honestly Dislikes These Reve-
latory Stories About His Struggles and Triumphs," New
York Post, Apr. 2, 1937.

440. Deutsch, Helen. "A Playwright and Poet," New York Herald
Tribune, Sept. 22, 1935, 1, 5. Making use of one of the
very few personal interviews that MA ever gave, Deutsch
gives some biographical details not available elsewhere about
the playwright's upbringing, the father's activities, the un-
dergraduate education at Univ. of North Dakota, and many
other bits and pieces that help round out what was for 1937
a most obscure life. Deutsch errs where she says that MA
went from Whittier directly to the copy desk of the San
Francisco Bulletin. He actually went first into teaching,
at Polytechnic High School in San Francisco. Deutsch was
a press agent.

441. _____. "When Drama and Poetry Wed, Was It to Last Forever After?" New York Herald Tribune, May 31, 1936, 1-2.

442. Dickinson, Thomas H. "The Theatre of Maxwell Anderson,"
Theatre Time, II (Spring, 1950), 93-97.

443. Downes, Alan S. (ed.). The American Theatre Today. New
York: Basic Books, 1967, pp. 18, 26-27, 29, 36, 44, 47,
155.

444. _____. Fifty Years of American Drama. Chicago: Henry
Regnery, 1951, pp. 105-10.

445. _____. Recent American Drama. Minneapolis: Univ. of
Minnesota Press, 1964, pp. 13, 18-19, 21.

446. Driver, Tom F. Romantic Quest and Modern Query. New
York: Delacorte Press, 1970, pp. 296, 299, 302-03.

447. Duffus, Robert Luthur. The Tower of Jewels[:] Memories
of San Francisco. New York: W. W. Norton, 1960, pp.
205-09. Duffus tells about a walking trip that he and MA

and Herman Rosse took together in the summer of 1917,
starting at the Mission of San Juan Batista, west of San
Jose, to the coast and thence up to Santa Cruz. Duffus
was at the time a San Francisco journalist; Rosse, an archi-
tect.

448. Durham, Frank. Elmer Rice. New York: Twayne, 1970, pp.
      108, 119.

449. Dukore, Bernard, et al. (eds.). "Maxwell Anderson (1888-
      1959)," McGraw-Hill Encyclopedia of World Drama, Vol. I.
      New York: McGraw-Hill, 1972, pp. 49-56.

450. Dusenbury, Winifred L. "Myth in American Drama Between
      the Wars," Modern Drama, VI (Dec., 1963), 294-308.

451. _____. The Theme of Loneliness in Modern American Drama.
      Gainesville: Univ. of Florida Press, 1960, pp. 119-25.

452. Eastman, Max. "By the Eternal," Stage, XIV (Apr., 1937),
      51-52. Eastman seriously claims that MA is a better play-
      wright than Shakespeare. But whereas the audience goes
      away from Shakespeare's tragedies feeling greater as mem-
      bers of the human race, it senses at the end of MA's
      tragedies a spiritual defeat. Even High Tor ends in gen-
      eral surrender for the hero (and by implication, for the
      audience).

453. Eaton, Walter Prichard. The Drama in English. New York:
      Charles Scribner's Sons, 1930, pp. 170, 315-16, 263.

454. _____. "The Drama in 1933," American Scholar, III (Win-
      ter, 1934), 96-101.

455. _____. "He Put Poetry Back on the Stage," New York
      Herald Tribune, Jan. 28, 1934, 12-13, 21.

456. _____. "Revolt from Realism," Virginia Quarterly Review,
      X (Oct., 1934), 515-28.

457. Fields, William. "Authors Who Have Made Stage History,"
      New York Herald Tribune, Nov. 6, 1940. Fields was the
      public relations man for the Playwrights Producing Company.

458. _____. "Maxwell Anderson: Some Fond Memories," The
      New York Times, Mar. 8, 1959, II, 3. As an associate and
      friend of MA's for many years in the Playwrights Producing
      Company, Fields wrote soon after the man's death that no
      one could be luckier than to have had the playwright call
      him a friend; that Fields was often appalled at the "spectac-
      ular scope" of MA's philanthropies, which far exceeded his
      means; that his friend was a hardy and humble and good man.

459. Flexner, Eleanor. American Playwrights: 1918-1938 The
      Theatre Retreats from Reality. Freeport, N.Y.: Books
      for Libraries, 1969, pp. 78-129. Discusses many of the
      plays in a perceptive manner.

460. Fleischmann, Wolfgang Bernard (ed.). "Maxwell Anderson,"
      Encyclopedia of World Literature in the 20th Century. New
      York: Frederick Ungar, 1967, Vol. I, p. 47.

461. Fort, Alice Buchanan, and Herbert S. Kates. "Maxwell An-
      derson and Laurence Stallings," Minute History of the Drama.
      New York: Grosset & Dunlap, 1935, p. 136.

462. Foster, Edward. "Core of Belief: An Interpretation of the
      Plays of Maxwell Anderson," Sewanee Review, L (Jan.,
      1942), 87-100.

463. Freedley, George, and John A. Reeves. A History of the
      Theatre. New York: Crown, 1968, pp. 643, 651, 834, 879,
      890.

464. Freedman, Morris. American Drama in Social Contest. Car-
      bondale: Southern Illinois Univ. Press, 1971, pp. 19, 61,
      82.

465. Frenz, Horst (ed.). American Playwrights on Drama. New
      York: Hill and Wang, 1968, pp. 16-21, 43-51.

466. Gagey, Edmond McAdoo. Revolution in American Drama. New
      York: Columbia Univ. Press, 1947, pp. 77-88.

467. Gard, Robert E., et al. (eds.). Theater in America[:] Ap-
      praisal and Challenge. New York: Theatre Arts Books,
      1968, pp. 59, 136.

468. Garfield, David. A Player's Place[:] The Story of the Actors
      Studio. New York: Macmillan, 1980, pp. 23, 67, 144-45.

469. Gassner, John. "Anchors Aweigh: Maxwell Anderson and
      Tennessee Williams," Theatre Time, I (Spring, 1949), 5-11.
      Also published in Gassner's Dramatic Soundings (see below).

470. _____. Dramatic Soundings. New York: Crown, 1968,
      pp. 43, 114, 149, 151, 298, 301-02, et passim.

471. _____. Form and Idea in Modern Theatre. New York:
      Dryden Press, 1956, pp. 6, 12, 73, 102, 143, 254.

472. _____. "Maxwell Anderson, Realist and Romancer," Masters
      of the Drama, 3rd ed. New York: New Directions, 1954,
      pp. 65, 665, 678-83.

473. _____. "The Possibilities and Perils of Modern Tragedy,"
     Tragedy[:] Vision and Form. 2nd ed. New York:
     Harper & Row, 1982, p. 304. Article originally published
     in Tulane Drama Review (1957).

474. _____. "Prospectus on Playwrights," Theatre Arts Monthly,
     XXXVIII (Nov., 1954), 31-32, 93.

475. _____. "The Theatre at the Crossroads," One-Act Play
     Magazine, I (July, 1937), 271-81.

476. _____. The Theatre in Our Times. New York: Crown,
     1954, pp. 233-39, et passim.

477. _____. "The Theatre in Praise of New York," One-Act
     Play Magazine, I (Mar., 1938), 941-51.

478. _____, and Edward Quinn. "Anderson, Maxwell," The
     Reader's Encyclopedia of World Drama. New York: Thomas
     Y. Crowell, 1969, p. 16.

479. _____, and Ralph G. Allen. Theatre and Drama in the
     Making. Boston: Houghton Mifflin, 1964, pp. 824, 826-27,
     829, 984.

480. Geiger, Louis G., and J. R. Ashton. "UND in the Era of
     Maxwell Anderson," The North Dakota Quarterly, XXV
     (Spring, 1957), 55-60. A description of the University of
     North Dakota campus, its faculty, its student body, and so
     forth during the period 1908-1911.

481. Geisinger, Marion. Plays, Players, & Playwrights. New York:
     Hart Publishing Co., 1975, pp. 509, 532, 534, 536, et pas-
     sim.

482. Gerstenberger, Donna. "Verse Drama in America: 1916-1939,"
     Modern Drama, VI (Dec., 1963), 309-22.

483. Gilder, Rosamond, et al. (eds.). Theatre Arts Monthly[:]
     A Record and a Prophecy. New York: Theatre Arts Books,
     1948, pp. 457, 632-34, 649.

484. Goldberg, Isaac. "The Later Maxwell Anderson," The One-
     Act Play Magazine, I (May, 1937), 89-90.

485. Goldman, William. The Season[:] A Candid Look at Broadway.
     New York: Harcourt, Brace & World, 1969, p. 413.

486. Goldstein, Malcolm. The Political Stage[:] American Drama
     and Theater of the Great Depression. New York: Oxford
     Univ. Press, 1974, pp. 8-9, 113-16, 342-43, et passim.

487. Goodman, Randolph. *Drama on Stage*. New York: Holt,
      Rinehart & Winston, 1961, pp. 12-13, 280.

488. Gordon, Max, and Lewis Funke. *Max Gordon Presents*. New
      York: Bernard Geis Associates, 1963, pp. 181, 269.

489. Gottfried, Martin. *A Theatre Divided[:] The Postwar Ameri-
      can Stage*. Boston: Little, Brown, 1967, p. 189.

490. Gould, Jean R. *Modern American Playwrights*. New York:
      Dodd Mead, [1966], pp. 118-34. Interestingly written sum-
      mary of MA's life and career.

491. Gray, [Henry] David. "Anderson at Stanford," *Prompter*,
      Vol. IV, No. 3 (Mar., 1938), p. 7 (Palo Alto Community
      Players, Palo Alto, Calif.). MA's former teacher at Stan-
      ford gives an unflattering picture of what the student was
      like. "... I confess, to my chagrin, that I saw little prom-
      ise of a Broadway success in Anderson when he took the
      course in Playwriting at Stanford." He says he recalls the
      work of a dozen to twenty students there which showed
      more promise than did MA's! See MA's essay "The Scholar
      Too Late" for what is surely a satirical picture of Gray.

492. Gregory, Horace. "Poets in the Theatre," *Poetry*, IIL (July,
      1936), 221-28.

493. Guernsey, Otis L., Jr. *Playwrights, Lyricists, Composers on
      Theater*. New York: Dodd, Mead, 1974, pp. 62, 283, 401.

494. Hagan, John P. "Frederick H. Koch and North Dakota:
      Theatre in the Wilderness," *North Dakota Quarterly*,
      XXXVIII (Winter, 1970), 75-87. MA took Shakespeare un-
      der Prof. Koch at the Univ. of North Dakota; he also be-
      longed to the Sock and Buskin dramatic society, which Koch
      sponsored. He spoofed the loveable Professor in one of his
      university plays. After leaving the Univ. of North Dakota,
      where he had begun to teach the writing of folk plays,
      Koch went on to another illustrious career at the Univ. of
      North Carolina.

495. Hage, Sylvia. "Anderson Festival Ends This Week," *Dakota
      Student* (Univ. of North Dakota student newspaper), Nov.
      6, 1958, p. 1.

496. Halline, Allan G. "American Drama and World War II," *Buck-
      nell University Studies*, II (Oct., 1950), 71-73, 79.

497. _____. "Maxwell Anderson's Dramatic Theory," *American
      Literature*, XVI (May, 1944), 68-81. Obtaining the theory
      from MA's critical essays, this study outlines the important

features and compares them with what goes on in his plays.
Halline correctly concludes that the theory achieved its first
full development in Mary of Scotland. Also, that the use
of the theory did not guarantee artistic or commercial success.

498. Halsey, William D., et al. (eds.). "Anderson, Maxwell,"
     Collier's Encyclopedia. New York: Macmillan Corp., 1978,
     Vol. II, pp. 183-84.

499. Hand, Ramond T. B. "Maxwell Anderson's New House,"
     House Beautiful, LXXVIII (Aug., 1936), 36-37. Hand gives
     left-handed praise to MA's expensive new house that he had
     built for himself at 170 S. Mountain Rd. in New City, N.Y.
     Local artisans and craftsmen had wrought such things as
     the stained glass, the furniture, the paintings, the ceramic
     tile. Hand omits to mention that this big house--what Elmer
     Rice had described as "hideous"--represented an enlargement
     of a simple, idyllic cottage that MA had first built on the
     property. The motif in the new house is functionalism and
     simplicity of design.

500. Hargrove, Marion. "Mr. Maxwell Anderson, Legendary Genius,
     Refuses to Act the Part," The Charlotte [N.C.] News (Mar.
     9, 1942). Hargrove, a brilliant young writer that MA met
     at Fort Bragg, N.C., in the spring of 1942 while he was
     gathering materials for Eve of St. Mark, gives his amusing
     impressions of the man whose friendship and encouragement
     were about to change the course of his life. Hargrove does
     not mention it in this article, but MA had just recently
     read some of Hargrove's ms. about soldier life in an army
     camp and recommended the work to a publisher. By the
     end of that year See Here, Private Hargrove would be a
     national best-seller.

501. _____. "Poor Sergeant Donald Bishop Is Broken on the
     Wheel of Fortune," The Charlotte [N.C.] News (Apr., 1942).
     Another sample of Hargrove's wit. Sergeant Bishop, un-
     aware that the famous MA was occupying a barrack cot at
     Fort Bragg overnight, and thinking him to be someone else,
     brusquely roused him from his sleep the next morning.
     Both men were embarrassed. The incident was so magnified
     out of proportion that it finally reached the pages of Time
     magazine and The New York Times.

502. Harris, Ainslie. "Maxwell Anderson[:] Poet and Playwright,"
     The Madison Quarterly, IV (Jan., 1944), 30-44. Excellent
     criticism. Harris is one of a tiny handful of critics who
     penetrate to the real meaning of Esdras' speech over the
     fallen lovers at the end of Winterset. Most critics either
     misunderstand the speech or consider it boring.

503. Hassan, Ihab. Contemporary American Literature 1945-1972.
New York: Frederick Ungar, 1973, p. 138.

504. Hatcher, Harlan. "Drama in Verse: Anderson, Eliot, Mac-
Leish," English Journal, XXV (Jan., 1936), 1-9.

505. _____. Modern American Dramas. New Edition. New York:
Harcourt, Brace, 1949, pp. 65-71.

506. Healey, Robert C. "Anderson, Saroyan, Sherwood: New Directions," Catholic World, CLII (Nov., 1940), 174-80.

507. Heffner, Hubert C.; Samuel Selden; and Hunton D. Sellman
(eds.). Modern Theatre Practice[:] A Handbook of Play
Production, 4th ed. New York: Appleton-Century-Crofts,
1959, pp. 47, 77, 96, 472.

508. Heiney, Donald. Recent American Literature. Woodbury,
N.Y.: Barron's Educational Series, 1958, pp. 369-76, 589.

509. _____, and Lenthiel H. Downs. Recent American Literature
After 1930. Woodbury, N.Y.: Barron's Educational Series,
1974, pp. 277-85, 429.

510. Helburn, Theresa. A Wayward Quest[:] The Autobiography
of Theresa Helburn. Boston: Little, Brown, 1960, pp.
239, 240-43. Helburn, long associated with the Theatre
Guild, was one of its prime directors. The Guild produced
all these Anderson plays: Elizabeth the Queen, Mary of
Scotland, Both Your Houses, Valley Forge, and The Masque
of Kings. Unlike MA, Helburn did not believe that the
playwright should have anything to do with the production
of the play except make occasional revisions in the script
as needed. Her attitude, made a Guild policy, helped drive
MA and some of his colleagues to leave the Guild, an otherwise admirable organization that did much to raise the level
of Broadway fare, and create the Playwrights Producing
Company, in which the member dramatists had considerable
freedom in planning each production.

511. Henderson, Mary C. The City and the Theatre. Clifton,
N.J.: James T. White, 1973, p. 257.

512. Herbst, Josephine. Money for Love. New York: Coward-
McCann, 1929. According to Herbst's biographer, Elinor
Langer, this early novel has a plot that "bears a marked
resemblance to her [Herbst's] recent attempt to get money
from Maxwell Anderson to begin a new life with John [Herr-
mann]" (p. 71 of Josephine Herbst). The novelist had recently had a love affair with Anderson that resulted in her
pregnancy. She paid for the expense of the abortion her-

self and then proceeded to blackmail the playwright, who
cheerfully gave her money in return for the love letters
that he had sent.

513. _____. "Unmarried" (retitled "Following the Circle"). Unpublished novel whose ms. is at Yale University. According
to Elinor Langer, this novel "follows her recent experiences
so closely that it is literally impossible to tell whether a
notebook labeled 'New York' among her papers [at Yale] is
a diary of her affair with Maxwell Anderson or a workbook
for the novel. It could be either or both" (Josephine
Herbst, p. 71). The story in the novel parallels the known
facts of Herbst's life quite closely: an unwed woman falls
in love with a married man, gets pregnant by him, has an
abortion, and her sister has an abortion too, after which
the sister dies. But the story remains incomplete. Written
c.1920.

514. Hewes, Henry. "American Playwrights Self-Appraised," Saturday Review of Literature, XXXVIII (Sept. 3, 1955), 18-19.

515. Hill, Frank Ernest. "Reminiscences of Frank Ernest Hill."
Transcript from interviews conducted by Dr. Donald F.
Shaughnessay in 1960 and 1961. Oral History Research Office at Columbia University. Runs to 611 pages. Refer-
ences to MA occur on pp. 134-36, 160-61, 163-71, 176-77,
205-07, 268-70, 288-92, et passim. Of all of MA's friends
who left written memoirs, Hill devotes the most space to
him, even though their association seems to wane after
1936, probably owing to the snobbery of the playwright's
companion Mab Maynard, who evidently thought Hill un-
qualified to move in her illustrious "husband's" circle. Hill
worked with MA on the Globe, lived across the road from
him in New City, read his friend's poems and plays and
offered criticism, and showed a good understanding of MA's
talents and limitations. But Hill himself, like his friend,
was not a great poet. Nevertheless, he wrote numerous
books, including a modern English translation of The Can-
terbury Tales (1940).

516. Himelstein, Morgan Yale. Drama Was a Weapon[:] The Left-
Wing Theatre in New York 1929-1941. New Brunswick,
N.J.: Rutgers Univ. Press, 1963, pp. 129-30, 133, 140,
et passim.

517. Hoffman, Frederick J. The Twenties[:] American Writing in
the Postwar Decade. New York: Viking, 1955, pp. 80,
360, 396.

518. Hogan, Robert C. The Independence of Elmer Rice. Carbon-
dale: Southern Illinois Univ. Press, 1965, pp. 5, 90, 143-
44, 148, 150.

519. Hollingsworth, Harry. "A Man Without a Country[:] James
     Peterson, Sr. Alias James Sutton of Crawford County,
     Pennsylvania," The American Genealogist, LI (July, 1975),
     158-61. The article records the search for an MA ancestor.

520. Houghton, Norris. The Exploding Stage. New York: Wey-
     bright and Talley, 1971, pp. 54, 100, 102.

521. Houseman, John. Run-Through[:] A Memoir. New York:
     Simon and Schuster, 1972, pp. 88n, 135, 136-42.

522. Hulme, Kathryn C. Undiscovered Country[:] A Spiritual
     Adventure. Boston: Little, Brown, 1966, pp. 6, 16.
     Hulme was a student in MA's English class at Polytechnic
     High School in San Francisco. Later, she attended the
     premiere performance of What Price Glory in Stamford,
     Connecticut. One of her novels is the best-seller The
     Nun's Story.

523. Isaacs, Edith J. R. "Maxwell Anderson," The English Jour-
     nal, XXV (Dec., 1936), 795-804.

524. _____. "Range of Life in One Man's Plays," The Theatre
     Arts Monthly, XVIII (Aug., 1934), 601-06.

525. Jackson, Esther M. "Maxwell Anderson: Poetry and Morality
     in the American Drama," Educational Theatre Journal, XXV
     (Mar., 1973), 15-33.

526. Johnson, Alvin. Pioneer's Progress. Lincoln: Univ. of
     Nebraska Press, 1960, p. 272. On this page Johnson tells
     that he hired MA for editorial work on The New Republic
     mainly on the basis of having read one spirited and daring
     poem by the future playwright: "Sic Semper."

527. Kaufman, Julian M. Appreciating the Theater: Cues for
     Theatergoers. New York: David McKay, 1971, p. 312.

528. Ker, Walter. Journey to the Center of the Theater. New
     York: Alfred Knopf, 1979, p. 46.

529. Kernodle, George R. Invitation to the Theatre. New York:
     Harcourt, Brace & World, 1967, pp. 76, 106-07, 221, 228,
     307, 427.

530. Koch, F[rederick] H[enry]. "The Dakota Playmakers: An
     Historical Sketch," The Quarterly Journal of the University
     of North Dakota, IX (Oct., 1918), 14-30. The article is a
     revelation of the kind of innovative theater professor that
     Koch (who had taught MA) was. Koch had organized the
     Dakota Playmakers at the Univ. of North Dakota, a group

devoted to writing folk plays and performing them. Two of
MA's plays, Sea-Wife and High Tor, contain folk elements.

531.   _____. "Making a Regional Drama," Bulletin of The American Library Association, XXVI (Aug., 1932), 468.

532.   _____. "Towards a New Folk Theatre," The Quarterly
Journal, XX (May, 1930), 167-68.

533. Koebel, Mary McGavran. "Anderson Tips 'Inside' of Playwright's Trade," Ohio State Journal (Columbus, Ohio),
Oct. 21, 1950.

534. Krutch, Joseph Wood. The American Drama Since 1918. New
York: George Braziller, 1957 (originally published 1939),
pp. 286-318.

535.   _____. "An American Drama," Literary History of the
United States. Edited by Robert E. Spiller et al. New
York: Macmillan, 1953, pp. 1320-23.

536.   _____. "The Meaning of the Modern Drama," The Nation,
CXLI (Sept. 18, 1935), 320-23.

537.   _____. "Modernism" in Modern Drama. New York: Cornell University, 1966, pp. 102, 109, 112, 117-24, 129.

538.   _____. "The New American Drama," The Nation, CXXX
(June 11, 1930), 678-79.

539.   _____. "The Theatre," America Now[:] An Inquiry into
Civilization in the United States. Edited by Harold Edmund Stearns. New York: Scribner's Sons, 1938, pp. 72-
81.

540. Kulp, Margaret Becker. "Chatterbox" column, The Patriot
(Harrisburg, Pa.), Jan. 16, 1942.

541. Kunitz, Stanley J., and Howard Haycraft (eds.). "Anderson, Maxwell," Twentieth Century Authors. New York :
H. W. Wilson, 1942, pp. 23-24.

542. Langer, Elinor. Josephine Herbst. New York: Little,
Brown, 1984, pp. 10, 55-58, 60-62, 65-66, et passim.
This book is significant in that it reveals for the first time
MA's affair in 1920 with the left-winger novelist Josephine
Herbst. The book also contains two of MA's poems that are
not published elsewhere.

543. Langner, Lawrence. The Magic Curtain. New York: E. P.
Dutton, 1951, pp. 252-53, 256-57, 268, 335. Like Helburn,

Langner was one of the dominant figures in the Theatre
Guild, which produced several MA plays.

544. Lee, Henry G. "Maxwell Anderson's Impact on the Theatre,"
North Dakota Quarterly, XXXV (Spring, 1957), 49-52.

545. Leifur, Barbara. "Leading American Playwright UND Graduate," Dakota Student (Univ. of North Dakota student newspaper), Mar. 7, 1956, p. 6.

546. Leonard, Baird. "Theatre." Life, XCVI (Nov. 21, 1930), 14.

547. Leonard, William Torbert (ed.). Theatre: Stage to Screen
to Television. Metuchen, N.J.: Scarecrow Press, 1981.
2 volumes. Contains detailed surveys of the following as
they appeared on the stage, the screen, and TV: Elizabeth
the Queen, Mary of Scotland, Key Largo, Masque of Kings,
Winterset, Knickerbocker Holiday, Saturday's Children, and
A Christmas Carol (play written expressly for TV).

548. Lerner, Alan Jay. The Street Where I Live. New York:
W. W. Norton, 1978, p. 35. Lerner, composer of musicals
for Broadway and Hollywood, was a neighbor of MA's in
New City.

549. Lewis, Allan. American Plays and Playwrights of the Contemporary Theatre. New York: Crown, 1965, pp. 100, 130,
140, 141-42, 222, and 225.

550. Lewis, Emory. Stages[:] The Fifty-Year Childhood of the
American Theatre. Englewood Cliffs, N.J.: Prentice-Hall,
1969, pp. 38, 42, 50, 59-60, 70, 83, 218.

551. Littell, Robert. "Where Are the New Playwrights?" Theatre
Arts Monthly, XIII (Jan., 1929), 11-12.

552. Little, Stuart W., and Arthur Cantor. The Playmakers. New
York: W. W. Norton, 1970, pp. 136, 243-44, 292.

553. Logan, Joshua. Josh: My Up and Down, In and Out Life.
New York: Delacorte, 1976, pp. 133-34. As a young
Broadway director he helped bring Knickerbocker Holiday
to the stage.

554. Loggins, Vernon. I Hear America ... Literature in the
United States Since 1900. New York: Biblo and Tannen,
1967 (originally published 1937), pp. 12, 71, 100-03, et
passim.

555. Luccock, Halford E. (ed.). Contemporary American Literature
and Religion. New York: AMS Press, 1970 (reprint of the
1934 edition), pp. 13, 119, 257, 338, et passim.

556. _____, and Frances Brentano. The Questing Spirit[:]
     Religion in the Literature of Our Time. New York:
     Coward-McCann, 1947, pp. 279-80, 477-88, 570-79, 597-98.

557. Lumley, Frederick. Trends in 20th Century drama. Fair-
     lawn, N.J.: Essential Books, 1956, pp. 125, 225.

558. McCalmon, George, and Christian Moe. Creating Historical
     Drama. Carbondale: Southern Illinois Univ. Press, 1965,
     pp. 5, 146, 185, 204-07.

559. McCarthy, John F. X. "Anderson, Maxwell," Record of Amer-
     ica[:] A Reference History of the United States. New
     York: Charles Scribner's Sons, 1974, Vol. I, p. 100.

560. McCarthy, Mary Therese. Sights and Spectacles 1937-1956.
     New York: Farrar, Straus and Cudahy, 1956, pp. 6-8, 48,
     69, et passim.

561. _____. Theatre Chronicles, 1937-1962. New York: Far-
     rar, Straus, 1963, pp. 7-8, 77-78, 166.

562. Macgowan, Kenneth. The Living Stage[:] A History of the
     World Theater. Englewood Cliffs, N.J.: Prentice-Hall,
     1955, pp. 429, 487.

563. MacLeish, Archibald. "The Poet as Playwright," The Atlantic,
     CXCV (Feb., 1955), 49-52.

564. _____. "A Stage for Poetry," Stage, XIII (Nov., 1935),
     38-39.

565. McCord, Bert. "Play About Charles II," New York Herald
     Tribune, Sept. 5, 1952. MA announces a new play under-
     way (title not revealed, but it will be Cavalier King).

566. McGrath, Thomas, and Marian Points. "Maxwell Anderson:
     Portrait in Pencil," The Shaft: A Literary Magazine, IV
     (Spring, 1938), 19. McGrath and Points, who were students
     at the Univ. of North Dakota during this era, derived some
     of their information from Prof. Gottfried Hult (who had
     been one of MA's teachers). Because they did not take the
     trouble to interview or correspond with MA or any of his
     relatives, certain errors crept into this sketch. For in-
     stance the authors claimed that MA worked in the Commons,
     but quit after only a day because he could not remember
     the orders given to him. MA's sister Lela, who was there
     at the time, told me that her brother worked there quite a
     while ("I used to eat at the Commons and he was there").
     Otherwise, the portrait that McGrath and Points give is
     highly appreciative, even rhapsodic.

567. _____, and _____. "Maxwell Anderson: Portrait in Pen-
     cil," The North Dakota Quarterly, XXXIII (Winter, 1965),
     10-13. Reprint of the preceding article.

568. Magill, Frank N. (ed.). "Maxwell Anderson," Cyclopedia of
     World Authors. Rev. ed. Englewood Cliffs, N.J.: Salem
     Press, 1974, Vol. I, pp. 55-56.

569. Maney, Richard. Fanfare; The Confessions of a Press Agent.
     New York: Harper & Brothers, 1957, pp. 73, 123, 179, et
     passim.

570. Mantle, Burns. "Maxwell Anderson," American Playwrights of
     Today. New York: Dodd, Mead, 1930, pp. 65-72. As
     one of the early champions of MA, he frequently printed
     MA plays in the Best Plays series that he edited.

571. _____. Contemporary American Playwrights. New York:
     Dodd, Mead, 1938, pp. 37-46.

572. _____. "How 5 Playwrights Decided on Benefits for German
     Refugees," New York News, Nov. 19, [1938]. The five
     dramatist members of the Playwrights Producing Company,
     having been stirred into action by MA's concern for the
     plight of German refugees who were pouring into America
     from Nazi Germany, decided on a way to provide these peo-
     ple with economic assistance. During an intermission in the
     production of Knickerbocker Holiday, MA stood up before
     the audience and asked for contributions. He also an-
     nounced that the Company and all who were involved in the
     production were waiving that night's earnings for the sake
     of the refugees. Robert E. Sherwood, over at the Plymouth
     Theatre that same night, made a similar speech.

573. Markowitz, Robert. "Anderson Believed America Is Growing
     Wiser with Age," The New York Times, Mar. 24, 1959.
     MA's last public interview.

574. Marsh, George. "The American Theatre Since the War," Sat-
     urday Review (London), CXLIX (June 21, 1930), 779-80.

575. Matlaw, Myron (ed.). "Anderson, Maxwell," Modern World
     Drama[:] An Encyclopedia. New York: E. P. Dutton,
     1972, pp. 23-24.

576. "Maxwell Anderson (1888-1959)," Encyclopedia International.
     Fairfax, Va.: Lexicon Publications, 1982, Vol. I, pp. 389-
     90.

577. Maxwell, Elsa. "Elsa Maxwell's Week-End Round-Up" column.
     New York Post, May 11, 1946.

108   Part II: Secondary Works

578. Mersand, Joseph E. The American Drama Since 1930[:] Es-
     says on Playwrights and Plays. Port Washington, N.Y.:
     Kennikat Press, 1961 (originally published 1949), pp. 23,
     47, 89, et passim.

579. _____. "Maxwell Anderson: Dramatist of the Future,"
     The High School Thespian (Nov., 1939), 8, 13.

580. _____. "Maxwell Anderson: Dramatist of the Future,"
     The Play's the Thing. Port Washington, N.Y.: Kennikat
     Press, 1968, pp. 49-54. Reprint of the above article.

581. _____. "Speech in the New Plays[:] The Poetic Dramas
     of Shakespeare and Maxwell Anderson Dominate the New
     York Stage," Correct English, XXXVII (Mar., 1937), 68-
     69, 94; continued in Part II (Apr., 1937), 117-18.

582. Meserve, Walter J. Robert E. Sherwood[:] Reluctant Moral-
     ist. New York: Pegasus, 1970, pp. 38-39, 50, 77, 102,
     et passim.

583. Miller, Jordan Y. "Maxwell Anderson: Gifted Technician,"
     The Thirties: Fiction, Poetry, Drama. Edited by Warren
     French. Deland, Fla.: Everett Edwards, 1967, pp. 183-92.
     Condescending treatment of MA's plays.

584. Miller, J. William. Modern Playwrights at Work. London:
     Samuel French, 1968, Vol. I, pp. 392, 397, 402, et passim.

585. Millett, Fred B., and Gerald Eades Bentley. The Art of the
     Drama. New York: Appleton-Century-Crofts, 1935, p. 77.

586. Milstead, John. "The Structure of Modern Tragedy," West-
     ern Humanities Review, XII (Aug., 1958), 365-69.

587. Mordden, Ethan. The American Theatre. New York: Oxford
     Univ. Press, 1981, pp. 101-07, 121-22, 151-54, et passim.

588. Morehouse, Ward. Matinee Tomorrow[:] Fifty Years of Our
     Theatre. New York: Whittlesey House, 1949, pp. 19, 197-
     99, 241, et passim.

589. Morris, Lloyd R. "Across the Footlights," Postscript to Yes-
     terday; America: The Last Fifty Years. New York: Ran-
     dom House, [1947], pp. 195-99.

590. Morton, Frederick. "Playwright's Craft," Theatre Arts Month-
     ly, XXIII (Aug., 1939), 612. Favorable review of The Es-
     sence of Tragedy.

591. Moses, Montrose J. "The Emancipation of the American Dra-
     ma," Current History, XXVI (Aug., 1927), 733-40.

592. _____. "The Theatre in America," North American Review, CCXIX (Jan., 1924), 82-91.

593. Muller, Herbert J. The Spirit of Tragedy. New York: Alfred A. Knopf, 1968, pp. 315-16.

594. Nannes, Caspar Harold. Politics in the American Drama. Washington, D.C.: Catholic Univ. Press of America, 1960, pp. 92-96.

595. Nathan, George Jean. The Magic Mirror. New York: Alfred A. Knopf, 1960, p. 224.

596. _____. The Theatre of the Moment. Cranbury, N.J.: Fairleigh Dickinson Univ. Press, 1970 (originally published in 1936), pp. 233-38.

597. The National Cyclopedia of American Biography. Clifton, N.J.: James T. White, 1981, pp. 323-25.

598. Nichols, Lewis. "Talk with a Self-Critical Author," The New York Times, Jan. 18, 1959, II, 5.

599. Nicoll, Allardyce. World Drama. Rev. edition. New York: Harper & Row, 1976, pp. 702, 735-38, 741-42.

600. Norton, Elliot. "Theatre: A Tribute," New York Herald Tribune, July 15, 1951.

601. Nyren, Dorothy (ed.). "Anderson, Maxwell (1888-1959)," A Library of Literary Criticism[:] Modern American Literature. 3rd edition. New York: Frederick Ungar, 1964, pp. 15-17.

602. O'Hara, Frank Hurbert. "Tragedies Without Finality," Today in American Drama. New York: Greenwood Press, 1969, pp. 1-52.

603. _____, and Margueritte Harmon. Invitation to the Theater. New York: Harper & Brothers, 1951, pp. 34, 59, 96, 133, 187.

604. Olson, Elder. Tragedy and the Theory of Drama. Detroit: Wayne State Univ. Press, 1961, p. 257.

605. Ormsbee, Helen. "From Bothwell to George Washington," New York Herald Tribune, Dec. 9, 1934.

606. Palmieri, Anthony F. R. Elmer Rice: A Playwright's Vision of America. Cranbury, N.J.: Associated Univ. Presses, 1980, pp. 23, 95, 168.

607. Parks, E. W. "Maxwell Anderson," Revista do Instituto Brasil-
      Estados Unidos (Rio de Janeiro), VII (Jan.-Feb., 1949),
      18-21.

608. Paxton, John. "The Finding of the Golden Fleece," Stage,
      XVI (Jan., 1939), 27-30, 73. About the members of the
      Playwrights Producing Company.

609. Phodna, Joe. "New Rules for Picking Plays," New York Her-
      ald Tribune, Aug. 3, 1947, p. 2.

610. _____. "Theatre News: Playwrights Company Are Again
      Active," New York Herald Tribune, Nov. 14, 1948.

611. Pickering, Jerry V. Theatre[:] A Contemporary Introduc-
      tion. St. Paul, Minn.: West Publishing Co., 1975, p. 21.

612. Poggi, Jack. Theater in America[:] The Impact of Economic
      Forces 1870-1967. Ithaca, N.Y.: Cornell Univ. Press,
      1968, pp. 131, 133, 271, 274.

613. Pollock, Arthur. "Mr. Anderson and Words," Brooklyn Daily
      Eagle, Feb. 14, 1937, section C.

614. Porter, Thomas E. Myth and the Modern Drama. Detroit:
      Wayne State Univ. Press, 1969, p. 181.

615. Poynter, Henry. "Pulitzer Prize Stirs Drama Row," New York
      Post, May 2, 1934.

616. Price, Julia S. The Off-Broadway Theater. New York:
      Scarecrow Press, 1962, pp. 17, 34, 44, 148-49, 203, 233.

617. Prior, Moody E. The Language of Tragedy. Bloomington:
      Indiana Univ. Press, 1966 (first published in 1947), pp.
      317-26.

618. Quinn, Arthur Hobson. A History of the American Drama
      from the Civil War to the Present Day. New York: Apple-
      ton-Century-Crofts, 1936, pp. 233-35, 266-71.

619. _____. "Real Hope for the American Theatre," Scribner's
      Magazine, XCVII (Jan., 1935), 30-35.

620. Quinn, Kerker. "Poets into Playwrights," Virginia Quarterly
      Review, XIII (Autumn, 1937), 616-20.

621. Rabkin, Gerald. Drama and Commitment Politics in the Amer-
      ican Theatre of the Thirties. Bloomington: Indiana Univ.
      Press, 1964, pp. 28, 30, 32, 38, et passim.

622. Rahv, Philip. "The Men Who Write Our Plays," American
      Mercury, L (Aug., 1940), 463-69.

623. Reed, Edward. "Playwrights Afield," Theatre Arts Monthly,
      XVIII (June, 1934), 453-54.

624. Rice, Elmer. The Living Theatre. New York: Harper &
      Row, 1959, pp. 126-28, 137, 141, et passim. Rice was a
      friend and a fellow member in the Playwrights Producing
      Company.

625. _____. Minority Report: An Autobiography. New York:
      Simon & Schuster, 1963, pp. 374-75, 378-80, 383-84, et
      passim.

626. Rice, Patrick J. "Maxwell Anderson and the Eternal Dream,"
      Catholic World, CLXXVII (Aug., 1953), 364-70. Rice finds
      fault with MA as a tragedian for not having a clear religious
      or philosophical faith, because the possession of such a faith
      has been the inspiration of the great artists of the past.
      MA has also mistakenly tried to make art take the place of
      the religion that he has lost or never had. His so-called
      tragedies deviate too much from what Aristotle prescribed,
      accepting only the "recognition scene" and the "hamartia,"
      and uses these for purposes that Aristotle had not intended.
      Therefore, MA manages to create glorious spectacles but not
      tragedies.

627. Rice, Robert. "Maxwell Anderson[:] A Character Study of
      the Most Talked of Playwright in America Based on the First
      Interview He Has Granted Since 1937," PM's Sunday Picture
      News, III (Nov. 29, 1942), 23-27. This is the most accurate
      and detailed newspaper interview about his life and work that
      reached print. Notable in the coverage of the early days:
      the character of MA's father, the Rev. Anderson; school
      days; marriage; teaching; motive for writing first play (de-
      sire for money!); the unforgettable public response to What
      Price Glory. Rice caught MA during one of his rare con-
      fidential moods, for there is much in the article that is not
      found elsewhere.

628. Richardson, Kenneth, and R. Clive Willis (eds.). "Anderson,
      Maxwell," Twentieth Century Writing[:] A Reader's Guide
      to Contemporary Literature. Levittown, N.Y.: Transatlan-
      tic Arts, 1967, p. 19.

629. Riepe, Dale. "The Philosophy of Maxwell Anderson," The
      North Dakota Quarterly, XXIV (Spring, 1956), 45-50.

630. Roberts, C. L. "In the Days of Peg Top Trousers," The
      North Dakota Quarterly, XXV (Spring, 1957), 52-54. A

nostalgic account of student life at the Univ. of North Dakota during MA's era, written by a friend and fellow-
student.

631. Roberts, Vera Moury. On Stage: A History of the Theatre.
      2nd ed. New York: Harper & Row, 1962, pp. 426, 436-37.

632. _____. The Nature of Theatre. New York: Harper &
      Row, 1971, pp. 141, 164, 208.

633. Rodell, John S. "Maxwell Anderson: A Criticism," Kenyon
      Review, V (Spring, 1943), 272-77.

634. Rosenberg, Harold. "Poetry and the Theatre," Poetry: A
      Magazine of Verse, LVII (Jan., 1941), 258-63.

635. Rowe, Kenneth Thorpe. A Theater in Your Head. New York:
      Funk & Wagnalls, 1960, pp. 10, 146-48, 151-52, 179.

636. Samachson, Dorothy, and Joseph Samachson. Let's Meet the
      Theatre. New York: Abelard-Schuman, 1954, pp. 147-48,
      152.

637. Sampley, Arthur M. "Theory and Practice in Maxwell Ander-
      son's Poetic Tragedies," College English, V (May, 1944),
      412-18.

638. Sanders, Ronald. The Days Grow Short: A Life and Music
      of Kurt Weill. New York: Holt, Rinehart and Winston,
      1980, pp. 373-75, 392-95, 313, et passim.

639. Sandoe, James L. "The Case for Maxwell Anderson," Colorado
      College Publications: Studies Series. No. 30 (Apr. 1,
      1940), 73-82.

640. Sedgwick, Ruth Woodbury. "Maxwell Anderson, Playwright
      and Poet," Stage, XIV (Oct., 1936), 54-56. Several bits
      of firsthand information about MA's life not otherwise avail-
      able in print, such as the detailed description of the study
      cabin. But Sedgwick errs where she says that MA does
      not revise his plays.

641. Seldes, Gilbert. "The People and the Arts," Scribner's Maga-
      zine, CI (Mar., 1937), 68-70. The author calls MA the
      "second most significant of our serious playwrights."

642. Sheaffer, Louis. O'Neill[:] Son and Artist. Boston: Little,
      Brown, 1973, p. 660.

643. Sherwood, Robert E. "'White Desert' to 'Bad Seed,'" Theatre
      Arts Monthly, XXXIX (Mar., 1955), 28-29, 93.

644. Shivers, Alfred S. Maxwell Anderson. Boston: Twayne,
      1976, pp. 176. The first chapter provides the most bio-
      graphical information on MA to see print until the Life
      (see next item) came out seven years later. Chapters 2-4
      contain discussions of the individual plays. Chapter 5
      draws conclusions about MA's dramatic literature.

645. _____. The Life of Maxwell Anderson. Briarcliff Manor,
      N.Y.: Stein and Day, 1983, pp. 397. Along with the
      biographical materials there are discussions of the individual
      plays and the significance of these in the context of the
      author's total work and the times in which he lived. Back-
      grounds of the individual works. Many descriptions of MA's
      friends and colleagues, especially those in the Playwrights
      Company. There is also a discussion of MA's novel Morning
      Winter and Night. Hardly anything at all about his short
      stories; a little more about his poems. Photographs. Fam-
      ily genealogy. Appendixes.

646. Sievers, Wieder David. Freud on Broadway. New York:
      Heritage House, 1955, pp. 171-79.

647. Skinner, Richard Dana. "Man and His Bootstraps," The In-
      dependent, CXIII (Oct. 11, 1924), 263.

648. _____. "The Pulitzer Award," Commonweal, XVIII (May
      19, 1933), 73-74.

649. _____. "Pulitzer Prize Drama Winner," Literary Digest,
      CXV (May 20, 1933), 15.

650. _____. "The Theatre--Ten Years," Commonweal, XXI
      (Nov. 2, 1934), 19-20.

651. Sper, Felix. From Native Roots[:] A Panorama of Our Re-
      gional Drama. Caldwell, Ida.: Caxton Printers, 1948, pp.
      60, 211.

652. Steinberg, M. W. Aspects of Modern Drama. New York:
      Holt Rinehart & Winston, 1960, pp. 1-2, 72-78.

653. Steiner, George. Death of Tragedy. New York: Alfred A.
      Knopf, 1961, p. 312.

654. Stevenson, Philip. "Concerning M. Anderson: A Word About
      the Career and Thoughts of the War Dramatist," The New
      York Times, Jan. 9, 1944, II, 1.

655. _____. "Maxwell Anderson: Thursday's Child," New
      Theatre, III (Sept. 3, 1936), 5-7, 25-27.

656. Szeliski, John von. Tragedy and Fear[:] Why Modern Drama
      Fails. Chapel Hill: Univ. of North Carolina Press, 1971,
      pp. 36, 42-43, 224-26, et passim.

657. Taubman, Howard. The Making of the American Theatre.
      New York: Coward McCann, 1965, pp. 178-79, 265, 273,
      et passim.

658. Taylor, William Edwards. "Maxwell Anderson: Traditionalist
      in a Theatre of Change," Modern American Drama: Essays
      in Criticism. Deland, Fla.: Everett/Edward, 1968, pp. 47-
      57.

659. Tees, Arthur T. "Legal and Poetic Justice in Maxwell Ander-
      son's Plays," North Dakota Quarterly, XXXVIII (Winter,
      1970), 25-31.

660. _____. "Maxwell Anderson's Changing Attitude Toward
      War," North Dakota Quarterly, IIL (Fall, 1980), 5-11.

661. _____. "Maxwell Anderson's Liberated Women," North
      Dakota Quarterly, XXXXII (Spring, 1974), 53-59.

662. Thompson, Alan Reynolds. The Anatomy of Drama. Berke-
      ley: Univ. of California Press, 1946, pp. 385-91.

663. Tietjens, Eunice. The World at My Shoulder. New York:
      Macmillan, 1938, pp. 257-58. Tietjens was briefly MA's
      neighbor in New City. She was consoled by him in the
      theater when her play Arabesque failed on the stage in
      1925 and left her disconsolate.

664. Tynan, Kenneth. Curtains. New York: Atheneum, 1961,
      p. 257.

665. Unsigned. Obituaries.

          on Gertrude (Mab) Maynard (MA's companion):

          a) The New York Times, Mar. 23, 1953.

          b) New York Daily Mirror, Mar. 23, 1953.

          c) Time, XLI (Mar. 30, 1953), 82.

          d) Newsweek, XLI (Mar. 30, 1953), 70.

          on Margaret Ethel Anderson (MA's first wife):

          e) The New York Times, Feb. 7, 1930, p. 21.

on Maxwell Anderson:

f) The New York Times, Mar. 1, 1959, I, 84.

g) Newsweek, LIII (Mar. 9, 1959), 82.

h) Time, LXXIII (Mar. 9, 1959), 84.

i) "Rites Held for Greenwood Township Native Son," The
Meadville [Pa.] Tribune, Oct. 21, 1963. Refers to the
final disposition of MA's ashes: burial in the old Anderson family cemetery near Geneva, Pa. Error in obitu-
ary: MA was not born in, nor did he ever live in the
Greenwood Township; instead, in the East Fallowfield
Township, just west of there.

666. _____. "About the Author," Theatre Arts Monthly, XXX
(June, 1949), 58.

667. _____. "Academy of Arts Adds 6 Members," The New
York Times, Dec. 10, 1955.

668. _____. "Anderson Asks $100,000," The New York Times,
May 21, 1949. This is the amount of the countersuit that
MA lodged against Francis Hackett for libel. Hackett had
charged him with plagiarizing materials from Hackett's works
to write Anne of the Thousand Days.

669. _____. "Anderson Calls Drama Critics 'Jukes Family,'"
New York Herald Tribune, Mar. 4, 1946. One of several
broadsides leveled by MA against the Broadway drama critics,
who, he claimed, had a life-or-death stranglehold on all
plays presented there.

670. _____. "Anderson Files Action Against Francis Hackett,"
Publisher's Weekly, CLV (June 4, 1949), 2301.

671. _____. "Anderson Going to Africa," The New York Times,
Jan. 24, 1943. The trip to North Africa during WWII
helped him obtain materials for Storm Operation.

672. _____. "Anderson Has Avoided the Spotlight," Brooklyn
Daily Eagle, Jan. 12, 1936.

673. _____. "Anderson Is Cool to Pulitzer Prize," The New
York Times, Apr. 6, 1936. On the previous day he had
received the Drama Critics' Circle Award for Winterset, an
award which he said he preferred to the Pulitzer because it
comes from judges who are more qualified in their area of
expertise.

674. _____. "Anderson on Broadway," Prompter, Vol. IV, No.
     3 (Mar., 1938), 3-7 (Palo Alto Community Players, Palo
     Alto, Calif.).

675. _____. "Anderson's Drama to Go On in Britain," The New
     York Times, May 1, 1943.

676. _____. [Anderson sells part of New City estate], The
     New York Times, July 11, 1953, p. 9.

677. _____. "Anderson, Stefansson Among Noted Alumni on
     Program," Dakota Student (Univ. of North Dakota student
     newspaper), Oct. 24, 1958, p. 1. Because of illness, MA
     did not attend this 75th anniversary conference of alumni.

678. _____. "Authors, Actors Fight Propaganda," New York
     World-Telegram, Jan. 31, 1941.

679. _____. "Benefit Performance for German Refugees," The
     New York Times, Nov. 21, 1938, I, 4. MA, the Playwrights
     Producing Company, the actors, and the stagehands putting
     on Knickerbocker Holiday donated the money from one night's
     performance to help the refugees fleeing Nazi Germany.

680. _____. [Biographical note], Scholastic, XXXVII (Jan. 13,
     1941), 20.

681. _____. "The Box Office," Theatre Arts Monthly, XXI
     (July, 1937), 576-77.

682. _____. "British Benefit Won't Say Hitler Is Dog and Ape,"
     New York Herald Tribune, Feb. 20, 1941.

683. _____. [Court approves '54 handwritten will made in Calif.;
     rejects two others made in Conn. and N.Y.; bequests],
     The New York Times, Sept. 29, 1959, p. 36.

684. _____. [Court rejects handwritten unwitnessed '57 will],
     The New York Times, Apr. 9, 1959, p. 26.

685. _____. "The Critic's Award," Christian Science Monitor
     Monthly, XXIX (Mar. 31, 1937), 14.

686. _____. "Dialogue Poetical...," Pasadena Playhouse News
     (April, 1938), 5, 11, 15.

687. _____. "Drama Critics Choose Anderson's Drama for Sea-
     son's Honors," New York World-Telegram, Mar. 27, 1936.

688. _____. "Drama for an Hour," Time, LIX (May 5, 1952),
     88, 91. Reports that Celanese Theatre, the TV program

that Gertrude (Mab) Maynard worked on, won the 1952 Peabody Award this week for plays done with "fidelity, intelligence, and scrupulous regard for the intentions of the playwright." The adapting work was being done under Mab's supervision.

689. _____. "Dramatist and Poet," The New York Times, Mar. 2, 1959.

690. _____. "Dramatist Wins Point in Protest Against Piggery," New York Herald Tribune, Aug. 14, 1940. MA had protested against the foul odors emanating from a piggery in his neighborhood at New City, N.Y.

691. _____." "Five Playwrights Organize Own Producing Unit," New York Herald Tribune, Mar. 8, 1938. This marked the formation of the Playwrights Producing Company, of which MA was now a member.

692. _____. "Francis Hackett Sees His Books in 'Anne' Play," New York Herald Tribune, May 18, 1949, p. 19. Hackett, a former colleague of MA's on the New Republic, had sued Anderson claiming plagiarism from three of his works: a biography, Henry the Eighth (1929); a novel, Queen Anne Boleyn (1939); and a play, Anne Boleyn, completed in 1942 but neither published nor produced.

693. _____. "Franklin's Ideas Seem Lost Today," The New York Times, May 27, 1954.

694. _____. "Get Interfaith Awards," New York Herald Tribune, Feb. 3, 1950. MA received the Brotherhood Award from the National Conference of Christians and Jews for his contribution to racial relations as embodied in the play Lost in the Stars.

695. _____. "High Tide in American Plays," Literary Digest, LXXVII (Apr. 7, 1923), 35.

696. _____. "Hollywood Gets Drubbing from the Dramatists," New York Herald Tribune, May 27, 1927.

696a. _____. "Institute Gives Drama Medal to Anderson," New York World-Telegram, Apr. 1, 1954. On May 26th, MA had received in absentia the Gold Medal for Drama from the American Academy and National Institute of Arts and Letters in New York.

697. _____. "Jury Selects Prize Play; Award Barred by Advisers," New York Journal, May 2, 1934. MA received the Pulitzer Prize for Both Your Houses.

698. _____. "Little Tor Area Given to State by Huntington,"
     New York Herald Tribune, Mar. 10, 1948. This area ad-
     joins High Tor, which inspired MA's play by that name.

699. _____. [Making money is incentive for MA writing his
     plays], The New York Times, Dec. 5, 1954, II, 7.

700. _____. "Many New Faculty Members Are Appointed This
     Year," The Quaker Campus (Whittier College student news-
     paper), Sept. 20, 1917, p. 1. Includes notice that MA is
     joining the English department; later he will become depart-
     ment head.

701. _____. "Maxwell Anderson," Current Biography Who's
     News and Why. New York: H. W. Wilson, 1942, pp. 18-21.

702. _____. "Maxwell Anderson," Scholastic, XXVI (Feb. 16,
     1935), 11.

703. _____. "Maxwell Anderson," Stage, Aug. 3, 1939, p. 11.

704. _____. "Maxwell Anderson," Theatre Arts Monthly, XI
     (July, 1927), 532.

705. _____. "Maxwell Anderson," Vogue, CI (Feb. 1, 1943),
     80-83.

706. _____. "Maxwell Anderson: Young Dramatist," Stage
     (London newspaper), Aug. 3, 1939, p. 11.

707. _____. "Maxwell Anderson Demanded and Got 'House One
     Could Live In,'" New York Herald Tribune, Aug. 2, 1936,
     X, 1, 6. Refers to the building of the new house on South
     Mountain Road in New City, N.Y.

708. _____. [Maxwell Anderson elected to membership in Na-
     tional Institute of Arts and Letters] The New York Times,
     Jan. 17, 1935, p. 21.

709. _____. "Maxwell Anderson Files Libel Action," New York
     Herald Tribune, May 21, 1949. A countersuit against Fran-
     cis Hackett, who had accused him of plagiarism.

710. _____. [Maxwell Anderson gets Columbia University honor-
     ary degree; speaks at alumni luncheon], The New York
     Times, June 5, 1946, p. 16.

711. _____. "Maxwell Anderson Gets Drama Critics' Plaque,"
     New York Herald Tribune, Apr. 2, 1937. This concerns
     MA's award for High Tor.

712. _____. [Maxwell Anderson gives mss. to Univ. of North
Dakota], The New York Times, Nov. 12, 1957, p. 45.

713. _____. "Maxwell Anderson Has Avoided the Spotlight,"
Brooklyn Daily Eagle, Jan. 12, 1936.

714. _____. "Maxwell Anderson Hits Race Policy at George
Washington Auditorium," The Washington Daily News, Oct.
28, 1946. The auditorium was excluding blacks from attend-
ing plays.

715. _____. [Maxwell Anderson inducted into American Academy
and National Institute of Arts and Letters], The New York
Times, May 24, 1956, p. 25.

716. _____. [Maxwell Anderson hospitalized after stroke], The
New York Times, Feb. 27, 1959, p. 3.

717. _____. "Maxwell Anderson, in Verse, Doubts If We Face
Air Raids," New York Herald Tribune, Aug. 14, 1943. He
argues for disbanding the airplane spotter unit at Pomona.

718. _____. [Maxwell Anderson interview], The New York
Times, Jan. 18, 1959, II, 5.

719. _____. "Maxwell Anderson Is Honored Again," Brooklyn
Daily Eagle, Jan. 10, 1943.

720. _____. "Maxwell Anderson Loses No Sleep Over Libel Law,"
New York Post, Feb. 20, 1937.

721. _____. "Maxwell Anderson: Poet and Realist," New York
Herald Tribune, Jan. 28, 1934.

722. _____. [Maxwell Anderson scores isolationism, Rutgers
Univ. event], The New York Times, Oct. 11, 1941, p. 20.

723. _____. [Maxwell Anderson speaks at hearing on New City,
N.Y., camp's pig problem], The New York Times, Aug. 14,
1940, p. 21.

724. _____. [Maxwell Anderson to get American Academy and
National Institute of Arts and Letters gold medal], The New
York Times, Apr. 1, 1954, p. 40.

725. _____. "Maxwell Anderson Will Tour Africa Front for Play
Material," New York Herald Tribune, Jan. 24, 1943. Refers
to his preparations for Storm Operation.

726. _____. "Miss Haskett Won First Prize," The Student
(Univ. of North Dakota student newspaper), May 10, 1911,

p. 1. Margaret Ethel Haskett, MA's future wife, won a prize in a university essay writing contest. She wrote on the topic: "The Value of a Total Abstinance [sic] Life."

727. _____. "News, Plans, Reports and a Rumor or So About the Theatre," The New York Times, Oct. 15, 1942.

728. _____. "New York Drama Critics Circle Awards First Annual Prize to M. Anderson's Winterset," Theatre Arts Monthly, XX (May, 1936), 326.

729. _____. [Maxwell Anderson's medical condition following a stroke], The New York Times, Feb. 28, 1959, p. 21. MA died that evening.

730. _____. "The O. P. Goes to a Party," The Observation Post, n.d., but circa World War II; p. 4. This paper was issued by the civil defense people, including MA, who lived in and around New City, N.Y. MA and his friend Kurt Weill were airplane spotters. Copy at the Univ. of Texas.

731. _____. "People," Review of Reviews, XCV (May, 1937), 24.

732. _____. "Play About Charles II," New York Herald Tribune, Sept. 5, 1952. Refers to Cavalier King, completed in 1952.

733. _____. "Play Recorded for Blind," New York World-Telegram, Feb. 5, 1941.

734. _____. "Plays and People," Newsweek, XXXVIII (Oct. 15, 1951). Concerns Celanese Theatre, which is scheduling Winterset and Saturday's Children for TV presentation.

735. _____. "Playwright Buys Home," The New York Times, July 24, 1955. MA bought a large house at 141 Downes Ave., Stamford, Conn.

736. _____. "Playwright in Serious Condition," Olean [N.Y.] Herald, Feb. 27, 1959. MA is deathly ill in the Stamford Hospital suffering from a stroke.

737. _____. "Playwrights, Producers and Critics," New York Sun, Mar. 9, 1946.

738. _____. "Playwrights Produce Three New Plays," New York Herald Tribune, May 8, 1954.

739. _____. "Playwright to Receive Art Institute Medal," The New York Times, Apr. 1, 1954.

740. _____. "Playwright to Visit Europe," Illinois State Register, Jan. 27, 1943.

741. _____. "Poetic Drama Spun for Air by Anderson," New York Herald Tribune, Aug. 22, 1937.

742. _____. "Portrait," Newsweek, XXII (Aug. 23, 1943), 10. Reports some doggerel by MA about the absurdity of wasting time on air raid precautions in America.

743. _____. "Producer Bites Critic," Newsweek, XXVII (Mar. 11, 1946), 82.

744. _____. "Range of Life in One Man's Plays," Theatre Arts Monthly, XVIII (Aug., 1934), 601-06.

745. _____. "Received $1000 for All Rights," New York Morning Telegraph, Oct. 3, 1925. About MA's sale of his rights to the play that became A Holy Terror.

746. _____. "Some Playwright Biographies," Theatre Arts Monthly, XI (July, 1927), 532.

747. _____. "The Stage Hero," New York Herald Tribune, Sept. 24, 1939.

748. _____. "Those Producer Playwrights," New York Herald Tribune, Mar. 10, 1936. About the Playwrights Producing Company.

749. _____. "Three or Four Dramas May Be Placed on Trial," New York World, Feb. 28, 1925.

750. _____. "To All Who Love the Theatre," New York Herald Tribune, Mar. 8, 1946. A notice from the Playwrights Producing Company.

751. _____. "A Tribute to Talent," New York Herald Tribune, Mar. 20, 1937.

752. _____. "Two Art Groups Make 24 Awards," The New York Times, May 24, 1956.

753. _____. "Union of Playwrights for Joint Producing," Theatre Arts Monthly, XXII (May, 1938), 323. About the formation of the Playwrights Producing Company.

754. _____. "West Bank," New York World Telegram, Oct. 3, 1937.

755. _____. "The World and the Theatre," Theatre Arts Monthly, XVII (June, 1933), 405-06.

756. _____. "The World and the Theatre," Theatre Arts Monthly, XX (May, 1936), 326.

757. Van Druten, John. Playwright at Work. New York: Harper
      & Brothers, 1953, pp. 8, 49.

758. Wadeau, Roy S. Vintage Years of the Theatre Guild 1928-
      1939. Cleveland, Ohio: Case Western Reserve Univ., 1972,
      pp. 26, 55, 62, et passim. The Theatre Guild produced
      several MA plays.

759. Waldorf, Wilella. "Maxwell Anderson Returning with Two
      Broadway Plays," New York Post, July 5, 1939.

760. Wall, Vincent. "Maxwell Anderson: The Last Anarchist,"
      American Drama and Its Critics. Edited by Alan Seymour
      Downer. Chicago: Univ. of Chicago, 1965, pp. 157-70.
      Originally published in Sewanee Review in 1941.

761. Ward, A. C., and Maurice Hussey. Longman Companion to
      Twentieth Century Literature. 3rd ed. Burnt Hill, Harlow,
      England: Longman Group Limited, 1981, p. 18.

762. Watts, Harold H. "Maxwell Anderson: The Tragedy of Attri-
      tion," College English, IV (Jan., 1943), 220-30.

763. Watts, Richard, Jr. "Rungs on the Ladder of Maxwell Ander-
      son," New York Herald Tribune, Feb. 10, 1929.

764. Waugh, Jennie. Das Theater als Spiegel der Amerikanischen
      Demokratie. Berlin: Junker und Dunnhaupt, 1936.

765. Weales, Gerald Clifford. American Drama Since World War II.
      New York: Harcourt, Brace & World, 1962, pp. 58, 84-86,
      122, et passim.

766. Wharton, John F. Life Among the Playwrights[:] Being
      Mostly the Story of the Playwrights Producing Company.
      New York: Quadrangle, 1974, pp. 14-15, 25-27, 39-42, et
      passim. Wharton, the stagestruck lawyer for the Company,
      relates in an informal and sometimes amusing way the long
      history of this remarkable organization that critics said was
      doomed from the start because, after all, artists with their
      prickly and idiosyncratic personalities simply wouldn't be
      able to work together in close association. But the Company
      managed to prosper for over 20 years. The founding mem-
      bers consisted of MA, Sidney Coe Howard, Elmer Rice,
      Robert E. Sherwood, and S. N. Behrman. Howard died be-
      fore he could finish his first play for the group. Behrman
      resigned after a few years. Then Kurt Weill joined, and
      later, Robert Woodruff Anderson. The policy of producing
      plays only by its members had to be changed to include
      works by outsiders as the original playwrights aged and
      turned out fewer stageable plays. But Wharton makes it

clear that the fellowship enjoyed by its members was most valuable in itself--particularly so in a lonely profession like writing. Almost all the works for which MA will be remembered, however, were written before he joined the Playwrights Producing Company in the spring of 1938.

767. Whipple, Sidney B. "Maxwell Anderson Ignores Box Office," New York World-Telegram, July 20, 1940.

768. Whitaker, Pamela. "Up-Hudson Artist," Park East[:] The Magazine of New York, XII (July, 1952), 6-13.

769. Whiting, Frank M. An Introduciton to the Theatre. 4th ed. New York: Harper & Row, 1978, pp. 149, 159. The second and third editions of this book are worth consulting also.

770. Who's Who in America. Vol. XXX (1958-59). Chicago: A. N. Marquis, 1958, p. 69.

771. Wilkins, Robert P. "Editor's Notes," The North Dakota Quarterly, XXXVIII (Winter, 1970), 4, 91-92.

772. Wilson, Edmund. "Prize Winning Blank Verse," New Republic, XCI (June 23, 1937), 193-94.

773. Wilson, Garff B. Three Hundred Years of American Drama and Theatre. Englewood Cliffs, N.J.: Prentice-Hall, 1973, pp. 379, 415, 452, et passim.

774. Witham, W. Tasker. Panorama of American Literature. New York: Stephen Daye, 1947, pp. 293-96.

775. Woltman, Fred. "Law and Dogs Tough on Maxwell Anderson," New York World-Telegram, Nov. 19, 1938, p. 8. A neighbor across the road from MA brought suit against him because Mab's two whippets, who never barked to give warning, would dart out of hiding and terrorize people, including nipping them on the heels.

776. Woodbridge, Homer E. "Maxwell Anderson," South Atlantic Quarterly, XLIV (Jan., 1945), 55-68.

777. Wright, Edward A. A Primer for Playgoers. New York: Prentice-Hall, 1958, pp. 34, 64-68, 72, et passim.

778. Wright, Edward A., and Lenthiel H. Downs. A Primer for Playgoers. 2nd ed. Englewood Cliffs, N.J.: Prentice-Hall, 1969, pp. 254-55.

779. Wyatt, Euphemia Van Rensselaer. "Post-War Poets and the Theatre," Catholic World, CXLV (Aug., 1937), 598-604.

780. Yoset, Thomas L. "Maxwell Anderson, the Playwright,"
     Crawford County [Pa.] Genealogy, I (July, 1978), 79-84.
     The first and only MA genealogy drawn up by a professional
     genealogist.

781. Young, Stark. "Fourth Theatre Guild," New Republic, XC
     (Mar. 3, 1937), 111-12.

782. _____. "Poetic Chances," New Republic, LXXXIV (Dec. 6,
     1935), 365.

783. _____. "'Valley Forge' and 'High Tor and Highty Tighty,'"
     Immortal Shadows. New York: Charles Scribner's Sons,
     1948, pp. 165-68, 185-88.

784. Zabel, W. D. "Poetry for the Theatre," Poetry, XLV (Dec.,
     1934), 152-58.

785. Zhito, Lee (ed.). American Entertainment[:] A Unique His-
     tory of Popular Show Business. New York: Billboard Pub-
     lications, 1978, pp. 230-31.

786. Zolotow, Maurice. Stagestruck: The Romance of Alfred Lunt
     and Lynn Fontanne. New York: Harcourt, Brace & World,
     1965, pp. 177-79, 269. Zolotow, drawing upon Fontanne's
     recollections, gives a distorted picture of MA's character,
     calling him an "old man" who chased "young girls." The
     first "young girl" mentioned, Mab Maynard, was all of 26
     by the fall of 1930 when MA was dating her. The second
     such girl that he was supposed to be chasing, this time in
     the spring of 1953, was said to be "sixteen or seventeen";
     this was Gilda Hazard, and she was 39 at the time. Zolotow
     omits mentioning that it was Mab Maynard who was first un-
     faithful to MA, and not vice versa; moreover, that they were
     not legally married at the time.

787. Zolotow, Sam. "Richard III Seen as Hero in Play," The New
     York Times, Aug. 19, 1955. This notice refers to MA's un-
     acted and unpublished Richard and Anne.

■ REVIEWS AND OTHER WRITINGS
ABOUT THE LONGER WORKS

Works are listed alphabetically by first word, including
the initial article "the."

ANNE OF THE THOUSAND DAYS

788. Alford, Walter. New York Herald Tribune, Jan. 2, 1949.

789. Anderson, Maxwell. "How a Play Gets Written: Diary Retraces the Steps," New York Herald Tribune, Aug. 21,
1949, V, 1-2.

790. Atkinson, Brooks. "At the Theatre," The New York Times,
Dec. 9, 1948.

791. _____. The New York Times, Dec. 19, 1948, II, 3.

792. _____. The New York Times, May 18, 1949, p. 32.

793. Barnes, Howard. New York Herald Tribune, Dec. 9, 1948.

794. _____. New York Herald Tribune, Dec. 19, 1948.

795. Barron, Mark. The Houston Post, Dec. 12, 1948.

796. Beaufort, John. The Christian Science Monitor, Dec. 19,
1948.

797. Bronson, Arthur. Variety, Jan. 19, 1949.

798. Brown, John Mason. "Harrison Rex," Saturday Review of
Literature, XXXI (Dec. 25, 1948), 24-26.

799. _____. Still Seeing Things. New York: McGraw-Hill,
1950, pp. 207-13.

800. Chapman, John. "Harrison and Redman Splendid in a Stir-
ring Historical Drama," New York Daily News, Dec. 9, 1948.

801. Clark, Norman. The Baltimore News Post, Nov. 30, 1948.

802. Clurman, Harold. "Maxwell Anderson," Lies Like Truth. New
      York: Macmillan, 1958, pp. 33, 34-35.

803. Coleman, Robert. "'Anne of Thousand Days' a Sure Hit at
      Shubert," New York Daily Mirror, Dec. 9, 1948.

804. Crosby, John. "Great Show," New York Herald Tribune,
      Nov. 14, 1952, p. 21. Deals with "The Trial of Anne
      Boleyn," a TV play made from MA's drama. The play
      starred Rex Harrison and Lilli Palmer. It was broadcast on
      the Ford Foundation show called "Omnibus" on Nov. 9, 1952.

805. Currie, George. Brooklyn Daily Eagle, Dec. 9, 1948.

806. _____. Brooklyn Daily Eagle, Dec. 12, 1948.

807. _____. Brooklyn Daily Eagle, Dec. 26, 1948.

808. _____. Brooklyn Daily Eagle, Aug. 26, 1948.

809. _____. Brooklyn Daily Eagle, Aug. 28, 1948.

810. Davis, Richard. New York Journal-American, Mar. 26, 1949.

811. Dickstein, Martin. Brooklyn Daily Eagle, Aug. 21, 1948.

812. Downing, Margot. The Detroit News, Nov. 29, 1949.

813. Fields, William. Evening Sun (Hanover, Pa.), Jan. 15, 1949.

814. Foldes, Peggy. The Northside News (New York City), Dec.
      18, 1948.

815. Gabriel, Gilbert W. "Playgoing," Theatre Arts Monthly,
      XXXIII (Mar., 1949), 52, 54-56.

816. Gaghan, Jerry. Philadelphia Daily News, Nov. 10, 1948.

817. Garland, Robert. New York Journal-American, Apr. 13, 1948.

818. _____. "Anderson at His Best and an Elegant Cast," New
      York Journal-American, Dec. 9, 1948.

819. Gassner, John. Forum, CXI (Feb., 1949), 92-93.

820. Gibbs, Wolcott. The New Yorker, XXIV (Dec. 18, 1948), 48,
      50.

821. Green, Mawbry. Theatre World, XLV (Feb., 1949), 30.

822. Hawkins, William. "Two Stars Light up New Anderson Play,"
      New York World-Telegram, Dec. 9, 1948.

823. "hobe" [signature]. Variety, Dec. 15, 1948.

824. "H. R." [signature]. The Christian Science Monitor, Oct. 11,
      1949.

825. Kanour, Gilbert. The Evening Sun (Baltimore, Md.), Nov.
      23, 1948.

826. _____. The Evening Sun (Baltimore, Md.), Nov. 30, 1948.

827. Kelley, Marion. Philadelphia Inquirer, Nov. 7, 1948.

828. Kirkley, Donald. The Baltimore Sun, Nov. 21, 1948.

829. _____. The Baltimore Sun, Nov. 30, 1948.

830. Koebel, Mary McGavran. Ohio State Journal (Columbus, Ohio),
      Nov. 15, 1949.

831. Krutch, Joseph Wood. The Nation, CLXVIII (Jan. 1, 1949),
      24-25.

832. _____. New York Star, Dec. 5, 1948.

833. _____. New York Times Book Review, Dec. 12, 1948, 4,
      20.

834. Lardner, John. "Mr. Anderson in a Tudor Mood," New York
      Star, Dec. 10, 1948.

835. Logan, Floyd. The News-Sentinel (Fort Wayne, Ind.), Mar.
      12, 1949.

836. McCord, Bert. New York Herald Tribune, Sept. 19, 1955.

837. Mace, Louise. The Springfield Sunday Republican (Spring-
      field, Mass.), Feb. 20, 1949.

838. McLauchlin, Russell. Detroit News, Nov. 29, 1949, pp. 22-23.

839. Martin, Linton. Philadelphia Inquirer, Nov. 14, 1948.

840. Matlaw, Myron (ed.). Modern World Drama[:] An Encyclo-
      pedia. New York: E. P. Dutton, 1972, p. 30.

841. Morehouse, Ward. "A Robust and Vivid Play," The New York
      Daily Sun, Dec. 9, 1948.

842. _____. The New York Daily Sun, Dec. 11, 1948.

843. _____. The New York Daily Sun, Feb. 22, 1949.

844. Nadel, Norman. The Columbus Citizen (Columbus, Ohio),
     Feb. 1, 1949.

845. _____. The Columbus Citizen (Columbus, Ohio), Nov. 15,
     1949.

846. Nathan, George Jean. Theatre Book of the Year, 1948-1949.
     New York: Alfred A. Knopf, 1949, pp. 197-99.

847. Norton, Elliot. Boston Sunday Post, Jan. 9, 1949.

848. Palmer, Rollin. Buffalo Courier Express, Oct. 27, 1949.

849. Perry, Lawrence. The Hartford Daily Courant (Hartford,
     Conn.), Dec. 12, 1948.

850. Phelan, Kappo. Commonweal, XLVIII (Dec. 24, 1948), 281.

851. Radcliffe, E. B. Cincinnati Enquirer, Nov. 23, 1949.

852. Ranney, Omar. The Cleveland Press (Cleveland, Ohio), Dec.
     13, 1948.

853. Sensenderfer, R. E. P. The Evening Bulletin (Philadelphia,
     Pa.), Nov. 10, 1948.

854. Shank, Theodore J. (ed.). A Digest of 500 Plays[:] Plot
     Outlines and Production Notes. New York: Crowell-
     Collier Press, 1963, p. 301.

855. Sherman, John K. The Minneapolis Star, Feb. 22, 1949.

856. Shivers, Alfred S. Maxwell Anderson. Boston: Twayne,
     1976, pp. 76-80.

857. _____. The Life of Maxwell Anderson. Briarcliff Manor,
     N.Y.: Stein and Day, 1983, pp. 227-28.

858. Soanes, Wood. Oakland Tribune (Oakland, Calif.), Feb. 1,
     1949.

859. Unsigned. America, Jan. 1, 1949.

860. _____. Catholic World, CLXVIII (Jan., 1949), 321-22.

861. _____. Cue, Dec. 18, 1948.

862. _____. Cue, Dec. 11, 1949.

863. _____. Forum, CXI (Feb., 1949), 92-93.

864. _____. Life, XXVI (Jan. 17, 1949), 74-76.

865. _____. New Republic, CXIX (Dec. 27, 1948), 29.

866. _____. Newsweek, XXXII (dec. 20, 1948), 72.

867. _____. New York Times Magazine, (Nov. 28, 1948), 40-41.

868. _____. Saturday Review of Literature, XXXI (Dec. 25, 1948), 24-26.

869. _____. Standard Times (New York City), Oct. 12, 1949.

870. _____. Theatre Arts Monthly, XXXII (Oct., 1948), 11-12.

871. _____. Theatre Arts Monthly, XXXIII (Mar., 1949), 52.

872. _____. The Nation, CLXVIII (Jan. 1, 1949), 24-25.

873. _____. The New Yorker, XXIV (Dec. 18, 1948), 48.

874. _____. The New York Times, Sept. 18, 1949, II, 1.

875. _____. Time, LII (Dec. 20, 1948), 60.

876. _____. Vogue, CXIII (Jan., 1949), 113.

877. Wahls, Robert. New York Daily News, Dec. 19, 1948.

878. Warner, A. J. Rochester Times-Union, Oct. 25, 1949.

879. "Waters" [signature]. Variety, Nov. 17, 1948.

880. Waters, Arthur B. Vierte Seite (Philadelphia, Pa.), Nov. 11, 1948.

881. _____. Vierte Seite (Philadelphia, Pa.), Nov. 14, 1948.

882. Watts, A. E. Boston Traveler, Oct. 11, 1949.

883. Watts, Richard, Jr. "New American Tragedy Aided by Rex Harrison," New York Post, Dec. 9, 1948.

884. Wharton, John F. Life Among the Playwrights[:] Being Mostly the Story of the Playwrights Producing Company. New York: Quadrangle, 1974, pp. 169-73. Wharton, a friend and colleague of MA, served as the legal counsel for the Playwrights Producing Company.

885. Wilson, Samuel T. Columbus Dispatch (Columbus, Ohio), Nov. 15, 1948.

886. Wyatt, Euphemia Van Rensselaer. Catholic World, CLXVIII
     (Jan., 1949), 321-22.

                              BAD SEED

887. Atkinson, Brooks. The New York Times, Dec. 9, 1954, 41.

888. _____. The New York Times, Dec. 19, 1954, II, 3.

889. Bailey, Mabel Driscoll. Maxwell Anderson[:] The Playwright
     as Prophet. New York: Abelard-Schuman, 1957, pp. 172-
     82.

890. Bass, Milton R. The Berkshire Evening Eagle (Berkshire,
     Mass.), Jan. 11, 1955.

891. Bentley, Eric. New Republic, CXXXI (Dec. 27, 1954), 21.

892. Bolton, Whitney. New York Morning Telegram, Dec. 10, 1954.

893. Carberry, Edward. Cincinnati Post, Jan. 31, 1956.

894. Carmody, Jay. The Evening Star (Washingotn, D.C.), Nov.
     16, 1954, B-14.

895. Chapman, John. New York Daily News, Dec. 9, 1954.

896. _____. The Wall Street Journal, Dec. 10, 1954.

897. Clark, Norman. Baltimore News-Post, Nov. 23, 1954.

898. Clurman, Harold. The Nation, CLXXIX (Dec. 25, 1954), 556-
     57.

899. Coe, Richard L. "'The Bad Seed' Next at Shubert," Washing-
     ton Post and Times Herald, Nov. 14, 1954.

900. _____. Washington Post and Times Herald, Nov. 17, 1954.

901. _____. New York Herald Tribune, Dec. 5, 1954.

902. Colby, Ethel. New York Journal of Commerce, Dec. 10, 1954.

903. Coleman, Robert. New York Daily Mirror, Dec. 9, 1954, p.
     46.

904. Cone, Theresa Loeb. Oakland Tribune (Oakland, Calif.),
     Mar. 20, 1956.

905. Crosby, John. New York Herald Tribune, Dec. 27, 1954.

906. Crossland, Philip F. Journal Every Evening (Wilmington, Dela.), Dec. 2, 1956.

907. Dash, Thomas. Women's Wear Daily (New York City), Dec. 9, 1954.

908. Davis, Richard S. The Milwaukee Journal, Apr. 24, 1956.

909. Denham, Reginald. "Fruit of a Bad Seed," Theatre Arts, XXXIX (Dec. 1955), 33-34.

910. Dettmar, Roger. Chicago American, May 27, 1956, p. 41.

911. Donnelly, Tom. The Washington Daily News, Nov. 16, 1954, p. 34.

912. Fall, Kingsley R. The Berkshire Evening Eagle (Berkshire, Mass.), Nov. 15, 1954.

913. _____. "Maxwell Anderson Fashions a Blood-Curdling Melodrama," Pittsfield Eagle (Pittsfield, Mass.), Nov. 15, 1954.

914. Fanning, William. Pittsburgh Post Gazette, Jan. 3, 1956.

915. F. F. F. [signature]. Kansas City Times, Feb. 24, 1956.

916. Field, Rowland. Newark Evening News, Dec. 9, 1954.

917. Finnegan, Thomas. Long Island Star-Journal, Jan. 21, 1955.

918. Foldes, Peggy. The Northside News (New York City), Dec. 15, 1954.

919. Freedley, George. New York Morning Telegraph, Dec. 21, 1954.

920. Freeman, Charles K. Reporter Dispatch (White Plains, N.Y.), Jan. 21, 1955.

921. Gaghan, Jerry. Philadelphia Daily News, Dec. 6, 1956.

922. Gardner, R. H. "'Bad Seed' Going Good," The Baltimore Sun, Nov. 21, 1954. About rehearsals in progress.

923. _____. The Evening Sun (Baltimore, Md.), Nov. 30, 1954.

924. Gibbs, Wolcott. The New Yorker, XXX (Dec. 18, 1954), 54, 56.

925. Glacklin, William C. Sacramento Bee, Mar. 22, 1956.

926. Glover, William. Times-Picayune (New Orleans, La.), Dec. 19, 1954.

927. Goodspeed, John. The Evening Sun (Baltimore, Md.), Nov. 23, 1954.

928. Greene, Patterson. Los Angeles Examiner, Feb. 29, 1956, III, 6.

929. Halliday, Robert S. Salt Lake City Tribune, Apr. 11, 1956.

930. Halline, Edward P. Milwaukee Sentinel, Apr. 24, 1956.

931. Harris, Sydney J. Chicago Daily News, May 1, 1956, p. 23.

932. Harrison, Carroll. Los Angeles Herald Express, Feb. 29, 1956.

933. Hawkins, William. New York World Telegram and Sun, Dec. 9, 1954.

934. Hayes, Richard. Commonweal, LXI (Dec. 31, 1954), 358-59.

935. Herridge, Frances. New York Post, Dec. 15, 1954.

936. Hewes, Henry. "How Many Inches to the Heart of a Child?" Saturday Review of Literature, XXXVII (Dec. 25, 1954), 22.

937. _____. "Critics on a Hot Tin Roof," Saturday Review of Literature, XXXVIII (Apr. 30, 1955), 26. Hewes, who was one of the judges on the New York Critics Circle Award panel, selected as his first choice the play Bad Seed. But he was out-voted, and the award went instead to Tennessee Williams for his Cat on a Hot Tin Roof.

938. Hodel, Emilia. San Francisco News, Mar. 20, 1956.

939. Houk, Norman. Minneapolis Tribune, Mar. 18, 1956.

940. Hughes, Elinor. Boston Herald, Dec. 20, 1955.

941. Humphreys, Henry. Cincinnati Times-Star, Jan. 31, 1956.

942. Hurren, Kenneth A. What's On in London, Apr. 22, 1955, p. 6.

943. Hutchings, Harold. Chicago Tribune Magazine, Mar. 13, 1955.

944. Kanour, Gilbert. The Evening Sun (Baltimore, Md.), Nov. 24, 1954.

945. _____. The Evening Sun (Baltimore, Md.), Nov. 29, 1954.

946. Keating, John. Cue, Dec. 18, 1954.

947. Kerr, Walter F. New York Herald Tribune, Dec. 9, 1954.

948. _____. New York Herald Tribune, Dec. 19, 1954.

949. Klepfer, Donald I. Wilmington News (Wilmington, Del.), Dec. 2, 1955.

950. Knickerbocker, Paine. San Francisco Chronicle, Mar. 21, 1956.

951. Kogan, Herman. Chicago Sun Times, May 1, 1956, p. 41.

952. Kronenberger, Louis. Time, LIV (Dec. 20, 1954), 59.

953. Krug, Karl. Pittsburgh Telegram, Jan. 3, 1956.

954. Krutch, Joseph Wood. "The Playwright Is Still a Poet," Theatre Arts Monthly, XXXIX (Apr., 1955), 26-27, 92-93.

955. Le Roy, Mervyn. "On Transplating the 'Bad Seed,'" The New York Times, Sept. 9, 1956, X, 7.

956. Lubeck, Robert E. Detroit News, Jan. 17, 1956.

957. McClain, John. New York Journal-American, Dec. 9, 1954.

958. McCord, Bert. "Anderson Is Dramatizing Bad Seed," New York Herald Tribune, July 29, 1954.

959. McDermott, William F. Cleveland Plain Dealer, Apr. 24, 1955.

960. _____. Cleveland Plain Dealer, Jan. 10, 1956.

961. Mace, Louise. The Springfield Union (Springfield, Mass.), Nov. 13, 1954.

962. _____. Springfield Sunday Republican (Springfield, Mass.), Nov. 21, 1954.

963. Martz, Maxine. Deseret News (Salt Lake City, Utah), Apr. 11, 1956.

964. Melrose, Frances. Rocky Mountain News (Denver, Colo.), Apr. 14, 1956.

965. Millstein, Gilbert. "Books of the Times," The New York Times, July 30, 1954.

966. Monahan, Nancy. The Pittsburgh Press, Jan. 3, 1956.

967. Monk, Herbert L. St. Louis Globe-Democrat, Feb. 14, 1956.

968. Morehouse, Ward. Cleveland Plain Dealer, Dec. 12, 1954.

969. Morton, Hortense. San Francisco Examiner, Mar. 21, 1956.

970. Naden, Norman. The Columbus Citizen, Jan. 15, 1955.

971. _____. The Columbus Citizen, Feb. 10, 1956, p. 16.

972. Nathan, George Jean. New York Journal American, Dec. 24, 1954.

973. Norton, Elliot. Boston Post, Dec. 20, 1955.

974. Nourse, Joan Thellusson. Roman Catholic News, Dec. 18, 1954.

975. Oliver, John L. Detroit Free Press, Jan. 18, 1956.

976. Patrick, Corbin. Indianapolis Star, Feb. 7, 1956.

977. Piet, Creighton. Virginian-Pilot (Norfolk, Va.), Dec. 9, 1954.

978. Polier, Rex. New York Sunday Mirror, Feb. 20, 1955, p. 15.

979. Radcliffe, E. B. Cincinnati Enquirer, Jan. 31, 1956, p. 18.

980. Ranney, Omar. Cleveland Press, Feb. 7, 1955.

981. Raven, Seymour. Chicago Daily Tribune, May 1, 1956.

982. Rudkin, W. Harley. "Murder in Pigtails Holds First Nighters Spellbound," The Springfield Daily News (Springfield, Mass.), Nov. 13, 1954.

983. Ryan, Dorothy D. Oregonian, Dec. 19, 1954.

984. Schallert, Edwin. Los Angeles Times, Feb. 29, 1956.

985. Schumach, Murray. "Private Lives of Child Thespians," New York Magazine, Jan. 16, 1955.

986. Sensenderfer, R. E. P. The Evening Bulletin (Philadelphia, Pa.), Dec. 6, 1955.

987. Sheaffer, Louis. Brooklyn Daily Eagle, Dec. 9, 1954.

988. _____. Brooklyn Daily Eagle, Jan. 2, 1955.

989. Sherman, John K. Star-Journal, Mar. 18, 1956.

990. _____. Star-Journal, Apr. 18, 1956.

991. Shivers, Alfred S. Maxwell Anderson. Boston: Twayne,
      1976, pp. 125-30.

992. _____. The Life of Maxwell Anderson. Briarcliff Manor,
      N.Y.: Stein and Day, 1983, pp. 254-55.

993. Standish, Myles. St. Louis Post-Dispatch, Feb. 14, 1956.

994. Stuckey, William. "Being a Little Monster Isn't Hurting
      Patty McCormack's Style," Courier-Journal (Louisville,
      Ky.), Jan. 16, 1955.

995. Taylor, Harvey. Detroit Times, Jan. 17, 1956.

996. Trewin, J. C. Illustrated London News, CXXXVI (Apr. 30,
      1955), 794.

997. Trump, Glenn. Omaha World Herald, Feb. 22, 1956.

998. Tucker, Ernest E. Chicago American, May 2, 1956.

999. Tweedell, Bob. Denver Post, Mar. 14, 1956.

1000. Unsigned. America, XCII (Dec. 25, 1954), 346.

1001. _____. Baltimore News Post, Nov. 30, 1954.

1002. _____. Catholic World, CLXXX (Feb., 1955), 387-88.

1003. _____. Chicago American, May 1, 1956, p. 12.

1004. _____. Cincinnati Inquirer, Jan. 30, 1956.

1005. _____. Courier-Journal (Louisville, Ky.), Dec. 12, 1954.

1006. _____. Evening Express (Portland, Maine), Dec. 14, 1954.

1007. _____. Indianapolis Times, Feb. 7, 1956, p. 10.

1008. _____. Kansas City Times, Feb. 24, 1956.

1009. _____. Life, XXXVIII (Jan. 10, 1955), 53-54, 56.

1010. _____. Long Island Star Journal, Dec. 9, 1954.

1011. _____. Newsweek, XXXXIV (Dec. 20, 1954), 57.

1012. _____. New York Journal-American, Dec. 18, 1954.

1013. _____. Ohio State Journal (Columbus, Ohio), Feb. 10,
        1956.

1014. _____. Rochester Times Union, Mar. 26, 1955.

1015. _____. San Francisco Call Bulletin, Mar. 20, 1956.

1016. _____. Spectator, CXCIV (Apr. 22, 1955), 502.

1017. _____. Springfield Daily News (Springfield, Mass.), Nov.
        13, 1954.

1018. _____. Theatre Arts Monthly, XXXIX (Feb., 1955), 18-20.

1019. _____. The New York Times, Dec. 9, 1954, p. 42.

1020. _____. The New York Times, Dec. 19, 1954, II, 3.

1021. _____. The New York Times, Jan, 16, 1955, VI, 22.

1022. _____. The New York Times, May 1, 1955, II, 3.

1023. _____. The Washington Daily News, Nov. 16, 1954.

1024. _____. Times (London), Apr. 22, 1955.

1025. _____. Times-Picayune (New Orleans), Feb. 6, 1955.

1026. _____. Variety, Dec. 15, 1954.

1027. _____. Variety, July 25, 1956.

1028. Wahls, Robert. Brooklyn Daily Eagle, Dec. 15, 1954.

1029. Watts, Richard, Jr. New York Post, Dec. 9, 1954.

1030. _____. New York Post, Dec. 19, 1954.

1031. Whitworth, Walter. Indianapolis News, Feb. 7, 1956.

1032. Williams, Dick. Los Angeles Mirror News, Feb. 29, 1956.

1033. Wilson, Samuel T. Columbus Dispatch, Feb. 10, 1956.

1034. Winchell, Walter. New York Daily Mirror, Dec. 10, 1954.

1035. Wyatt, Euphemia Van Rensselaer. Catholic World, CLXXX
        (Feb., 1955), 387-88.

1036. Zolotow, Maurice. Theatre Arts Monthly, XXXIX (Feb.,
      1955), 20-21.

                    BAREFOOT IN ATHENS

1037. Allerup, Paul R. Miami Daily News, Nov. 3, 1951.

1038. Atkinson, Brooks. The New York Times, Nov. 1, 1951.

1039. _____. The New York Times, Nov. 11, 1951, II, 1.

1040. Bailey, Mabel Driscoll. Maxwell Anderson[:] The Playwright
      as Prophet. New York: Abelard-Schuman, 1957, pp. 84-
      97.

1041. Barron, Mark. News & Courier (Charleston, S.C.), Nov.
      11, 1951.

1042. Barry, Virginia. The Asbury Park Press, Nov. 18, 1951.

1043. Briney, Nancy Wells. Junior League Magazine, Dec., 1951.

1044. Brown, John Mason. As They Appear. New York: McGraw-
      Hill, 1952, pp. 199-206.

1045. _____. "Socrates Without Plato," Saturday Review of Lit-
      erature, XXXIV (Nov. 24, 1951), 26-28.

1046. Chapman, John. New York Daily News, Nov. 1, 1951.

1047. _____. New York Daily News, Nov. 11, 1951.

1048. Coleman, Robert. New York Daily Mirror, Nov. 1, 1951.

1049. _____. New York Sunday Mirror, Nov. 4, 1951.

1050. Cooke, Richard P. The Wall Street Journal, Nov. 2, 1951.

1051. Field, Rowland. Newark News, Nov. 1, 1951.

1052. Garland, Robert. New York Journal-American, Nov. 1, 1951.

1053. Gibbs, Wolcott. New Yorker, XXVII (Nov. 10, 1951), 66,
      68.

1054. Hawkins, William. New York World-Telegram and Sun, Nov.
      1, 1951.

1055. Hershbell, Jackson K. "The Socrates and Plato of Maxwell

Anderson," North Dakota Quarterly, XXXVIII (Winter,
1970), 45-59.

1056. Hewes, Henry. Saturday Review of Literature, XXXV (Feb.
       23, 1952), 28.

1057. Highet, Gilbert. "A Socratic Dialogue," New York Herald
       Tribune, Oct. 28, 1951.

1058. Kerr, Walter F. New York Herald Tribune, Nov. 1, 1951.

1059. _____. "When the Director Saves the Day," New York
       Herald Tribune, Nov. 11, 1951.

1060. Krutch, Joseph Wood. The Nation, CLXXIII (Nov. 17,
       1951), 430-31.

1061. McCord, Bert. New York Herald Tribune, Oct. 31, 1951.

1062. Martin, Linton. Philadelphia Inquirer, Oct. 21, 1951.

1063. Morehouse, Ward. New York World Telegram and Sun, Nov.
       3, 1951.

1064. Murdock, Henry T. Philadlephia Inquirer, Oct. 14, 1951.

1065. Nathan, George Jean. Theatre Arts Monthly, XXXVI (Jan.
       1952), 81.

1066. _____. Theatre in the Fifties. New York: Alfred A.
       Knopf, 1953, pp. 40-42.

1067. Phelan, Kappo. Commonweal, LV (Nov. 16, 1951), 142-43.

1068. Rice, Vernon. New York Post, Oct. 30, 1951.

1069. Sheaffer, Louis. Brooklyn Daily Eagle, Nov. 1, 1951.

1070. _____. Brooklyn Daily Eagle, Nov. 11, 1951.

1071. Shipley, Joseph T. The New Leader, Nov. 26, 1951.

1072. Shivers, Alfred S. Maxwell Anderson. Boston: Twayne,
       1976, pp. 66-71.

1073. _____. The Life of Maxwell Anderson. Briarcliff Manor,
       N.Y.: Stein and Day, 1983, pp. 236-39.

1074. Stern, Harold. The American Hebrew, Nov. 23, 1951.

1075. Unsigned. AUFBAU, Nov. 9, 1951. [In German.]

1076. _____. Brooklyn Daily Eagle, Oct. 28, 1951.

1077. _____. Cue, Nov. 10, 1951.

1078. _____. Newsweek, XXXVIII (Nov. 12, 1951), 92.

1079. _____. The New York Times, Oct. 28, 1951, II, 1.

1080. _____. The New York Times, Nov. 11, 1951, II, 1.

1081. _____. Time, LVIII (Nov. 12, 1951), 60.

1082. "Waters" [signature]. Variety, Oct. 18, 1951.

1083. Watts, Richard, Jr. New York Post, Nov. 1, 1951.

1084. _____. New York Post, Nov. 11, 1951.

1085. Winchell, Walter. New York Sunday Mirror, Nov. 4, 1951.

1086. Wyatt, Euphemia Van Rensselaer. Catholic World, CLXXIV
      (Dec., 1951), 226-27.

BASTION ST. GERVAIS

1087. Shivers, Alfred S. The Life of Maxwell Anderson. Briar-
      cliff Manor, N.Y.: Stein and Day, 1983, pp. 52, 165.

1088. _____. Maxwell Anderson. Boston: Twayne, 1976, p.
      181.

1089. Unsigned. "Writes Radio Drama, Bastion St. Gervais," The
      New York Times, May 22, 1938, XI, 10.

BOTH YOUR HOUSES

1090. Anderson, John. New York Evening Journal, Mar. 7, 1933.

1091. Atkinson, Brooks. "Maxwell Anderson Attacking Politics in
      Both Your Houses," The New York Times, Mar. 7, 1933.
      p. 20.

1092. _____. "Sins of Both Your Houses," The New York Times,
      Mar. 12, 1933, IX, 1.

1093. Atkinson, Brooks, and Albert Hirschfeld. The Lively Years
      1920-1973. New York: Association Press, 1973, pp. 80-84.

1094. Avery, Laurence G. "Maxwell Anderson and Both Your
       Houses," North Dakota Quarterly, XXXVIII (Winter, 1970),
       5-24.

1095. Bailey, Mabel Driscoll. Maxwell Anderson[:] The Playwright
       as Prophet. New York: Abelard-Schuman, 1957, pp.
       58-61.

1096. Bonin, Jane F. Major Themes in Prize-Winning American
       Drama. Metuchen, N.J.: Scarecrow Press, 1975, pp.
       102-05.

1097. Broun, Heywood. New York World-Telegram, Mar. 15, 1933.

1098. _____. New York World-Telegram, May 8, 1933.

1099. Brown, John Mason. New York Evening Post, Mar. 11, 1933.

1100. _____. New York Evening Post, May 8, 1933.

1101. _____. Two on the Aisle: Ten Years of the American
       Theatre in Performance. New York: W. W. Norton, 1938,
       pp. 208-11.

1102. Burr, Eugene. Billboard, XLV (Mar. 18, 1933), 17.

1103. Caldwell, Cy. New Outlook, CLXI (Apr., 1933), 46.

1104. Carb, David. Vogue, LXXXI (May 1, 1933), 84.

1105. Clark, Barrett H. Maxwell Anderson[:] The Man and His
       Plays. Ann Arbor, Mich.: University Microfilms, 1968
       (originally published in 1933), pp. 28-29.

1106. Dukore, Bernard, et al. (eds.). "Anderson, Maxwell, 1888-
       1959," McGraw-Hill Encyclopedia of World Drama. Vol. I.
       New York: McGraw-Hill, 1972, pp. 53-54; 2nd edition,
       1984.

1107. Eaton, Walter Prichard. New York Herald Tribune Books,
       IX (May 21, 1933), 9.

1108. Eustis, Morton. Theatre Arts Monthly, XVII (May, 1933),
       338-40.

1109. Flexner, Eleanor. American Playwrights: 1918-1938 The
       Theatre Retreats from Reality. Freeport, N.Y.: Books
       for Libraries, 1969, pp. 125-26. Typical left-wing criticism.

1110. French, Samuel. Sunday Oregonian, May 14, 1933.

1111. Gabriel, Gilbert W. New York American, Mar. 7, 1933.

1112. Garland, Robert. New York World-Telegram, Mar. 4, 1933.

1113. _____. New York World-Telegram, Mar. 7, 1933.

1114. _____. New York World-Telegram, Apr. 5, 1933.

1115. _____. New York World-Telegram, May 23, 1933.

1116. Gaul, Harvey. Pittsburgh Post-Gazette, Feb. 28, 1933.

1117. Goldstein, Malcolm. "The Playwrights of the 1930's," The American Theatre Today. Edited by Alan S. Downer. New York: Basic Books, 1967, pp. 26-27.

1118. Hammond, Percy. New York Herald Tribune, Mar. 7, 1933.

1119. _____. New York Herald Tribune, May 14, 1933.

1120. Hart, James D. (ed.). Oxford Companion to American Literature. 5th edition. New York: Oxford Press, 1983, p. 89.

1121. Heiney, Donald. Recent American Literature. Great Neck, N.Y.: Barron's Educational Series, 1958, pp. 373-74.

1122. _____, and Lenthiel H. Downs. Recent American Literature After 1930. Woodbury, N.Y.: Barron's Educational Series, 1974, pp. 282-83.

1123. Herzberg, Max J. (ed.). Reader's Encyclopedia of American Literature. New York: Thomas Y. Crowell, 1962, p. 99.

1124. Himmelstein, Morgan Yale. Drama Was a Weapon[:] The Left-Wing Theatre in New York 1929-1941. New Brunswick, N.J.: Rutgers Univ. Press, 1963, pp. 129-30.

1125. "Ibee" [signature]. Variety, CX (Mar. 14, 1933), 42.

1126. Krutch, Joseph Wood. "The Minutes Stand Approved," The Nation, CXXXVI (Mar. 29, 1933), 355-56.

1127. Lawson, John H. Theory and Technique of Playwriting and Screenwriting. New York: G. P. Putnam's Sons, 1949, pp. 146-51. Lawson lived across the road from MA in New City during the 1920's. It was Lawson's play Roger Bloomer that prompted MA to write his first full-length dramatic work.

1128. Lockridge, Richard. The New York Daily Sun, Mar. 7, 1933.

1129. _____. The New York Daily Sun, Apr. 3, 1933.

1130. McKean, Kenneth. "Congress Has Burlesque Session in Maxwell Anderson's Both Your Houses," Stage, X (Apr., 1933),
16-17.

1131. Mantle, Burns. New York Daily News, Mar. 6, 1933.

1132. _____. New York Daily News, Mar. 7, 1933, p. 31.

1133. Matlaw, Myron (ed.). Modern World Drama[:] An Encyclopedia. New York: E. P. Dutton, 1972, pp. 99-100.

1134. Morris, Lloyd R. Postscript to Yesterday; America: The
Last Fifty Years. New York: Random House, 1947, p.
199.

1135. Nathan, George Jean. Vanity Fair, XL (May, 1933), 31-32.

1136. Pollock, Arthur. Brooklyn Daily Eagle, Mar. 7, 1933.

1137. Rabkin, Gerald. Drama and Commitment; Politics in the
American Theatre of the Thirties. Bloomington: Indiana
Univ. Press, 1964, pp. 270-72.

1138. Ruhl, Arthur. New York Herald Tribune, Mar. 19, 1933.

1139. Shepard, Oscar. The Bangor Daily News (Bangor, Maine),
Jan. 4, 1939. Review of new production by a little theater
group.

1140. Shivers, Alfred S. Maxwell Anderson. Boston: Twayne,
1976, pp. 96-100.

1141. _____. The Life of Maxwell Anderson. Briarcliff Manor,
N.Y.: Stein and Day, 1983, pp. 125-26.

1142. Skinner, Richard Dana. Commonweal, XVIII (Mar. 22, 1933),
582.

1143. _____. Commonweal, XVIII (May 19, 1933), 73-74.

1144. Thornton, Noel. Los Angeles Herald Express, Mar. 11, 1933.

1145. Toohey, John L. A History of the Pulitzer Prize Plays. New
York: Citadel Press, 1967, pp. 109-11.

1146. Unsigned. Booklist, XXIX (July, 1933), 335.

1147. _____. Books (May 21, 1933), 9.

1148. _____. "Both Your Houses," Catholic World, CXXXVII (Apr., 1933), 80-81.

1149. _____. Cleveland Open Shelf (Nov., 1933), 11.

1150. _____. Commonweal, XVII (Mar. 22, 1933), 582.

1151. _____. "Congress Pilloried on the Stage," Literary Digest, CXV (Mar. 25, 1933), 15.

1152. _____. "The Drama," Catholic World, CXXXVII (Apr., 1933), 81-82.

1153. _____. (London) Times, May 17, 1933.

1154. _____. New Outlook, CLXI (Apr., 1933), 46.

1155. _____. Newsweek, I (Mar. 18, 1933), 29.

1156. _____. New York Herald Tribune, May 28, 1933.

1157. _____. New York World-Telegram, Mar. 3, 1933.

1158. _____. New York World-Telegram, May 15, 1933.

1159. _____. New York World-Telegram, May 20, 1933.

1160. _____. Pasadena Star News (Pasadena, Calif.), July 25, 1939.

1161. _____. "Pulitzer Prize Play," Theatre Arts Monthly, XVII (June, 1933), 405-06.

1162. _____. "Pulitzer Prize Won by Anderson Drama," The New York Times, May 5, 1933.

1163. _____. Stage, X (Apr., 1933), 6.

1164. _____. The Nation, CXXXVI (Mar. 29, 1933), 355.

1165. _____. The New York Times, May 23, 1933, p. 22.

1166. _____. "The Pulitzer Prize Drama Winner," Literary Digest, CXV (May 20, 1933), 15-16.

1167. _____. Time, XXI (Mar. 13, 1933), 40.

1168. _____. Wisconsin Library Bulletin, XXIX (June, 1933), 161.

1169. Wadeau, Roy S. Vintage Years of the Theatre Guild 1928-

1939. Cleveland, Ohio: Case Western Reserve Univ.,
1972, pp. 150-52.

1170. Wyatt, Euphemia Van Rensselaer. Catholic World, CXXXVII
       (Apr., 1933), 80-81.

1171. Young, Stark. "Both Your Houses," New Republic, LXXIV
       (Mar. 29, 1933), 188.

CANDLE IN THE WIND

1172. Allen, Kelcey. Woman's Wear Daily (New York City), Oct.
       23, 1941.

1173. Anderson, John. New York Journal-American, Oct. 23,
       1941.

1174. _____. New York Journal-American, Nov. 2, 1941.

1175. Atkinson, Brooks. The New York Times, Oct. 23, 1941, p.
       26.

1176. _____. The New York Times, Nov. 2, 1941, IX, 1.

1177. Azrael, Louis. Baltimore News Post, Oct. 1, 1941.

1178. Bailey, Mabel Driscoll. Maxwell Anderson[:] The Playwright
       as Prophet. New York: Abelard-Schuman, 1957, pp. 114-
       17.

1179. Bell, Nelson. Washington Post, Oct. 7, 1941.

1180. _____. Washington Post, Oct. 10, 1941.

1181. _____. Washington Post, Oct. 14, 1941.

1182. Bessie, Alvah. New Masses, Nov. 4, 1941.

1183. Brown, John Mason. New York World-Telegram, Oct. 23,
       1941.

1184. _____. New York World-Telegram, Nov. 1, 1941.

1185. Byrnes, Garrett D. Pasadena Evening Bulletin, Sept. 17,
       1941.

1186. Carmody, Jay. Washington Star, Oct. 5, 1941.

1187. _____. Washington Star, Oct. 7, 1941.

1188. Clark, Norman. Baltimore News Post, Sept. 30, 1941.

1189. Clarke, George W. Boston Post, Sept. 27, 1941.

1190. Coleman, Robert. New York Daily Mirror, Oct. 23, 1941.

1191. Cooke, Richard P. "Miss Hayes and the Nazis," The Wall Street Journal, Oct. 24, 1941.

1192. Craig, Don. Washington Daily News, Oct. 7, 1941.

1193. Doyle, Peggy. Boston Evening American, Sept. 16, 1941, p. 30.

1194. Drutman, Irving. New York Herald Tribune, Nov. 16, 1941.

1195. _____. New York Herald Tribune, Dec. 28, 1941.

1196. Eager, Helen. Boston Traveler, Sept. 16, 1941.

1197. Fagin, Bryllion. New Dealer, Nov. 1, 1941.

1198. Field, Rowland. "Broadway," Newark Evening News, Aug. 9, 1941.

1199. _____. Newark Evening News, Oct. 23, 1941.

1200. "Fox" [signature]. Variety, Sept. 17, 1941.

1201. Freedley, George. New York Morning Telegraph, Oct. 24, 1941.

1202. Gaffney, Leo. Boston Daily Record, Sept. 17, 1941.

1203. Gibbs, Wolcott. The New Yorker, XVII (Nov. 1, 1941), 45-46.

1204. Gilder, Rosamond. Theatre Arts Monthly, XXV (Dec., 1941), 861-66.

1205. _____. Theatre Arts Monthly, XXVI (Feb., 1942), 80, 85.

1206. Green, Mawbry. Theatre World, XXXVII (Jan., 1942), 29-30.

1207. Harrison, Bernie. New York Herald Tribune, Oct. 7, 1941.

1208. Himmelstein, Morgan Yale. Drama Was a Weapon[:] The Left-Wing Theatre in New York 1929-1941. New Brunswick, N.J.: Rutgers Univ. Press, 1963, p. 151.

1209. Hughes, Elinor. The Boston Herald, Sept. 16, 1941, p. 12.

1210. _____. The Boston Herald, Sept. 21, 1941.

1211. "Ibee" [signature]. Variety, Oct. 29, 1941.

1212. Jordan, Elizabeth. America, Nov. 8, 1941.

1213. Kanour, Gilbert. Baltimore Evening Sun, Sept. 30, 1941.

1214. Kaplan, Mike. Billboard, Sept. 27, 1941.

1215. Kirkley, Donald. The Baltimore Sun, Sept. 30, 1941.

1216. Kronenberger, Louis. PM (New York City), Oct. 23, 1941.

1217. _____. PM (New York City), Nov. 2, 1941.

1218. Krutch, Joseph Wood. The Nation, CLIII (Nov. 8, 1941), 462-63.

1219. Lang, Daniel. New York Post, Nov. 29, 1941.

1220. Lawrence, David. Washington Star, Oct. 13, 1941.

1221. Lockridge, Richard. The New York Daily Sun, Oct. 23, 1941.

1222. _____. The New York Daily Sun, Nov. 8, 1941.

1223. Mace, Louise. Springfield Sunday Union and Republican (Springfield, Mass.), Sept. 28, 1941.

1224. Mantle, Burns. New York Daily News, Oct. 23, 1941.

1225. _____. New York Sunday News, Nov. 2, 1941, p. 82.

1226. Martin, Linton. Philadelphia Inquirer, Nov. 1, 1943.

1227. Morehouse, Ward. New York Sun, Oct. 18, 1941.

1228. Norton, Elliot. Boston Post, Sept. 16, 1941.

1229. _____. Boston Post, Sept. 21, 1941.

1230. O'Hara, John. Newsweek, XVIII (Nov. 3, 1941), 58.

1231. Ormsbee, Helen. New York Herald Tribune, Oct. 26, 1941.

1232. Pollock, Arthur. Brooklyn Daily Eagle, Oct. 23, 1941.

1233. _____. Brooklyn Daily Eagle, Oct. 26, 1941.

1234. Pollock, J. H. Congress Weekly, Dec. 26, 1941.

1235. Price, Edgar. Brooklyn Citizen, Oct. 23, 1941.

1236. Quick, Dorothy. The East Hampton star, Nov. 27, 1941, p. 6.

1237. Quinn, Arthur Hobson. The New York Times, Nov. 14, 1941. [Letter about Candle in the Wind.]

1238. Radcliffe, E. B. Cincinnati Enquirer, Oct. 5, 1941.

1239. Sensenderfer, Robert. Philadelphia Bulletin, Nov. 13, 1942.

1240. Shivers, Alfred S. Maxwell Anderson. Boston: Twayne, 1976, p. 56.

1241. _____. The Life of Maxwell Anderson. Briarcliff Manor, N.Y.: Stein and Day, 1983, pp. 187-88.

1242. Sloper, L. A. The Christian Science Monitor, Sept. 16, 1941.

1243. Unsigned. The Baltimore Sun, Sept. 30, 1941. [Editorial.]

1244. _____. Billboard, Nov. 1, 1941.

1245. _____. Boston Globe, Sept. 16, 1941.

1246. _____. "Boston Lauds 'Candle in the Wind,'" New York Herald Tribune, Sept. 17, 1941.

1247. _____. Bronx Home News, Oct. 23, 1941.

1248. _____. "Burst of Activity Promised by the Guild and the Playwrights," New York Post, Oct. 14, 1941.

1249. _____. "'Candle in the Wind' Released," New York Post, Aug. 18, 1941.

1250. _____. Current History, I (Dec., 1941), 379-80.

1251. _____. "Former Player in Reich Prized as Stage Nazi," New York Herald Tribune, Oct. 19, 1941, VI, 2. This item is about the German immigrant actor Tonio Selwart, who played the Nazi lieutenant in Candle in the Wind.

1252. _____. "'Hals und Beinbruch' Greets a Forgotten Hero of Bundling," New York Herald Tribune, Nov. 2, 1941. (See the foregoing news item.)

1253. _____. "Helen Hayes Gives Up Playing Queens," Brooklyn Daily Eagle, Oct. 19, 1941.

1254. _____. "Helen Hayes Here in 'Candle in the Wind,'" The New York Times, Oct. 22, 1941.

1255. _____. The Kansas City Star, Dec. 7, 1941.

1256. _____. New Leader, Nov. 1, 1941.

1257. _____. "Occupied France Is Scene of New Anderson Play," Boston Herald, Aug. 24, 1941.

1258. _____. Players Magazine, XVIII (Jan., 1942), 11.

1259. _____. "Staged by Lunt," Cue, Oct. 18, 1941.

1260. _____. The New York Times, Sept. 16, 1941.

1261. _____. Where to Go in New York, Nov. 1, 1941.

1262. Vernon, Grenville. Commonweal, XXXV (Nov. 7, 1941), 71-72.

1263. Wadeau, Roy S. Vintage Years of the Theatre Guild 1928-1939. Cleveland, Ohio: Case Western Reserve Univ., 1972, pp. 374-75.

1264. Waldorf, Wilella. New York Post, Sept. 15, 1941.

1265. _____. New York Post, Oct. 23, 1941.

1266. _____. New York Post, Oct. 25, 1941.

1267. _____. New York Post, Nov. 8, 1941.

1268. _____. New York Post, Dec. 16, 1941.

1269. Warner, Ralph. Daily Worker, Oct. 25, 1941.

1270. _____. "Playwrights Take Half a Step Towards Reality," Sunday Worker, Nov. 2, 1941.

1271. Watts, Richard, Jr. New York Herald Tribune, Oct. 23, 1941.

1272. _____. New York Herald Tribune, Nov. 2, 1941.

1273. Winchell, Walter. New York Sunday Mirror, Oct. 26, 1941.

1274. Wyatt, Euphemia Van Rensselaer. Catholic World, CLIV (Dec., 1941), 334-35.

1275. Young, Stark. New Republic, CV (Nov. 10, 1941), 621.

1276. Zunser, Jesse. Cue, Nov. 1, 1941.

ELIZABETH THE QUEEN

1277. Atkinson, Brooks. The New York Times, Nov. 3, 1930.

1278. Avery, Laurence G. "Maxwell Anderson," Twentieth-Century
American Dramatists, Part I: A-J. Edited by John Mac-
Nicholas. Detroit, Mich.: Gale Research Co., 1981, pp.
29-30.

1279. Bailey, Mabel Driscoll. Maxwell Anderson[:] The Playwright
as Prophet. New York: Abelard-Schuman, 1957, pp. 45-
54.

1280. Beach, Stewart. Theatre, LIII (Jan., 1931), 66, 68.

1281. Benchley, Robert. The New Yorker, VI (Nov. 5, 1930), 30.

1282. Brown, John Mason. New York Evening Post, Nov. 4, 1930.

1283. Carmer, Carl. "Maxwell Anderson, Poet and Champion,"
Theatre Arts Monthly, XVII (June, 1933), 443-45.

1284. Chatfield-Taylor, Otis. Outlook, CLVI (Nov. 19, 1930), 472.

1285. Clark, Barrett H. Maxwell Anderson[:] The Man and His
Plays. Ann Arbor, Mich.: Univ. Microfilms, 1968, pp.
21-25.

1286. Diez, Henry A. "Vienna Stages Anderson Play as U.S.
Classic," New York Herald Tribune, Nov. 9, 1935.

1287. Downer, Alan Seymour. Fifty Years of American Drama.
Chicago: Henry Regner, 1951, pp. 106-07.

1288. Dukore, Bernard, et al. (eds.). McGraw-Hill Encyclopedia
of World Drama. New York: McGraw-Hill, 1972, Vol. I,
p. 53.

1289. Eaton, Walter P. New York Herald Tribune Books, VII
(Jan. 11, 1931), 16.

1290. Fergusson, Francis. "The Theatre," Bookman, LXXII (Feb.,
1931), 628-29.

1291. Flexner, Eleanor. American Playwrights: 1918-1938. New
York: Simon and Schuster, 1938, pp. 88-93.

1292.   Foster, Edward.   "Core of Belief," Sewanee Review, L (Jan.,
        1942), 90-91.

1293.   Gabriel, Gilbert.   New York American, Nov. 4, 1930.

1294.   Gagey, Edmond McAdoo.   Revolution in American Drama.
        New York: Columbia Univ. Press, 1947, pp. 77-78.

1295.   Gassner, John (ed.).   A Treasury of the Theatre, rev. ed.
        New York: Simon and Schuster, 1951, Vol. III, pp. 864-
        65.

1296.   Hammond, Percy.   New York Herald Tribune, Nov. 4, 1930.

1297.   Harrison, Carroll.   Los Angeles Evening Herald, Apr. 7,
        1931, p. B-8.

1298.   Heiney, Donald.   Recent American Literature.   Great Neck,
        N.Y.:   Barron's Educational Series, 1958, p. 373.

1299.   _____, and Lenthiel H. Downs.   Recent American Litera-
        ture After 1930.   Woodbury, N.Y.:   Barron's Educational
        Series, 1974, pp. 283-84.

1300.   Herzberg, Max (ed.).   The Reader's Encyclopedia of Ameri-
        can Literature.   New York: Thomas Y. Crowell, 1962, p.
        305.

1301.   Hutchens, John.   Theatre Arts Monthly, XV (Jan., 1931),
        10-12.

1302.   "Ibee" [signature].   Variety, C (Nov. 5, 1930), 62.

1303.   Knepler, Henry W.   "Maxwell Anderson: A Historical Paral-
        lel," Queen's Quarterly, LXIV (Summer, 1957), 250-63.

1304.   Lawrence, Florence.   Los Angeles Examiner, Apr. 7, 1931.

1305.   Langner, Lawrence.   The Magic Curtain.   New York: E. P.
        Dutton, 1951, pp. 252-53.

1306.   Leonard, Baird.   "Theatre," Life, XCVI (Nov. 21, 1930),
        14.

1307.   Littell, Robert.   New York World, Nov. 4, 1930.

1308.   Lockridge, Richard.   The New York Daily Sun, Nov. 4,
        1930.

1309.   Matthews, Rives.   Billboard, XLII (Nov. 15, 1930), 32.

1310. Miller, Jordan Y. "Maxwell Anderson: Gifted Technician,"
       The Thirties: Fiction, Poetry, Drama. Edited by Warren
       French. Deland, Fla.: Everett/Edwards, 1967, pp. 186-
       87.

1311. Nathan, George Jean. Judge, XCIX (Nov. 29, 1930), 16.

1312. _____. New Freeman, II (Dec. 3, 1930), 279-80.

1313. _____. Vanity Fair, XXXV (Jan., 1931), 30.

1314. Pollock, Arthur. Brooklyn Daily Eagle, Nov. 4, 1930.

1315. Quinn, Arthur Hobson. A History of the American Drama
       from the Civil War to the Present Day. New York:
       Appleton-Century-Crofts, 1936, pp. 267-68.

1316. Rabkin, Gerald. Drama and Commitment Politics in the Amer-
       ican Theatre of the Thirties. Bloomington: Indiana Univ.
       Press, 1964, pp. 274-76.

1317. Schallert, Edwin. Los Angeles Times, Apr. 7, 1931.

1318. Shank, Theodore J. A Digest of 500 Plays[:] Plot Outlines
       and Production Notes. New York: Crowell-Collier, 1963,
       pp. 298-99.

1319. Shivers, Alfred S. Maxwell Anderson. Boston: Twayne,
       1976, pp. 85-89.

1320. _____. The Life of Maxwell Anderson. Briarcliff Manor,
       N.Y.: Stein and Day, 1983, pp. 114-20.

1321. Skinner, Richard Dana. Commonweal, XIII (Nov. 19, 1930),
       76.

1322. _____. Our Changing Theatre. New York: Dial Press,
       1931, pp. 25, 30, 69-71.

1323. Unsigned. Catholic World, CXXXII (Dec., 1930), 335.

1324. _____. Drama Magazine (Chicago), XXI (Dec., 1930), 11-
       12.

1325. _____. Literary Digest, CVII (Nov. 22, 1930), 17-18.

1326. _____. The Nation, CXXXI (Nov., 1930), 562.

1327. _____. New York Herald Tribune, Nov. 26, 1930.

1328. _____. The New York Times, Oct. 5, 1930, IX, 4.

1329. _____. The New York Times, Nov. 4, 1930, p. 37.

1330. _____. The New York Times, Nov. 9, 1930, IX, 1.

1331. _____. The New York Times, Nov. 9, 1935, p. 18.

1332. _____. The New York Times, July 28, 1936, p. 23.

1333. _____. The New York Times, Oct. 30, 1936, p. 25.

1334. _____. The New York Times, Aug. 25, 1937, p. 24.

1335. _____. The New York Times, Nov. 4, 1966, p. 30.

1336. _____. Woman's Journal, XV (Dec., 1930), 15.

1337. Wadeau, Roy S. Vintage Years of the Theatre Guild 1928-
       1939. Cleveland, Ohio: Case Western Reserve Univ.,
       1972, pp. 98-101.

1338. Wall, Vincent. "Maxwell Anderson: The Last Anarchist,"
       American Drama and Its Critics. Edited by Alan S.
       Downer. Chicago: Univ. of Chicago Press, 1965, pp.
       151-54.

1339. Warren, George C. San Francisco Chronicle, May 12, 1931.

1340. Watson, E. Bradlee, and Benfield Pressey (eds.). "Elizabeth
       the Queen," in Contemporary Drama[:] European[;] Eng-
       lish and Irish[;] American Plays. New York: Charles
       Scribner's Sons, 1966, pp. 1067-68.

1341. Watts, Richard, Jr. New York Herald Tribune, Nov. 7,
       1930.

1342. Wellman, Rita. Town and Country, LXXXV (Dec. 1, 1930),
       44.

1343. Woollcott, Alexander. Collier's, LXXXVII (Feb. 7, 1931),
       10, 62.

1344. Young, Stark. "Elizabeth," New Republic, LXV (Nov. 19,
       1930), 17-19.

1345. Zolotow, Maurice. Stagestruck: The Romance of Alfred
       Lunt and Lynn Fontanne. New York: Harcourt, Brace
       & World, 1965, pp. 178-79.

FIRST FLIGHT

1346. Anderson, John. New York Evening Post, Sept. 18, 1925.

1347. Bailey, Mabel Driscoll. Maxwell Anderson[:] The Playwright
       as Prophet. New York: Abelard-Schuman, 1957, p. 124.

1348. Brown, John Mason. Theatre Arts Monthly, IX (Nov., 1925),
       713-14.

1349. Clark, Barrett H. Maxwell Anderson[:] The Man and His
       Plays. Ann Arbor: Univ. of Michigan Press, 1968 (orig-
       inally published in 1933), pp. 14-15.

1350. Coleman, Robert. New York Daily Mirror, Sept. 18, 1925.

1351. Gabriel, Gilbert. The New York Daily Sun, Sept. 18, 1925.

1352. Hammond, Percy. New York Herald Tribune, Sept. 18, 1925.

1353. Krutch, Joseph Wood. The Nation, CXXI (Oct. 7, 1925),
       390-91.

1354. Mantle, Burns. American Playwrights of Today. New York:
       Dodd, Mead, 1930, pp. 68-69.

1355. _____. New York Daily News, Sept. 18, 1925.

1356. Nathan, George Jean. American Mercury, VI (Nov., 1925),
       377.

1357. _____. Judge, LXXXIX (Oct. 10, 1925), 16, 26.

1358. Parker, H. T. Boston Transcript, Sept. 28, 1925.

1359. Pollock, Arthur. Brooklyn Daily Eagle, Sept. 18, 1925.

1360. Quinn, Arthur Hobson. A History of the American Drama
       from the Civil War to the Present Day. New York: Apple-
       ton-Century-Crofts, 1936, p. 235.

1361. Shivers, Alfred S. Maxwell Anderson. Boston: Twayne,
       1976, p. 29.

1362. _____. The Life of Maxwell Anderson. Briarcliff Manor,
       N.Y.: Stein and Day, 1983, p. 104.

1363. Simon, Bernard. New York Telegraph, Sept. 18, 1925.

1364. Torres, H. Z. New York Commercial, Sept. 18, 1925.

1365. Unsigned. New York Amusements, Sept. 21, 1925.

1366. _____. New York Evening Post, Sept. 26, 1925.

1367. _____. New York Journal of Commerce, Sept. 18, 1925.

1368. _____. The New York Times, Sept. 18, 1925, p. 26.

1369. _____. The New York Times, Sept. 27, 1925, VII, 1.

1370. Vreeland, Frank. New York Telegram, Sept. 18, 1925.

1371. Winchell, Walter. New York Graphic, Sept. 18, 1925.

1372. Woollcott, Alexander. New York World, Sept. 18, 1925.

                          GODS OF THE LIGHTNING

1373. Atkinson, Brooks. The New York Times, Oct. 25, 1928.

1374. Avery, Laurence G. "Maxwell Anderson: A Changing Atti-
       tude Toward Love," Modern Drama, X (Dec., 1967), 241-
       42.

1375. Benchley, Robert. Life, LXXXVII (Nov. 16, 1928), 14.

1376. Block, Anita. The Changing World in Plays and Theatre.
       Boston: Little, Brown, 1939, pp. 230-39.

1377. Clark, Barrett H. Drama, XIX (Jan., 1929), 101.

1378. _____. Maxwell Anderson[:] The Man and His Plays.
       Ann Arbor, Mich.: University Microfilms, 1968 (originally
       published in 1933), pp. 17-19.

1379. Eaton, Walter Prichard. New York Herald Tribune Books,
       V (Feb. 17, 1929), 20.

1380. Ervine, St. John. New York World, Oct. 25, 1928.

1381. Flexner, Eleanor. American Playwrights: 1918-1938. Simon
       and Schuster, 1938, pp. 115-16.

1382. Gabriel, Gilbert. The New York Daily Sun, Oct. 25, 1928.

1383. Garland, Robert. New York Telegraph, Feb. 23, 1928.

1384. _____. New York Telegraph, Oct. 25, 1928.

1385. Gold, Michael. New Masses, IV (Dec., 1928), 15.

1386. Hammond, Percy. New York Herald Tribune, Oct. 25, 1928.

1387. Holmesdale, Jeffrey. New York World, Nov. 25, 1928.

1388. Isaacs, Edith J. R. Theatre Arts Monthly, XIX (Nov., 1935), 815-20.

1389. Krutch, Joseph Wood. "Melpomene on a Soap-Box," The Nation, CXXVII (Nov. 14, 1928), 528.

1390. Littell, Robert. New York Evening Post, Oct. 25, 1928.

1391. _____. "Where Are the New Playwrights?" Theatre Arts Monthly, XIII (Jan., 1929), 12, 17.

1392. Mantle, Burns. New York Daily News, Oct. 25, 1928, p. 39.

1393. Mordden, Ethan. The American Theatre. New York: Oxford Univ. Press, 1981, pp. 121-22, 126, 130.

1394. Morris, Lloyd R. Postscript to Yesterday; America: The Last Fifty Years. New York: Random House, 1947, pp. 197-98.

1395. Nannes, Caspar Harold. Politics in the American Drama. Washington, D.C.: The Catholic University of America Press, 1960, pp. 92-94.

1396. Nathan, George Jean. Judge, XCV (Nov. 17, 1928), 31.

1397. O'Hara, Frank Hurbert. Today in American Drama. New York: Greenwood Press, 1969 (first published in 1939), pp. 254-55.

1398. Osborn, E. W. New York Evening World, Oct. 25, 1928.

1399. Parker, H. T. Boston Transcript, Nov. 22, 1928.

1400. Pollock, Arthur. Brooklyn Daily Eagle, Oct. 25, 1928.

1401. Quinn, Arthur Hobson. A History of the American Drama from the Civil War to the Present Day. New York: Appleton-Century-Crofts, 1936, p. 266.

1402. Rabkin, Gerald. Drama and Commitment Politics in the American Theatre of the Thirties. Bloomington: Indiana University Press, 1964, pp. 266-68.

1403. Reed, Edward. Theatre Arts Monthly, XVIII (June, 1934), 453-54.

1404. Riley, Wilfred J. Billboard, XL (Nov. 3, 1928), 7.

1405. Seldes, Gilbert. The Dial, LXXXVI (Jan.; 1929), 80-83.

1406. Shivers, Alfred S. Maxwell Anderson. Boston: Twayne,
       1976, pp. 105-07.

1407. Unsigned. Booklist, XXV (Mar., 1929), 239-40.

1408. _____. "Boston Protects Itself," The Nation, CXXVII
       (Dec. 5, 1928), 593.

1409. _____. Survey, LXII (Apr. 1, 1929), 69.

1410. _____. Theatre Arts Monthly, XIII (May, 1929), 386-87.

1411. _____. The Dial, LXXXVI (Jan., 1929), 80-82.

1412. _____. The New York Times, Oct. 25, 1928, p. 27.

1413. _____. The New York Times, Nov. 27, 1935, p. 17.

1414. _____. Time, XXIV (Dec. 10, 1934), 46, 48-49.

1415. _____. "Travesty of Trials Offered as Drama," Boston
       Transcript, Nov. 26, 1935, p. 20.

1416. _____. Vogue, LXXII (Dec. 8, 1928), 99.

1417. _____. Wilson Library Bulletin, XXV (Feb., 1929), 71.

1418. Wyatt, Euphemia Van Rensselaer. Catholic World, CXXVIII
       (Dec., 1928), 338-39.

1419. Young, Stark. New Republic, LVI (Nov. 7, 1928), 326-27.

                              GYPSY

1420. Atkinson, Brooks. The Daily Telegraph (London), Feb. 21,
       1929.

1421. Bellamy, Francis R. Outlook, CLI (Jan. 30, 1929), 171, 197.

1422. Benchley, Robert. Life, XCIII (Feb. 1, 1929), 23.

1423. Brackett, Charles. The New Yorker, IV (Jan. 26, 1929),
       25.

1424. Carb, David. Vogue, LXXIII (Mar. 2, 1929), 73.

1425. Clark, Barrett H. Drama, XIX (Mar., 1929), 171.

1426. _____. Maxwell Anderson[:] The Man and His Plays.
       Ann Arbor, Mich." University Microfilms, 1968, pp. 19-21.

1427. _____. "Stallings and Anderson," An Hour of American
       Drama. Philadelphia: J. P. Lippincott, 1930, pp. 93-95.

1428. Dudley, Bide. New York World, Jan. 13, 1929.

1429. Ervine, St. John. New York World, Jan. 16, 1929.

1430. Flexner, Eleanor. American Playwrights: 1918-1938 The
       Theatre Retreats from Reality. Freeport, N.Y.: Books
       for Libraries, 1969 (originally published 1938), pp. 83-84.

1431. Hammond, Percy. New York Herald Tribune, Jan. 15, 1929.

1432. Jordan, Elizabeth. American, XL (Feb. 23, 1929), 484.

1433. Krutch, Joseph Wood. "Maxwell Anderson Goes Wrong,"
       The Nation, CXXVIII (Feb. 6, 1929), 168.

1434. Littell, Robert. New York Evening Post, Jan. 15, 1929.

1435. _____. Theatre Arts Monthly, XIII (Mar., 1929), 170-71.

1436. Mantle, Burns. New York Daily News, Jan. 19, 1929, p. 25.

1437. Nathan, George Jean. Judge, XCVI (Feb. 2, 1929), 18.

1438. Parker, H. T. Boston Transcript, Mar. 21, 1929.

1439. Parry, Florence Fisher. The Pittsburgh Press, Jan. 11,
       1929.

1440. Pollock, Arthur. Brooklyn Daily Eagle, Jan. 2, 1929.

1441. Quinn, Arthur Hobson. A History of the American Drama
       from the Civil War to the Present Day. New York: Apple-
       ton-Century-Crofts, 1936, pp. 266-67.

1442. Ruhl, Arthur. New York Herald Tribune, Feb. 3, 1929.

1443. Shivers, Alfred S. Maxwell Anderson. Boston: Twayne,
       1976, pp. 29-30.

1444. _____. The Life of Maxwell Anderson. Briarcliff Manor,
       N.Y.: Stein and Day, 1983, p. 107.

1445. Sievers, W. David. Freud on Broadway. New York: Hermi-
       tage House, 1955, pp. 173-74.

1446. Skinner, R. Dana. Commonweal, IX (Feb. 6, 1929), 406.

1447. Unsigned. Brooklyn Daily Eagle, Jan. 8, 1929.

1448. _____. Brooklyn Daily Eagle, Jan. 13, 1929.

1449. _____. Life, XCIII (Feb. 1, 1929), 23.

1450. _____. The New York Daily Sun, Mar. 3, 1929.

1451. _____. The New York Times, Jan. 15, 1929, p. 22.

1452. _____. The New York Times, Jan. 27, 1929, IX, 1.

1453. _____. The New York Times, Oct. 13, 1929, IX, 2.

1454. Wall, Vincent. "Maxwell Anderson: The Last Anarchist,"
       American Drama and Its Critics. Edited by Alan S.
       Downer. Chicago: Univ. of Chicago Press, 1965, p. 151.
       (Reprinted from the Sewanee Review, IL (1941), 340-69.)

1455. Wyatt, Catherine Van Rensselaer. Catholic World, CXXVIII
       (Dec., 1928), 338-39.

1456. _____. Catholic World, CXXVIII (Mar., 1929), 724-25.

HIGH TOR

1457. Anderson, John. New York Evening Journal, Jan. 11, 1937,
       p. 14.

1458. Atkinson, Brooks. The New York Times, Jan. 11, 1937, p.
       15.

1459. Bailey, Mabel Driscoll. Maxwell Anderson[:] The Playwright
       as Prophet. New York: Abelard-Schuman, 1957, pp. 146-
       49.

1460. Benet, Stephen Vincent. "New Grandeur in Our Theatre,"
       Stage, XIV (Jan., 1937), 39-41.

1461. Brown, John Mason. New York Post, Jan. 11, 1937.

1462. _____. Two on the Aisle: Ten Years of the American
       Theatre in Performance. New York: W. W. Norton, 1938,
       pp. 152-55.

1463. Clark, Barrett H., and George Freedley. A History of Mod-
       ern Drama. New York: Appleton-Century-Crofts, 1947,
       p. 697.

1464.   Coleman, Robert. New York Daily Mirror, Jan. 11, 1937.

1465.   Colum, Mary Maguire. Forum, IIIC (June, 1937), 353.

1466.   Dusenbury, Winifred L. "Myth in American Drama Between
        the Wars," Modern Drama, VI (Dec., 1963), 299.

1467.   Fadiman, Clifton. "Comedy with Errors," Stage, XIV (Mar.,
        1937), 41-44.

1468.   Flexner, Eleanor. American Playwrights: 1919-1938 The
        Theatre Retreats from Reality. Freeport, N.Y.: Books
        for Libraries, 1969 (originally published in 1938), pp. 126.

1469.   Gabriel, Gilbert W. New York American, Jan. 11, 1937.

1470.   Gassner, John. "Maxwell Anderson, Realist and Romancer,"
        Masters of the Drama. 3rd ed. New York: Dover Pub-
        lications, 1954, p. 683.

1471.   _____. "Theatre at the Crossroads," One Act Play Maga-
        zine, I (July, 1937), 273-74.

1472.   Gilbert, Douglas. "'High Tor' Is Set Up at the Martin Beck,"
        New York World-Telegram, Jan. 11, 1937, p. 14.

1473.   _____. New York World-Telegram, Jan. 18, 1937.

1474.   Goldstein, Malcolm. The Political Stage[:] American Drama
        and Theatre of the Great Depression. New York: Oxford
        Univ. Press, 1974, p. 393.

1475.   Green, Mawbry. Theatre World, XXVII (Apr., 1937), 185.

1476.   Hale, Wanda. New York Daily News, Jan. 11, 1937, p. 34.

1477.   Harkins, John. New York American, Mar. 30, 1937.

1478.   Heiney, Donald. Recent American Literature. Great Neck,
        N.Y.: Barron's Educational Series, 1958, pp. 375-76.

1479.   _____, and Lenthiel H. Downs. Recent American Litera-
        ture After 1930. Woodbury, N.Y.: Barron's Educational
        Series, 1974, pp. 284-85.

1480.   Herzberg, Max (ed.). The Reader's Encyclopedia of Amer-
        ican Literature. New York: Thomas Y. Crowell, 1962, p.
        466.

1481.   Hochman, Stanley, et al. (eds.). McGraw-Hill Encyclopedia
        of World Drama. 2nd ed. New York: McGraw-Hill, 1984,
        Vol. I, p. 142.

1482. Isaacs, Edith J. R. "A Young Race in Its Morning," The-
       atre Arts Monthly, XXI (Mar., 1937), 175-79.

1483. Kernodle, George R. "Playwrights and Ancestors," College
       English, II (Jan., 1941), 331-32.

1484. Krutch, Joseph Wood. The American Drama Since 1918.
       New York: George Braziller, 1957, pp. 301-04.

1485. _____. The Nation, CXXXXIV (Jan. 30, 1937), 136.

1486. Lockridge, Richard. The New York Daily Sun, Jan. 11,
       1937.

1487. Mantle, Burns. New York Daily News, Jan. 11, 1937.

1488. Matlaw, Myron (ed.). Modern World Drama[:] An Encyclo-
       pedia. New York: E. P. Dutton, 1972, p. 356.

1489. Miller, Jordan Y. "Maxwell Anderson: Gifted Technician,"
       The Thirties: Fiction, Poetry, Drama. Edited by Warren
       French. Deland, Fla.: Everett/Edwards, 1967, p. 190.

1490. Mordden, Ethan. The American Theatre. New York: Oxford
       Univ. Press, 1981, pp. 153-54.

1491. Nathan, George Jean. Scribner's Magazine, CI (June, 1937),
       65-66.

1492. Pollock, Arthur. Brooklyn Daily Eagle, Jan. 11, 1937.

1493. Rabkin, Gerald. Drama and Commitment Politics in the
       American Theatre of the Thirties. Bloomington: Indiana
       Univ. Press, 1964, pp. 284-86.

1494. Savell, Isabelle K. "High Tor on the Hudson Being Sought
       for as a Park," The New York Times, Nov. 15, 1942. The
       actual mountain High Tor, part of the Palisades along the
       Hudson River, looms 832 feet above the port of Haver-
       straw, and is about three miles from MA's house in New
       City. Elmer Van Orden (original for Van Van Dorn in the
       play) had lived on the mountain and owned it for many
       years until his death on Feb. 19, 1942. In order to pre-
       serve High Tor from the kinds of Biggs and Skimmerhorns
       shown in the play, various civic-minded people in the re-
       gion finally raised enough money to buy the mountain from
       Van Orden's heirs, and then they presented the mountain
       to the Palisades Interstate Park Commission.

1495. Shivers, Alfred S. Maxwell Anderson. Boston: Twayne,
       1976, pp. 114-22. Contains an earlier version of the ac-
       count given in The Life of Maxwell Anderson.

1496. _____. The Life of Maxwell Anderson. Briarcliff Manor,
N.Y.: Stein and Day, 1983, pp. 150-53. Contains an
extensive account of the mountain, its unusual owner (Elmer Van Orden, who was the model for the hero in the
play), local legends, and MA's relationship with Van Orden
and the mountain itself.

1497. Sievers, W. David. Freud on Broadway. New York: Hermitage House, 1955, pp. 176-77.

1498. Sugrue, Francis. "High Tor Sold with Its Ghosts and Old
House," New York Herald Tribune, Feb. 10, 1950.

1499. Tobias, Ravena Wilson. The News and Courier (Charleston,
S.C.), Nov. 2, 1938. About the Charleston production of
High Tor.

1500. Unsigned. "Anderson Wins Critics' Prize for High Tor,"
New York Herald Tribune, May 29, 1937. MA won the
Drama Critics Circle Award again.

1501. _____. "Elmer Van Orden, 79, Is Dead; High Tor Owner
Inspired Play," New York Herald Tribune, Feb. 20, 1942.

1502. _____. "High Tor Acclaimed at Opening in [Cleveland]
Ohio," The New York Times, Dec. 31, 1936, p. 20.

1503. _____. "'High Tor': Poetry on a Pinnacle," Literary Digest, CXXIII (Jan. 23, 1937), 21.

1504. _____. "'High Tor' Stages Real Fire After Award by
Critics," The New York Times, Apr. 3, 1937.

1505. _____. "Mounting High Tor," The New York Times, Feb.
14, 1937, X, 2.

1506. _____. "Neighbors Honor Owner of High Tor," The New
York Times, June 16, 1939, I, 25. For years, Elmer Van
Orden had resisted the enticements and pressures of quar-
riers to sell his beloved mountain to them and have it
razed for the sake of its trap rock. After the play had
made him famous, his neighbors began to appreciate, apparently for the first time, his contribution to local ecol-
ogy. He was no longer just "odd," a "queer fish," a
"peculiar, crusty old crank" who had held out against
progress and the advance of civilization, but was suddenly
elevated to the rank of being an eccentric and something
of a hero to boot.

1507. _____. Newsweek, IX (Jan. 16, 1937), 32.

1508. _____. New York Daily Mirror, Jan. 11, 1937, p. 20.

1509. _____. "Plans Are Drawn for High Tor Fund Raising
       Drive," The Journal News, Nov. 10, 1942.

1510. _____. "The Critics' Award," The Christian Science
       Monitor, XXIX (Mar., 1937), 14.

1511. _____. The News and Courier (Charleston, S.C.), Oct.
       30, 1938.

1512. _____. The Jersey Journal (Jersey City, N.J.), Mar. 31,
       1937.

1513. _____. The Journal News, Nov. 5, 1942, pp. 1-2. A
       fund drive was underway to save High Tor from quarriers.

1514. _____. The New York Times, Jan. 17, 1937, X, 1.

1515. _____. The New York Times, Feb. 21, 1937, X, 1.

1516. _____. The New York Times, Apr. 4, 1937, X, 1.

1517. _____. "The Savior of High Tor," The New York Times,
       June 17, 1939, I, 14.

1518. _____. Time, XXIX (Jan. 18, 1937), 47.

1519. _____. Variety, Jan. 13, 1937.

1520. Vernon, Grenville. Commonweal, XXV (Jan. 29, 1937), 388.

1521. _____. Commonweal, XXVI (May 28, 1937), 132.

1522. Walker, Danton. Spooks Deluxe[:] Some Excursions into
       the Supernatural. New York: Franklin Watts, 1956, pp.
       162-68. About the local ghost of a young woman who was
       supposed to have been Elmer Van Orden's long ago sweet-
       heart. Walker reports that MA denied knowing the ghost
       story until Walker told it to him. The story is interesting
       because High Tor contains the phantom of a young Dutch
       woman. Walker's remark that MA, prior to writing his
       play, had never met Van Orden and had not climbed High
       Tor mountain, is preposterous, according to what various
       Anderson relatives told me.

1523. Watts, Richard, Jr. New York Herald Tribune, Jan. 11,
       1937.

1524. _____. New York Herald Tribune, Jan. 17, 1937.

1525. _____. New York Herald Tribune, Apr. 4, 1937.

1526. Wilson, Edmund. New Republic, XCI (June 23, 1937), 193-
       94.

1527. Wyatt, Euphemia Van Rensselaer. Catholic World, CXXXXIV
       (Mar., 1937), 728-29.

1528. Young, Stark. "Best American Play," New Republic, XC
       (Apr. 14, 1937), 295.

1529. _____. "High Tor and Highty Tighty," Immortal Shadows.
       New York: Charles Scribner's Sons, 1948, pp. 187-88.

1530. _____. New Republic, LXXXIX (Feb. 3, 1937), 411-12.

                      JOAN OF LORRAINE

1531. Atkinson, Brooks. Broadway Scrapbook. Westport, Conn.:
       Greenwood Press, 1970, pp. 251-54.

1532. _____. The New York Times, Nov. 19, 1946, p. 40.

1533. _____. The New York Times, Nov. 24, 1946, II, 1.

1534. Bailey, Mabel Driscoll. Maxwell Anderson[:] The Playwright
       as Prophet. New York: Abelard-Schuman, 1957, pp. 155-
       69.

1535. Barnes, Howard. New York Herald Tribune, Nov. 19, 1946.

1536. _____. New York Herald Tribune, Nov. 24, 1946.

1537. Bentley, Eric. In Search of Theater. New York: Alfred
       A. Knopf, 1953, pp. 7-9, 267.

1538. Bergman, Ingrid, and Alan Burgess. Ingrid Bergman[:]
       My Story. New York: Delacorte Press, 1980, pp. 162-63,
       167, 169-71, 173, 178-79.

1539. Brent, Romney. Billboard (Cincinnati, Ohio), Nov. 30, 1946.

1540. Brown, John Mason. Saturday Review of Literature, XXIX
       (Dec. 21, 1946), 24-25.

1541. Caldwell, Lily May. The Birmingham News, Feb. 3, 1947.

1542. Carberry, Edward. New York Post, May 2, 1947.

1543. Chapman, John. New York Daily News, Nov. 19, 1946.

1544. _____. New York Sunday News, Nov. 24, 1946.

1545. _____. New York Daily News, Dec. 18, 1946.

1546. _____. New York Daily News, Feb. 1, 1947.

1547. Coleman, Robert. New York Daily Mirror, Nov. 19, 1946.

1548. Cooke, Richard P. The Wall Street Journal, Nov. 20, 1946.

1549. Craig, Don. New York Times Herald, Oct. 30, 1946.

1550. Doncour, Paul S. J. "Joan of Arc," The Sign, Nov., 1948,
      pp. 26-28. A promotion of the film version of the play.

1551. Donnelly, Tom. The Washington Daily News, Oct. 30, 1946.

1552. Downer, Alan Seymour. Fifty Years of American Drama.
      Chicago: Henry Regnery, 1951, pp. 109-10.

1553. Doyle, Louis F. America, Jan. 11, 1947, pp. 409-10.

1554. Drutman, Irving. New York Herald Tribune, Jan. 19, 1947.

1555. Durgin, Cyrus. Boston Sunday Globe, Feb. 23, 1947.

1556. Eaton, Walter Prichard. New York Herald Tribune, May 23,
      1947.

1557. Garland, Robert. New York Journal-American, Nov. 19,
      1946.

1558. Gaver, Jack. Columbia [S.C.] Record, Dec. 5, 1946.

1559. Gibbs, Wolcott. The New Yorker, XXII (Nov. 30, 1946), 58.

1560. Gilder, Rosamond. Theatre Arts Monthly, XXXI (Jan., 1947),
      12-13.

1561. Green, E. Mawbry. Theatre World, XLIII (Jan., 1947), 35-
      36.

1562. Halline, Edward P. Milwaukee Sentinel, Feb. 12, 1947, II,
      8.

1563. Hawkins, William. New York World-Telegram, Nov. 19, 1946.

1564. Hughes, Elinor. Boston Herald, Apr. 20, 1947.

1565. "Ibee" [signature]. Variety, Nov. 20, 1946.

1566. Kanin, Garson. Hollywood. New York: Viking, 1974, pp. 204-07.

1567. Kaye, Joseph. The Kansas City Star, Feb. 16, 1947.

1568. Kronenberger, Louis. PM (New York City), Nov. 20, 1946.

1569. Krutch, Joseph Wood. The Nation, CLXIII (Dec. 7, 1946), 671-72.

1570. Lind, Inez. The American Swedish Monthly (Jan., 1947), 13-14.

1571. Maxwell, Elsa. New York Post, Dec. 18, 1946, p. 12.

1572. Morehouse, Ward. The New York Daily Sun, Nov. 19, 1946.

1573. Morris, Frank. Winnipeg Free Press, Feb. 10, 1947.

1574. Morrison, Hobe. Boston Sunday Post, Nov. 24, 1946.

1575. Nathan, George Jean. New York Journal-American, Dec. 2, 1946.

1576. Neer, Betty R. News-Sentinel (Ft. Wayne, Ind.), [Jan., 1947].

1577. O'Brian, Jack. Houston Post, Nov. 24, 1946.

1578. _____. Journal-Courier (New Haven, Conn.), Nov. 19, 1946.

1579. Ormsbee, Helen. New York Herald Tribune, Dec.8, 1948.

1580. Phelan, Kappo. Commonweal, XLV (Dec. 6, 1946), 200.

1581. Phodna, Joe. New York Herald Tribune, Aug. 3, 1947.

1582. Pollock, Arthur. Brooklyn Daily Eagle, Nov. 19, 1946, p. 10.

1583. Rice, Vernon. New York Post, Jan. 15, 1947.

1584. Rose, Billy. PM (New York City), Feb. 27, 1947.

1585. Savery, Ronald. The Montreal Daily Star, Nov. 30, 1946.

1586. Scanlon, Ed. Buffalo Evening News, Feb. 19, 1947.

1587. Shipley, Joseph T. The New Leader, Nov. 30, 1946.

1588. Shivers, Alfred S. Maxwell Anderson. Boston: Twayne,
      1976, pp. 73-76.

1589. _____. The Life of Maxwell Anderson. Briarcliff Manor,
      N.Y.: Stein and Day, 1983, pp. 222-24.

1590. Sievers, W. David. Freud on Broadway. New York: Hermi-
      tage House, 1955, p. 179.

1591. Sillen, Samuel. Daily Worker, Nov. 22, 1946.

1592. Soanes, Wood. Oakland Tribune, Nov. 30, 1946.

1593. Unsigned. Cue, Jan. 25, 1947, p. 8.

1594. _____. Los Angeles Daily News, Oct. 30, 1946.

1595. _____. "'Joan of Lorraine' in Athens Premiere," New
      York Herald Tribune, Nov. 14, 1947.

1596. _____. Kirkeby Hotels Magazine (Feb., 1947), 20-21.

1597. _____. Life, XXI (Dec. 2, 1946), 51-52, 54.

1598. _____. Look, X (Dec. 10, 1946).

1599. _____. Newsweek, XXVIII (Dec. 2, 1946), 94.

1600. _____. Newsweek, XXIX (Jan. 27, 1947), 84.

1601. _____. New York Herald Tribune, Nov. 1, 1947.

1602. _____. Providence [R.I.] Sunday Journal, Dec. 1, 1946.

1603. _____. The New York Times, Oct. 30, 1946, p. 29.

1604. _____. The New York Times, Nov. 10, 1946, VI, 22.

1605. _____. The New York Times, Dec. 1, 1946, II, 3.

1606. _____. The New York Times, Nov. 14, 1947, p. 29.

1607. _____. The New York Times, Mar. 26, 1955, p. 12.

1608. _____. The New York Times Magazine, Nov. 10, 1946, pp.
      22-23.

1609. _____. The New York Times Magazine, Jan. 19, 1947 pp.
      20-21.

1610. _____. Time IIL (Dec. 2, 1946), 54.

1611. Watts, Richard, Jr. New York Post, Nov. 19, 1946.

1612. _____. New York Post, Nov. 23, 1946, p. 12.

1613. _____. New York Post, Apr. 12, 1947, p. 12.

1614. Wyatt, Euphemia Van Rensselaer. Catholic World, CLXIV
       (Jan., 1947), 357-58.

1615. Young, Stark. "Weaknesses," New Republic, CXV (Dec. 2,
       1946), 725-26.

                     JOURNEY TO JERUSALEM

1616. Allen, Kelcey. Women's Wear Daily, Oct. 7, 1940.

1617. Anderson, John. New York Journal of Commerce, Oct. 13,
       1940.

1618. Arthur, George K. Go, Oct. 19, 1940.

1619. Atkinson, Brooks. The New York Times, Oct. 7, 1940, p.
       21.

1620. Azrael, Louis. Baltimore American, Oct. 13, 1940.

1621. Bailey, Mabel Driscoll. Maxwell Anderson[:] The Playwright
       as Prophet. New York: Abelard-Schuman, 1957, pp. 154-
       55.

1622. Barron, Mark. Baltimore Sun, Oct. 13, 1940.

1623. Bessie, Alvah. New Masses, Oct. 22, 1940.

1624. Brown, John Mason. New York Post, Oct. 7, 1946.

1625. Claxton, Oliver. Cue, Oct. 12, 1940.

1626. Colby, Ethel. New York Journal of Commerce, Oct. 7, 1940.

1627. Coleman, Robert. New York Daily Mirror, Oct. 7, 1940.

1628. Dash, Thomas. Retailing, Home Furnishings, Oct. 14, 1940,
       p. 38.

1629. Field, Rowland. Newark Evening News, Oct. 7, 1940.

1630. Foster, Edward. "Core of Belief: An Interpretation of the
       Plays of Maxwell Anderson," Sewanee Review, L (Jan.,
       1942), 98-100.

1631. Freedley, George. New York Morning Telegraph, Oct. 8,
       1940.

1632. Gagey, Edmond McAdoo. Revolution in American Drama.
       New York: Columbia Univ. Press, 1947, pp. 87-88.

1633. Gibbs, Wolcott. The New Yorker, XVI (Oct. 12, 1940), 46.

1634. Gilder, Rosamond. Theatre Arts Monthly, XXIV (Dec.,
       1940), 850, 853.

1635. Hughes, Elinor. The Boston Herald, Oct. 7, 1940.

1636. "Ibee" [signature]. Variety, Oct. 9, 1940.

1637. "J. P. B." [signature]. The Wall Street Journal, Oct. 7,
       1940.

1638. Krutch, Joseph Wood. The Nation, CLI (Oct. 19, 1940), 373-
       74.

1639. Layman, Theodore. New York Herald Tribune, Dec. 29,
       1940.

1640. Lockridge, Richard. The New York Daily Sun, Oct. 7, 1940.

1641. Mantle, Burns. New York Daily News, Oct. 7, 1940.

1642. _____. New York Sunday News, Oct. 13, 1940.

1643. "M. M. M." [signature]. Gotham Life, Oct. 12, 1940.

1644. Nathan, George Jean. American Mercury, LI (Dec., 1940),
       481-83.

1645. O'Hara, John. Newsweek, XVI (Oct. 14, 1940), 74.

1646. Pollock, Arthur. Brooklyn Daily Eagle, Oct. 7, 1940.

1647. _____. Brooklyn Daily Eagle, Oct. 10, 1940.

1648. Price, Edgar. Brooklyn Citizen, Oct. 7, 1940.

1649. Roosevelt, Eleanor. New York World Telegram, Oct. 10,
       1940.

1650. Shivers, Alfred S. Maxwell Anderson. Boston: Twayne,
       1976, pp. 30, 136.

1651. _____. The Life of Maxwell Anderson. Briarcliff Manor,
       N.Y.: Stein and Day, 1983, pp. 186-87.

1652. Unsigned. Arts and Decoration, LII (Nov., 1940), 40.

1653. _____. Billboard, Oct. 19, 1940.

1654. _____. The New York Times, Sept. 29, 1940, IX, 1.

1655. _____. People's Press, Oct. 12, 1940.

1656. _____. Scholastic, XXXVII (Jan. 13, 1941), 17-20. Consists mostly of a reprint of the play's last scene.

1657. _____. PM's Weekly News of Theater, Oct. 6, 1940, 45-47.

1658. _____. Time, XXXVI (Oct. 14, 1940), 62.

1659. _____. Troy Observor Budget, Oct, 12, 1940.

1660. Vernon, Grenville. Commonweal, XXXII (Oct. 18, 1940), 530.

1661. Waldorf, Wilella. "Maxwell Anderson's Next Play on Biblical Subject," New York Post, Apr. 15, 1940.

1662. _____. New York Post, Oct. 17, 1940.

1663. Watts, Harold H. "Maxwell Anderson: The Tragedy of Attrition," College English, IV (Jan., 1943), 228-30.

1664. Watts, Richard, Jr. New York Herald Tribune, Oct. 6, 1940.

1665. _____. New York Herald Tribune, Oct. 7, 1940.

1666. _____. New York Herald Tribune, Oct. 20, 1940.

1667. Whipple, Sidney B. New York World Telegram, Oct. 7, 1940.

1668. Wray, Albert. New York Heights Daily News, Oct. 18, 1940.

1669. Wright, Edward A. A Primer for Playgoers. New York: Prentice-Hall, 1958, pp. 203-04.

1670. Wyatt, Euphemia Van Rensselaer. Catholic World, CLII (Nov., 1940), 216-17.

1671. Young, Stark. New Republic, CIII (Oct. 21, 1940), 557.

KEY LARGO

1672. Allen, Kelcey. Women's Wear Daily, Nov. 28, 1939.

1673. Anderson, John. New York Journal of Commerce, Oct. 7,
        1940.

1674. _____. New York Journal of Commerce, Nov. 28, 1939,
        p. 10.

1675. _____. New York Journal-American, Dec. 3, 1939.

1676. Atkinson, Brooks. The New York Times, Nov. 28, 1939, p.
        30.

1677. _____. The New York Times, Dec. 10, 1939, X, 3.

1678. Bailey, Mabel Driscoll. Maxwell Anderson[:] The Playwright
        as Prophet. New York: Abelard-Schuman, 1957, pp. 106-
        14.

1679. Barron, Mark. Miami Herald, Dec. 3, 1939.

1680. Beaufort, John D. The Christian Science Monitor, Nov. 28,
        1939.

1681. Benchley, Robert. The New Yorker, XV (Dec. 9, 1939),
        38.

1682. Bessie, Alvah. New Masses, Dec. 12, 1939.

1683. Brown, John Mason. Broadway in Review. New York:
        W. W. Norton, 1940, pp. 67-71.

1684. _____. New York Post, Nov. 28, 1939.

1685. Byrnes, Darrell D. Providence Evening Bulletin, Nov. 15,
        1939.

1686. Cassidy, Claudia. Chicago Journal of Commerce, Nov. 1,
        1939.

1687. Colby, Julius J. New York Journal of Commerce, Nov. 29,
        1939.

1688. Coleman, Robert. "'Key Largo's' Dress Rehearsal Wins Much
        Praise," New York Mirror, Oct. 28, 1939.

1689. Crawdus, Vincent. Lexington [Ky.] Herald, Mar. 26, 1939.
        Refers to the production of Key Largo at the Univ. of
        Kentucky.

1690. Cromwell, Leta Crews. "Bards of Passion and of Mirth,"
        Forum, CIII (Jan., 1940), 32.

1691. Cunningham, William S. Columbus Citizen (Columbus, Ohio),
      Nov. 3, 1939.

1692. Dana, Joyce. Boston Record, Nov. 15, 1939.

1693. Donahue, J. C., Jr. The Manhattan Quadrangle, Feb. 9,
      1940.

1694. Downer, Alan S. American Drama and Its Critics. Chicago:
      Univ. of Chicago Press, 1965, pp. 162-64.

1695. Doyle, Peggy. Boston American, Nov. 15, 1939.

1696. Dusenbury, Winifred L. "Myth in American Drama Between
      the Wars," Modern Drama, VI (Dec., 1963), 299-300.

1697. Eager, Helen. Boston Traveler, Nov. 14, 1939.

1698. Eikert, Harold C. Ohio State Journal (Columbus, Ohio),
      Nov. 3, 1939.

1699. Field, Rowland. Newark Evening News, Nov. 28, 1939.

1700. Foster, Edward. "Core of Belief: An Interpretation of the
      Plays of Maxwell Anderson," Sewanee Review, L (Jan.,
      1942), 95-97.

1701. Frazer, Frank. Long Island Daily Advocate, Dec. 26, 1939.

1702. French, Winsor. Cleveland Press, Nov. 3, 1939.

1703. Gaffney, Leo. Boston Sunday Advertiser, Nov. 19, 1939.

1704. Gagey, Edmond McAdoo. Revolution in American Drama.
      New York: Columbia Univ. Press, 1947, pp. 85-87.

1705. Gilbert, Douglas. New York World Telegram, Nov. 19, 1939.

1706. Gilder, Rosamond. Theatre Arts Monthly, XXIV (Feb.,
      1940), 81-83, 85-87.

1707. Grafton, Samuel. New York Post, Dec. 2, 1939.

1708. Graham, Marian. Butler County Record, Dec. 25, 1940.

1709. Himmelstein, Morgan Yale. Drama Was a Weapon[:] The
      Left-Wing Theatre in New York 1929-1941. New Bruns-
      wick, N.J.: Rutgers Univ. Press, 1963, p. 146.

1710. Hoffman, Calvin. Suffolk Bulletin, Dec. 18, 1940.

1711. Hughes, Elinor. Boston Herald, Nov. 14, 1939.

1712. _____. Boston Herald, Nov. 18, 1939.

1713. _____. Boston Herald, Nov. 19, 1939.

1714. Hutchins, John K. Boston Evening Transcript, Nov. 14, 1939.

1715. _____. Boston Evening Transcript, Nov. 18, 1939.

1716. _____. Boston Evening Transcript, Nov. 19, 1939.

1717. "Ibee" [signature]. Variety, Nov. 29, 1939.

1718. Kernodle, George R. "Playwrights and Ancestors," College English, II (Jan., 1941), 325-37.

1719. Krutch, Joseph Wood. "Key Largo," The Nation, CIL (Dec. 9, 1939), 656, 658.

1720. Levitt, Vic. People's Press, Dec. 9, 1939.

1721. Lewis, George D., Jr. Fordham Ram, Jan. 1, 1940.

1722. Lewis, Lloyd. Chicago Daily News, Nov. 3, 1939.

1723. Lockridge, Richard. The New York Daily Sun, Nov. 28, 1939.

1724. _____. The New York Daily Sun, Dec. 2, 1939.

1725. _____. The New York Daily Sun, Mar. 11, 1940.

1726. McDermott, William F. Cleveland Plain Dealer, Nov. 7, 1939.

1727. Mace, Louise. Springfield Sunday Union and Republican, Nov. 26, 1939.

1728. McIlhenney, Anne M. Buffalo Courier-Express, Nov. 10, 1939.

1729. Mantle, Burns. New York Daily News, Nov. 28, 1939.

1730. _____. New York Sunday News, Dec. 10, 1939.

1731. Martin, Boyd. Louisville [Ky.] Courier-Journal, Nov. 5, 1939.

1732. Martin, Linton. Philadelphia Inquirer, Feb. 27, 1940.

1733. Mason, Jeffrey D. "Maxwell Anderson's Dramatic Theory and
       Key Largo," North Dakota Quarterly, IIL (Summer, 1980),
       iii, 38-52.

1734. Matlaw, Myron (ed.). Modern World Drama[:] An Encyclo-
       pedia. New York: E. P. Dutton, 1972, p. 427.

1735. Meyer, Ernest L. New York Post, Dec. 4, 1939.

1736. _____. New York Post, Dec. 14, 1939.

1737. Miller, Jordan Y. "Maxwell Anderson: Gifted Technician,"
       The Thirties: Fiction, Poetry, Drama. Edited by Warren
       French. Deland, Fla.: Everett/Edwards, 1967, p. 191.

1738. Morehouse, Ward. The New York Daily Sun, Nov. 29, 1939.

1739. Nathan, George Jean. Newsweek, XIV (Dec. 11, 1939), 34.

1740. Neumann, Henry. "Keeping Our Ultimate Faith: The Prob-
       lem of 'Key Largo.'" A paper read for the Society for
       Ethical Culture, May 17, 1940. Mimeographed. New York
       Public Library.

1741. Norton, Elliot. Boston Post, Nov. 14, 1939.

1742. _____. Boston Post, Nov. 19, 1939.

1743. Ormsbee, Helen. New York Herald Tribune, Dec. 10, 1939.

1744. Piet, Creighton. Los Angeles Evening News, Dec. 2, 1939.

1745. Pollak, Robert. Chicago Daily Times, Oct. 31, 1939.

1746. _____. Chicago Sunday Times, Dec. 10, 1939.

1747. Pollock, Arthur. Brooklyn Daily Eagle, Nov. 28, 1939.

1748. _____. Brooklyn Daily Eagle, Dec. 3, 1939.

1749. Price, Edgar. Brooklyn Citizen, Nov. 28, 1939.

1750. Rabkin, Gerald. Drama and Commitment Politics in the Amer-
       ican Theatre of the Thirties. Bloomington: Indiana Univ.
       Press, 1964, pp. 286-88.

1751. Rice, Robert. New York Morning Telegraph, Nov. 29, 1939.

1752. _____. New York Morning Telegraph, Jan. 1, 1940, pp.
       2, 4.

1753. Rodell, John S.   "Maxwell Anderson: A Criticism," Kenyon
       Review, V (Spring, 1943), 275-76.

1754. Ryan, Dorothy D.   The Sunday Oregonian (Portland, Ore-
       gon), Dec. 10, 1939.

1755. Schloss, Edwin H.   Philadelphia Record, Feb. 27, 1940.

1756. Sensenderfer, R. E. P.   Philadelphia Bulletin, Feb. 27, 1940.

1757. Shipley, Joseph T.   The New Leader, Dec. 9, 1939.

1758. Shivers, Alfred S.   Maxwell Anderson.   Boston: Twayne,
       1976, pp. 52-56.

1759. _____.   The Life of Maxwell Anderson.   Briarcliff Manor,
       N.Y.:   Stein and Day, 1983, p. 184.

1760. Sievers, W. David.   Freud on Broadway.   New York: Hermi-
       tage House, 1955, pp. 177-78.

1761. Sloper, L. A.   The Christian Science Monitor, Nov. 14, 1939.

1762. Smart, Alexander.   Y.M.H.A. Bulletin, Feb. 9, 1940.

1763. Smith, Ardis.   Buffalo Evening News, Nov. 10, 1939.

1764. Smith, Cecil.   Chicago Daily Tribune, Oct. 31, 1939.

1765. Stevens, Ashton.   Chicago American, Oct. 31, 1939.

1766. Strauss, Theodore.   The New York Times, Dec. 17, 1939,
       pp. 3, 5.

1767. Thrasher, James.   Indiana Times, Oct. 31, 1939.

1768. Tucker, Robert G.   The Indianapolis Star, Oct. 31, 1939.

1769. Unsigned.   Booklist, XXXVI (Jan. 1, 1940), 173.

1770. _____.   Books, Jan. 21, 1940, p. 8.

1771. _____.   Boston Globe, Nov. 14, 1939.

1772. _____.   Bronx Home News, Oct. 7, 1940.

1773. _____.   Buffalo Courier-Express, Nov. 12, 1939.

1774. _____.   Chicago Herald-American, Oct. 31, 1939.

1775. _____.   Cue, Dec. 1, 1939.

1776. _____. Cue, Dec. 9, 1939.

1777. _____. Daily Worker, Nov. 30, 1939.

1778. _____. Indianapolis News, Oct. 31, 1939.

1779. _____. New Statesman and Nation, XXIII (Feb. 21, 1942),
      123.

1780. _____. Newsweek, XIV (Dec. 11, 1939), 34.

1781. _____. New York Herald Tribune, Dec. 3, 1939.

1782. _____. Ohio State Journal (Columbus, Ohio), Oct. 31,
      1939.

1783. _____. Sign, XIX (Jan., 1940), 364.

1784. _____. The New York Times, Oct. 31, 1939, p. 26.

1785. _____. The New York Times, Nov. 19, 1939, X, 3.

1786. _____. The New York Times, Nov. 28, 1939, p. 30.

1787. _____. The New York Times, Dec. 3, 1939, IX, 5.

1788. _____. The New York Times, Dec. 10, 1939, X, 3.

1789. _____. The New York Times, June 21, 1942, VIII, 1.

1790. _____. The New York Times, July 31, 1947, p. 17.
      Warner Bros. obtains film rights to the play.

1791. _____. Time, XXXIV (Dec. 11, 1939), 49.

1792. _____. Variety, Nov. 1, 1939.

1793. _____. The Wall Street Journal, Nov. 28, 1939.

1794. Vernon, Grenville. Commonweal, XXXI (Dec. 8, 1939), 163-
      64.

1795. Waldorf, Wilella. New York Post, July 5, 1939.

1796. Wall, Vincent. "Maxwell Anderson: The Last Anarchist,"
      American Drama and Its Critics. Edited by Alan Seymour
      Downer. Chicago: Univ. of Chicago Press, 1965, pp.
      162-64. [Originally published in Sewanee Review in 1941.]

1797. Watts, Harold H. "Maxwell Anderson: The Tragedy of At-
      trition," College English, IV (Jan., 1943), 220-30.

1798. Watts, Richard, Jr. New York Herald Tribune, Nov. 28,
        1939.

1799. _____. New York Herald Tribune, Dec. 3, 1939.

1800. "W. E. J. M." [signature]. Buffalo Courier-Express, Nov.
        10, 1939.

1801. Whipple, Sidney B. New York World-Telegram, Nov. 28,
        1939.

1802. _____. New York World-Telegram, Dec. 2, 1939.

1803. Whitworth, Walter. The Indianapolis News, Oct. 31, 1949.

1804. Wilson, Samuel T. Columbus Dispatch, Nov. 3, 1939.

1805. Winchell, Walter. New York Daily Mirror, Nov. 28, 1939.

1806. Wolfert, Ira. Dallas Morning News, June 16, 1940.

1807. _____. San Francisco Chronicle, Dec. 13, 1939.

1808. "W. T. C." [signature]. The Wall Street Journal, Nov. 29,
        1939.

1809. Wyatt, Euphemia Van Rensselaer. Catholic World, CL (Jan.,
        1940), 467-68.

1810. Young, Stark. New Republic, CI (Dec. 13, 1939), 230.

                        KNICKERBOCKER HOLIDAY

1811. Allen, Kelcey. Women's Wear Daily, Oct. 28, 1938.

1812. Anderson, John. "Anderson Pans a Columnist," New York-
        Journal American, Nov. 8, [1938].

1813. _____. "Our Five Leading Authors Unite to Produce Own
        Plays[.] Musical Comedy Group's First Opus," New York
        Journal-American, Aug. 28, 1938, p. E-9.

1814. _____. New York Journal-American, Oct. 20, 1938.

1815. Angoff, Charles. "Drama: Brief Reviews of This Season's
        Significant Productions," North American Review, CCXXXXVI
        (Winter, 1938-39), 374-75.

1816. Atkinson, Brooks. The New York Times, Oct. 20, 1938.

1817. _____. The New York Times, Nov. 20, 1938.

1818. Bailey, Mabel Driscoll. Maxwell Anderson[:] The Playwright
      as Prophet. New York: Abelard-Schuman, 1957, pp. 76-
      79, 82.

1819. Beebe, Lucius. "How Did Huston Do It? Posterity Will Ask,"
      New York Herald Tribune, Dec. 18, [1938]. Walter Huston
      played the important singing role of Peter Stuyvesant.

1820. Bell, Nelson B. "That Playwrights' Company Proves Power
      in the Theatre," Washington Post, Oct. 9, [1938].

1821. _____. Washington Post, Oct. 11, [1938].

1822. _____. Washington Post, Oct. 12, [1938].

1823. Braggiotti, Mary. New York Post, Oct. 20, 1938.

1824. Brown, John Mason. New York Post, Oct. 20, 1938.

1825. Burr, Eugene. Billboard, Mar. 18, [1939].

1826. Carmody, Jay. Washington Star, Oct. 11, [1938].

1827. Drake, Herbert. "Genius and Harmony Are Not, It Seems,
      Incompatible," New York Herald Tribune, Nov. 13, [1938].

1828. Eager, Helen. "'Knickerbocker Holiday' Opens," Boston
      Traveler, Sept. 28, 1938.

1829. "Fox" [signature]. Variety, Oct. 5, 1938.

1830. French, Winsor. Cleveland Press, Mar. 24, [1939].

1831. Gentry, Charles. Detroit Evening Times, Apr. 14, [1939].

1832. Gibbons, John. Boston Transcript, Oct. 1, [1938].

1833. Gilder, Rosamond. Theatre Arts Monthly, XXII (Dec., 1938),
      862.

1834. Goldstein, Malcolm. The Political Stage[:] American Drama
      and Theater of the Great Depression. New York: Oxford
      Univ. Press, 1974, pp. 394-96.

1835. Gutman, John. Modern Music, XVI (Nov.-Dec., 1938), 54-
      56.

1836. Hamilton, Clayton. "Art and Business Get Together," New
      York Herald Tribune, Oct. 30, [1938].

1837. Harkins, E. F. Boston Record, Sept. 28, [1938].

1838. Herzberg, Max (ed.). The Reader's Encyclopedia of Ameri-
       can Literature. New York: Thomas Y. Crowell, 1962, p.
       575.

1839. Hillyer, Katharine. Washington News, Oct. 11, [1938].

1840. Himmelstein, Morgan Yale. Drama Was a Weapon[:] The
       Left-Wing Theatre in New York 1929-1941. New Bruns-
       wick, N.J.: Rutgers Univ. Press, 1963, pp. 144-45.

1841. Hughes, Elinor. Boston Herald, Sept. 28, 1938.

1842. _____. Boston Herald, Oct. 2, [1938].

1843. Huston, Walter. "There's No Place Like Broadway Be It
       Ever So Noisy," Stage Magazine, XV (Oct., 1938), 22-26.

1844. Hutchins, John K. Boston Transcript, Oct. 1, [1938].

1845. Hynes, Betty. Washington Herald, Oct. 11, [1938].

1846. Keen, J. H. New York Daily News, Mar. 14, [1939].

1847. Kelley, Andrew R. Washington Times, Oct. 11, [1938].

1848. Krutch, Joseph Wood. The Nation, CXXXXVII (Nov. 5,
       1938), 487-89.

1849. "L. A. S." [signature]. "Musical Comedy, New Style," The
       Christian Science Monitor, Sept. 28, 1938, p. 11.

1850. Lockridge, Richard. The New York Daily Sun, Oct. 20,
       1938.

1851. _____. The New York Daily Sun, Dec. 17, 1938.

1852. Logan, Joshua. Josh: My Up and Down, In and Out Life.
       New York: Delacorte, 1976, pp. 128-33. The young
       Logan, having long been an admirer of MA and Weill, was
       asked to direct Knickerbocker Holiday and it became a hit.

1853. _____. Movie Stars, Real People and Me. New York:
       Delacorte, 1978, pp. 177-81.

1854. Lyons, L. New York Post, Oct. 20, 1938.

1855. McCarthy, Julia. "Actor Huston Gauges Self by His Audi-
       ence," New York Daily News, Feb. 3, [1939].

1856. McDermott, William F. Cleveland Plain Dealer, Mar. 24, [1939].

1857. Mace, Louise. Springfield [Mass.] Sunday Union, Oct. 9, [1938].

1858. McLauchlin, Russell. Detroit News, Apr. 14, [1939].

1859. Mantle, Burns. New York Daily News, Oct. 20, 1938.

1860. _____. New York Sunday News, Oct. 30, 1938, p. 82.

1861. Martin, Linton. Philadelphia Inquirer, Mar. 14, [1939].

1862. _____. Philadelphia Inquirer, Mar. 19, [1939].

1863. Matlaw, Myron (ed.). Modern World Drama[:] An Encyclopedia. New York: E. P. Dutton, 1972, p. 434.

1864. Mersand, Joseph E. The American Drama Since 1930[:] Essays on Playwrights and Plays. Port Washington, N.Y.: Kennikat Press, 1968 (originally published in 1941), p. 123.

1865. Mok, Michel. "From Song and Dance to Othello and Back, Huston's Just 'A Spadeful of Good Earth,'" New York Post, Feb. 13, 1939.

1866. Morehouse, Ward. The New York Daily Sun, Oct. 8, 1938.

1867. Murdock, Henry T. Philadelphia Ledger, Mar. 14, [1939].

1868. Nathan, George Jean. Encyclopedia of the Theatre. New York: Alfred A. Knopf, 1940, pp. 313-14.

1869. _____. Newsweek, XII (Oct. 31, 1938), 29.

1870. Norton, Elliot. "Second Thoughts of a First-Nighter," Boston Post, Oct. 2, 1938.

1871. O'Brien, Howard Vincent. Chicago News [in "All Things Considered" Column], May 4, 1939.

1872. O'Hara, Frank Hurbert. Today in American Drama. New York: Greenwood Press, 1969 (first published in 1939), pp. 101-02.

1873. Ormsbee, Helen. "Walter Huston, Plus a Wooden Leg," New York Herald Tribune, Sept. 18, 1938. Huston, playing the role of the dictatorial Peter Stuyvesant, put on a wooden leg for his performances.

1874. Parry, Florence Fisher. Pittsburgh Press, Oct. 24, [1938].

1875. Pollock, Arthur. Brooklyn Daily Eagle, Oct. 20, 1938.

1876. Rabkin, Gerald. Drama and Commitment Politics in the Amer-
       ican Theatre of the Thirties. Bloomington: Indiana Univ.
       Press, 1964, pp. 270-274.

1877. Rice, Elmer. Minority Report: An Autobiography. New
       York: Simon & Schuster, 1963, pp. 380, 383. Rice was
       a friend and colleague of MA's in the Playwrights Company.

1878. Rose, George. "Predict Anderson Smash," New York World-
       Telegram, Sept. 19, 1938.

1879. Sanders, Ronald. The Days Grow Short: A Life and Music
       of Kurt Weill. New York: Holt, Rinehart and Winston,
       1980, pp. 270-82.

1880. Schloss, Edwin H. Philadelphia Record, Mar. 14, 1939.

1881. Sensenderfer, R. E. P. Philadelphia Bulletin, Mar. 14,
       [1939].

1882. Shaw, Len G. Detroit Free Press, Apr. 14, [1939].

1883. Shivers, Alfred S. Maxwell Anderson. Boston: Twayne,
       1976, pp. 89-93.

1884. _____. The Life of Maxwell Anderson. Briarcliff Manor,
       N.Y.: Stein and Day, 1983, pp. 171-77.

1885. Sloper, L. A. The Christian Science Monitor, Oct. 11, 1938.

1886. Smith, Ardis. Buffalo News, Mar. 22, [1939].

1887. Smith, Cecil, and Glenn Litton. Musical Comedy in America.
       New York: Theatre Arts Books, 1950, pp. 194-95.

1888. Unsigned. "All Is Not Lost--Or Won" [an editorial], The
       New York Times, Nov. 13, [1938].

1889. _____. Boston Globe, Sept. 28, [1938].

1890. _____. "Celebrities in a New Venture," Boston Post, Sept.
       25, 1938. The "celebrities" are the five dramatist members
       of the fledgling Playwrights Producing Company: MA,
       Robert Sherwood, S. N. Behrman, Elmer Rice, Sidney
       Howard. Knickerbocker Holiday was one of the four plays
       that they were presenting that season. Howard died before
       he could get his first play ready for the group.

1891. _____. "Delay Opening of Musical Play," Boston Post,
         Sept. 26, 1938.

1892. _____. "Dutch in the Forties," The New York Times,
         Sept. 25, 1938, IX, 1-2. The "Forties" refers to the
         1640's.

1893. _____. "Hartford 'Holiday,'" Boston Herald, Sept. 27
         [1938]. Knickerbocker Holiday had its tryout opening in
         Hartford, Connecticut. It was the first musical that any
         of the Playwright Company dramatists had ever put on the
         professional stage.

1894. _____. "Hitler Depicted in Villain's Role," The New York
         Daily Sun, Oct. 10, 1941. Critics saw the dictatorial gov-
         ernor Peter Stuyvesant as a slap at Hitler, even though
         he is made halfway loveable and gets to court the heroine
         and even sings the now famous "September Song."

1895. _____. New York Daily Mirror [editorial], Oct. 17, [1938].

1896. _____. New York Herald Tribune, Nov. 27, 1938.

1897. _____. New York Herald Tribune, Jan. 29, 1939.

1898. _____. "Notes on Maxwell Anderson," New Masses, Nov.
         29, 1938, p. 27.

1899. _____. "Roosevelt Sees Operetta Which Pokes Fun at
         Peter Stuyvesant as Colonial Dictator," The New York
         Sunday Times, Oct. 15, [1938], p. 1. President Roose-
         velt, according to all reports, laughed a good deal during
         the performance in Washington, D.C., even though the
         play contained jabs at the New Deal administration and at
         him personally. There is even a Roosevelt in the play.

1900. _____. "Roosevelt, at Operetta, Laughs at Sallies of
         'Peter Stuyvesant' Twitting Government," The New York
         Times, Oct. 16, 1938, I, 3. For more information on
         Roosevelt and his connection with the play, see my book
         The Life of Maxwell Anderson, pp. 175-77.

1901. _____. "'Silver Legs' to Music" [editorial]. Boston Herald,
         Oct. 6, [1938].

1902. _____. Stage Magazine, XVI (Oct., 1938), 26-27.

1903. _____. Stage Magazine, XVI (Nov., 1938), 35.

1904. _____. "St. Mark's Sees Huston in Role of Stuyvesant,"
         New York Herald Tribune, Jan. 30, [1938].

1905. _____. "Stuyvesant Life Told in Services," The New York
       Times, Jan. 30, [1939].

1906. _____. "Theatre," Life, VI (Feb. 6, 1939), 29.

1907. _____. The New York Times, Oct. 2, [1938].

1908. _____. "The Presidency," Time, XXXII (Oct. 24, 1938).

1909. _____. Time, XXXII (Oct. 31, 1938), 55.

1910. _____. Variety, Oct. 9, [1938].

1911. _____. "Walter Huston Kids an Early American Dictator,"
       Life, V (Nov. 21, 1938), 37.

1912. Vernon, Grenville. Commonweal, XXIX (Nov. 4, 1938), 48-
       49.

1913. Waldorf, Wilella. "Five of Broadway's Leading Playwrights
       New Producers," New York Post, Sept. 6, 1938.

1914. Walker, Danton. "Broadway," New York News, Sept. 9,
       1938.

1915. Wall, Vincent. "Maxwell Anderson: The Last Anarchist,"
       American Drama and Its Critics[:]   A Collection of Critical
       Essays. Chicago: Univ. of Chicago Press, 1965, pp. 172-
       74.

1916. Whipple, Sidney B. New York World-Telegram, Oct. 20,
       1938.

1917. _____. "Playwrights' Company Theatre: Hope Today,"
       New York World-Telegram, Nov. 8, [1938].

1918. Winchell, Walter. New York Daily Mirror, Oct. 20, 1938.

1919. Wyatt, Euphemia Van Rensselaer. Catholic World,
       CXXXXVIII (Dec., 1938), 343-44.

1920. Young, Stark. New Republic, XCVII (Nov. 9, 1938), 18-19.

LOST IN THE STARS

1921. Atkinson, Brooks. The New York Times, Oct. 31, 1949, p.
       21.

1922. _____, and Albert Hirschfeld. The Lively Years[:] 1920-
       1973. New York: Association Press, 1973, pp. 213-15.

1923. Bailey, Mabel Driscoll. Maxwell Anderson[:] The Playwright
       as Prophet. New York: Abelard-Schuman, 1957, pp. 182-
       93.

1924. Barnes, Howard. New York Herald Tribune, Oct. 31, 1949.

1925. _____. New York Herald Tribune, Nov. 6, 1949.

1926. Barnes, Clive. The New York Times, Apr. 19, 1972, p. 38.
       About a revival on Broadway.

1927. Baro, Gene. Washington Post, Feb. 21, 1972.

1928. Barron, Mark. Post Gazette (Pittsburgh, Pa.), Nov. 4,
       1949.

1929. Bohle, Bruce. St. Louis Star-Times, Oct. 10, 1950.

1930. Brown, John Mason. "Lost in the Stars American Tragedy,"
       Saturday Review of Literature, XXXII (Aug. 6, 1949), 127-
       28.

1931. _____. Saturday Review of Literature, XXXII (Nov. 26,
       1949), 31-32.

1932. _____. Still Seeing Things. New York: McGraw-Hill
       Book Co., 1950, pp. 227-32.

1933. Bugbee, Emma. "Paton Arrives to See Novel Made into
       Play," New York Herald Tribune, Oct. 20, 1949.

1934. Buzek, Dorothy. Huntington Advertiser, Oct. 19, [1950].

1935. _____. "'Lost in the Stars' to Open Artists Series' 15th
       Season," The Herald Advertiser, Oct. 8, 1950. She refers
       to the Marshall College Artists Series.

1936. Cassidy, Claudia. Chicago Tribune, Oct. 31, 1950.

1937. Chapman, John. New York Daily News, Oct. 31, 1949.

1938. _____. New York Daily News, Nov. 6, 1949.

1939. _____. New York Daily News, Nov. 10, 1949.

1940. _____. New York Journal-American, Oct. 31, 1949.

1941. Clurman, Harold. "Lost in the Stars of Broadway," Saturday
       Review of Literature, XXXII (Dec. 31, 1949), 43-44.

1942. Coleman, Robert. New York Daily Mirror, Oct. 31, 1949.

1943. _____. "Anderson Should Have Gotten Nobel Prize," New
       York Daily Mirror, Nov. 13, 1949.

1944. Currie, M. Brooklyn Daily Eagle, Nov. 6, 1949.

1945. Daugherty, A. A. The Louisville Times, Oct. 17, 1950.

1946. Fried, Alexander. San Francisco Examiner, Aug. 9, 1950.

1947. Garland, Robert. New York Journal-American, Oct. 31, 1949.

1948. Gassner, John. Forum, CXII (Dec., 1949), 339-40.

1949. Getlein, Frank. The Evening Star (Washington, D.C.),
       Feb. 21, 1972.

1950. Gibbs, Wolcott. The New Yorker, XXV (Nov. 5, 1949), 64.

1951. Gill, Brendan. The New Yorker, XLVIII (Apr. 29, 1972),
       103.

1952. Gilroy, Harry. "Written in the Stars," The New York Times,
       Oct. 30, 1949.

1953. Goldberg, Albert. Los Angeles Times, Mar. 18, 1957.

1954. Green, Mawbry. Theatre World, XLV (Dec., 1949) 27.

1955. Harford, Margaret. Los Angeles Mirror News, Mar. 18, 1957.

1956. Harris, Sydney J. Chicago News, Oct. 31, 1950.

1957. Hawkins, William. New York World-Telegram, Oct. 31, 1949.

1958. Hewes, Henry. Saturday Review of Literature, LV (May 6,
       1972), 64-65.

1959. Hinton, James, Jr. Musical America, LXIX (Nov. 15, 1949),
       9.

1960. Hobart, John. The San Francisco Chronicle, Aug. 9, 1950.

1961. Hodel, Emilia. San Francisco News, Aug. 8, 1950.

1962. Jarrell, Boyd. Huntington Herald Dispatch, Oct. 19, 1950.

1963. Kelley, Bev. Chicago Sun-Times, Oct. 29, 1950.

1964. Koebel, Mary McGavran. Ohio State Journal (Columbus,
       Ohio), Oct. 21, 1950, p. 3. Concerns the opening at the
       Hartman Theatre on the coming Tuesday evening. Article

is based on interview with MA and his wife, who were in town.

1965. Leonard, William. Chicago Journal of Commerce, Oct. 31, 1950.

1966. "L. L." [signature]. The Kansas City Times, Oct. 6, 1950.

1967. Marshall, Margaret. The Nation, CLXIX (Nov. 12, 1949), 478.

1968. Martin, Boyd. The Courier-Journal (Louisville, Ky.), Jan. 1, 1950.

1969. _____. The Courier-Journal (Louisville, Ky.), Oct. 17, 1950.

1970. Masters, Ann. Chicago Herald American, Oct. 31, 1950.

1971. Matlaw, Myron. "Alan Paton's Cry, the Beloved Country and Maxwell Anderson's/Kurt Weill's 'Lost in the Stars': A Consideration of Genres," Arcadia, X (1975), 260-72.

1972. Monk, Herbert L. St. Louis Globe-Democrat, Oct. 10, 1950.

1973. Morehouse, Ward. The New York Daily Sun, Oct. 31, 1949.

1974. Morton, Hortense. San Francisco Examiner, Aug. 9, 1950.

1975. Nathan, George Jean. American Review, LXX (Feb., 1950), 170-72.

1976. Norton, Elliot. Boston Post, Oct. 31, 1949.

1977. Phelan, Kappo. Commonweal, LI (Nov. 25, 1949), 212.

1978. Phelan, Paul. The New York Daily Sun, Dec. 2, 1949.

1979. Pollak, Robert. Chicago Sun-Times, Oct. 31, 1950.

1980. Pollock, Arthur. The Daily Compass, Oct. 8 ,1949.

1981. _____. The Daily Compass, Dec. 1, 1949.

1982. Richman, Jake. Evening World Herald (Omaha, Nebr.), Oct. 5, 1950.

1983. Roosevelt, Eleanor. New York World-Telegram, Nov. 19, 1949.

1984. Sanders, Ronald. The Days Grow Short: A Life and Music

of Kurt Weill. New York: Holt, Rinehart and Winston,
1980, pp. 375-88, 391-92.

1985. Shivers, Alfred S. Maxwell Anderson. Boston: Twayne,
1976, p. 31.

1986. _____. The Life of Maxwell Anderson. Briarcliff Manor,
N.Y.: Stein and Day, 1983, pp. 228-31.

1987. Smock, Susan Wanless. "Lost in the Stars and Cry, the
Beloved Country: A Thematic Comparison," North Dakota
Quarterly, IIL (Summer, 1980), iii, 53-59.

1988. Soanes, Wood. Oakland Tribune, Aug. 8, 1950.

1989. Standish, Myles. St. Louis Post-Dispatch, Oct. 10, 1950.

1990. Start, Clarissa. St. Louis Post-Dispatch, Oct. 9, 1950.

1991. Stern, Harold. American Jewish Daily, Nov. [?], 1949.

1992. Taylor, F. Beatrice. The Free Press (London, Ontario),
Mar. 18, 1950, p. 4.

1993. Unsigned. AUFBAU, Nov. 18, 1949. [In German.]

1994. _____. Cue, Nov. 5, 1949.

1995. _____. Life, XXVII (Nov. 11, 1949), 143-44, 146, 149.

1996. _____. Life, XXVII (Nov. 14, 1949), 143-46, 149.

1997. _____. New York Morning Telegraph, Nov. 1, 1949.

1998. _____. Newsweek, XXXIV (Nov. 7, 1949), 80.

1999. _____. New York Herald Tribune, Aug. 5, 1949.

2000. _____. New York Herald Tribune, May 17, 1950.

2001. _____. New York Herald Tribune, June 24, 1950.

2002. _____. Rochester Democrat and Chronicle, Apr. 9, 1950.

2003. _____. Theatre Arts Monthly, XXXIV (Jan., 1950), 11.

2004. _____. The New York Times, Oct. 30, 1949, II, 3.

2005. _____. The New York Times, Dec. 11, 1949, VI, 14.

2006. _____. The New York Times, Feb. 18, 1972, p. 20. An

announcement that the play is scheduled for Broadway production again.

2007. _____. The New York Times, Apr. 30, 1972, II, 3. More about the Broadway revival of Lost in the Stars.

2008. _____. Time, LIV (Nov. 7, 1949), 80.

2009. _____. Variety, Nov. 2, 1949.

2010. Warfield, Polly. "The Weill-Anderson Collaboration Is Successful on Stage and Off," San Francisco Chronicle, Aug. 6, 1950.

2011. Watt, Douglas. New York Daily News, Apr. 19, 1972, p. 84.

2012. Watts, Richard, Jr. New York Post, Oct. 31, 1949.

2013. _____. New York Post, Nov. 13, 1949.

2014. _____. New York Post, Apr. 19, 1972.

2015. "W. C. G." [signature]. The Sacramento Bee, Aug. 12, 1950.

2016. White, Walter. New York Herald Tribune, Nov. 6, 1949.

2017. Wyatt, Euphemia Van Rensselaer. Catholic World, CLXX (Dec., 1949), 226.

MARY OF SCOTLAND

2018. Adams, F. P. New York Herald Tribune, Dec. 2, 1933.

2019. Allen, Kelcey. Women's Wear Daily, Nov. 28, 1933.

2020. Anderson, John. New York Evening Journal, Nov. 28, 1933, p. 22.

2021. Atkinson, Brooks. The New York Times, Nov. 28, 1933, p. 28.

2022. _____. The New York Times, Nov. 29, 1933.

2023. _____. The New York Times, Dec. 3, 1933, IX, 5.

2024. _____. The New York Times, Dec. 17, 1933.

2025. Bailey, Mabel Driscoll. Maxwell Anderson[:] The Playwright

as Prophet. New York: Abelard-Schuman, 1957, pp. 37-45.

2026. Barron, Mark. New York World Telegram, Dec. 8, 1933.

2027. Benet, William Rose. Saturday Review of Literature, X (Feb. 17, 1934), 496.

2028. Brandt, George. Review of Reviews, LXXXIX (Feb. 17, 1934), 39.

2029. Brown, John Mason. New York Evening Post, Nov. 28, 1933.

2030. _____. New York Evening Post, Dec. 2, 1933.

2031. _____. New York Evening Post, Dec. 16, 1933.

2032. Burr, Eugene. Billboard, XLV (Dec. 9, 1933), 17, 53.

2033. Caldwell, Cy. New Outlook, CLXIII (Jan., 1934), 42.

2034. Chamberlain, John. The New York Times, Dec. 19, 1933.

2035. Clark, Norman. The Baltimore News, Nov. 7, 1933.

2036. "Cohen" [signature]. Legitimate, Nov. 7, 1933.

2037. Crosby, Edward Harold. Boston Post, Nov. 14, 1933.

2038. Doherty, Brian. Canadian Forum, XV (Apr., 1935), 275.

2039. Dusenbury, Winifred L. "Myth in American Drama Between the Wars," Modern Drama, VI (Dec., 1963), 297-98.

2040. Eaton, Walter Prichard. New York Herald Tribune, Feb. 11, 1934.

2041. Flexner, Eleanor. American Playwrights: 1918-1938[:] The Theatre Retreats from Reality. Freeport, N.Y.: Books for Libraries Press, 1969, pp. 93-97.

2042. Gabriel, Gilbert W. New York American Nov. 28, 1933.

2043. _____. "Maxwell Anderson's Mary of Scotland," The American Theatre as Seen by Its Critics, 1752-1934. Edited by Montrose J. Moses and John Mason Brown. New York: Cooper Square, 1934, pp. 315-18.

2044. _____. New York American, Nov. 28, 1933.

2045. _____. Town and Country, Jan. 1, 1933, p. 19.

2046. Gagey, Edmond McAdoo. Revolution in American Drama. New York: Columbia Univ. Press, 1947, pp. 78-79.

2047. Garland, Robert. New York World-Telegram, Nov. 15, 1933.

2048. _____. New York World-Telegram, Nov. 28, 1933.

2049. _____. "'Mary of Scotland' Victim of Miscasting," New York World-Telegram, June 22, 1934, p. 18.

2050. _____. New York World-Telegram, Oct. 22, 1934.

2051. Gassner, John. "The Theatre at the Crossroads," One Act Play Magazine, I (July, 1937), 274-75.

2052. Gaul, Harvey. Pittsburgh Post-Gazette, Oct 31, 1933.

2053. Goodrich, Laurence B. Players Magazine, X (May-June, 1934), 32.

2054. Halline, Allan G. "Maxwell Anderson's Dramatic Theory," American Literature, XVI (May, 1944), 68-81.

2055. Hamilton, Clayton. The Washington Post, Oct. 24, 1933.

2056. Hammond, Percy. New York Herald Tribune, Nov. 28, 1933.

2057. _____. New York Herald Tribune, Nov. 29, 1933.

2058. _____. New York Herald Tribune, Dec. 3, 1933.

2059. Hayes, Helen, and Lewis Funke. A Gift of Joy. Philadelphia: M. Evans & Co., 1965, pp. 127-36.

2060. Helburn, Theresa. A Wayward Quest[:] The Autobiography of Theresa Helburn. Boston: Little, Brown, 1960, pp. 241-43.

2061. Hochman, Stanley, et al. (eds.). McGraw-Hill Encyclopedia of World Drama. 2nd ed. New York: McGraw-Hill Book Co., 1984, Vol. I, pp. 141-42.

2062. Hoffher, Fred G. "On joue à New-York, 'Marie d'Ecosse' un drame de M. Maxwell Anderson," Comoedia, Feb. 17, 1934.

2063. Isaacs, Edith J. R. "Good Playing A-Plenty," Theatre Arts Monthly, XVIII (Jan., 1934), 14-18.

2064. Kanour, Gilbert. Baltimore Evening Sun, Nov. 7, 1933.

2065. Kelley, Andrew R. The Wahsington Times, Oct. 24, 1933, p. 16.

2066. Kirkley, Donald. The Baltimore Sun, Nov. 7, 1933.

2067. Knepler, Henry W. "Maxwell Anderson: A Historical Paral-
       lel," Queen's Quarterly, LXIV (1957), 250-63.

2068. Krutch, Joseph Wood. The Nation, CXXXVII (Dec. 13, 1933),
       688-90.

2069. Lockridge, Richard. The New York Daily Sun, Nov. 28,
       1933.

2070. _____. The New York Daily Sun, Dec. 2, 1933.

2071. _____. The New York Daily Sun, May 12, 1934.

2072. MacDonald, Rose. The Evening Telegram (Toronto), Sept. 1,
       1942. About a new production of Mary of Scotland.

2073. Maguire, C. E. "The Divine Background," Drama Critique,
       II (Feb., 1959), 19-24.

2074. Mantle, Burns. New York Daily News, Nov. 28, 1933.

2075. _____. New York Daily News, June 7, 1934, p. 51.

2076. Matlaw, Myron (ed.). Modern World Drama[:] An Encyclo-
       pedia. New York: E. P. Dutton, 1972, pp. 509-10.

2077. Melcher, E. de S. The Evening Star (Toronto), Oct. 24,
       1933, p. C8.

2078. Miller, Jordan Y. "Maxwell Anderson: Gifted Technician,"
       The Thirties: Fiction, Poetry, Drama. Edited by Warren
       French. Deland, Fla.: Everett/Edwards, 1967, pp. 186-87.

2079. Morehouse, Ward. The New York Daily Sun, Dec. 4, 1933.

2080. _____. The New York Daily Sun, Oct. 16, 1937.

2081. Motherwell, Hiram. The Stage, XI (Dec., 1933), 10-11, 15-
       17.

2082. Nathan, George Jean. Vanity Fair, XLI (Feb., 1934), 41.

2083. Nicoll, Allardyce. The New York Times, Jan. 28, 1934.

2084. Paynter, Henry. "'Mary of Scotland' Is Sidetracked from
       'Men in White,'" New York Post, May 2, 1934.

2085. Perry, Henry Ten Eyck. Yale Review, XXIII (Summer, 1934),
       842-43. Review of the published play.

2086. Pollock, Arthur. Brooklyn Daily Eagle, Nov. 28, 1933.

2087. Quinn, Arthur Hobson. A History of the American Drama from the Civil War to the Present Day. New York: Appleton-Century-Crofts, 1936, pp. 268-70.

2088. Rabkin, Gerald. Drama and Commitment Politics in the American Theatre of the Thirties. Bloomington: Indiana Univ. Press, 1964, pp. 274-76.

2089. Ross, George. New York World-Telegram, Dec. 5, 1933.

2090. _____. New York World-Telegram, Dec. 7, 1933.

2091. Ruhl, Arthur. New York Herald Tribune, Feb. 11, 1934, V, 2.

2092. Schallert, Edwin. Los Angeles Times, Sept. 11, 1934.

2093. Seibel, George. Pittsburgh Sun, [c.Oct. 31, 1933].

2094. Shank, Theodore J. (ed.). A Digest of 500 Plays[:] Plot Outlines and Production Notes. New York: Crowell-Collier, 1963, pp. 299-300.

2095. Shivers, Alfred S. Maxwell Anderson. Boston: Twayne, 1976, pp. 80-85.

2096. _____. The Life of Maxwell Anderson. Briarcliff Manor, N.Y.: Stein and Day, 1983, pp. 119, 126, 128, 129.

2097. Skinner, Richard Dana. Commonweal, XIX (Dec. 15, 1933), 189-90.

2098. Unsigned. Booklist, XXX (Mar., 1934), 208-09.

2099. _____. Boston Globe, Nov. 14, 1933.

2100. _____. "Helen Mencken as Elizabeth in Her Youth," New York Herald Tribune, Nov. 26, 1933.

2101. _____. Literary Digest, CXXII (Aug. 8, 1936), 18. About movie version of the play.

2102. _____. London Times, Mar. 24, 1934.

2103. _____. Newsweek, II (Dec. 9, 1933), 32.

2104. _____. New York World-Telegram, Oct. 24, 1933.

2105. _____. New York World-Telegram, Dec. 2, 1933.

2106. _____. Nottingham Evening News (Nottingham, England),
      Feb. 8, 1934.

2107. _____. Players Magazine, X (May-June, 1934), 32.

2108. _____. Scholastic, XXIX (Sept. 19, 1936), 17. Review
      of the movie version starring Katharine Hepburn and Fred-
      ric March as Mary and Bothwell, respectively.

2109. _____. The New York Times, Sept. 18, 1933, p. 22. An-
      nounces that Helen Hayes is to have the lead role in the
      play.

2110. _____. The New York Times, Apr. 14, 1935, IX, 2.

2111. _____. The Wall Street Journal, Nov. 29, 1933.

2112. _____. Time, XXII (Dec. 4, 1933), 48-49.

2113. _____. Variety, Dec. 5, 1933, p. 54.

2114. Wadeau, Roy S. Vintage Years of the Theatre Guild 1928-
      1939. Cleveland, Ohio: Case Western Reserve Univ.,
      1972, pp. 167-71.

2115. Waldorf, Wilella. New York Evening Post, Jan. 6, 1934.

2116. Watts, Harold H. "Maxwell Anderson: The Tragedy of At-
      trition," College English, IV (Jan., 1943), 220-30.

2117. Winchell, Walter. New York Daily Mirror, Nov. 28, 1933.

2118. Wyatt, Euphemia Van Rensselaer. Catholic World, CXXXVIII
      (Jan., 1934), 473-74.

2119. Young, Stark. New Republic, LXXVII (Dec. 13, 1933), 130-
      31.

MORNING WINTER AND NIGHT

2120. "L. V." [signature]. Review in San Francisco Chronicle,
      July 27, 1952, p. 13.

2121. Parone, Edward. Review in The New York Times, July 13,
      1952, p. 17.

2122. Shivers, Alfred S. The Life of Maxwell Anderson. Briar-
      cliff Manor, N.Y.: Stein and Day, 1983, pp. 234-36.

2123.   Unsigned. Review in Kirkus, XX (Feb. 1, 1952), 85.

2124.   _____. Review in The Nation, CLXXV (Aug., 9, 1952),
        116.

2125.   _____. Review in Saturday Review of Literature, XXXV
        (June 7, 1952), 54-55.

2126.   Webster, Harvey Curtis. Review in New York Herald Tribune
        Book Review, Apr. 27, 1952, p. 11.

                        NIGHT OVER TAOS

2127.   Atkinson, Brooks. "On an American Theme," The New York
        Times, Mar. 10, 1932, p. 25.

2128.   Avery, Laurence G. "The Conclusion of 'Night Over Taos,'"
        American Literature, XXXVII (Nov., 1965), 318-21.

2129.   Bailey, Mabel Driscoll. Maxwell Anderson[:] The Playwright
        as Prophet. New York: Abelard-Schuman, 1957, pp. 128-
        31.

2130.   Benchley, Robert. The New Yorker, VIII (Mar. 19, 1932),
        30.

2131.   Brown, John Mason. New York Evening Post, Mar. 10, 1932,
        p. 13.

2132.   _____. New York Evening Post, Mar. 19, 1932, III, 8.

2133.   Brown, John Russell, and Bernard Harris (eds.). American
        Theatre Stratford Avon Studies #10. New York: St. Mar-
        tin's Press, 1967, pp. 74-77.

2134.   Burr, Eugene. Billboard, XLIV (Mar. 19, 1932), 16-17.

2135.   Carb, David. Vogue, LXXIX (May 15, 1932), 100.

2136.   Clark, Barrett H. Maxwell Anderson[:] The Man and His
        Plays. Ann Arbor, Mich.: University Microfilms, 1968,
        (originally published in 1933), pp. 25-27.

2137.   Clurman, Harold. The Fervent Years[:] The Story of the
        Group Theatre and the Thirties. New York: Alfred A.
        Knopf, 1945, pp. 79-81.

2138.   Flexner, Eleanor. American Playwrights: 1918-1938 The

Theatre Retreats from Reality. Freeport, N.Y.: Books
for Libraries, 1969, p. 98.

2139. Gabriel, Gilbert W. New York American, Mar. 10, 1932.

2140. _____. New York American, Mar. 20, 1932, p. E-7.

2141. Gagey, Edmond McAdoo. Revolution in American Drama.
New York: Columbia Univ. Press, 1947, p. 80.

2142. Garland, Robert. New York World-Telegram, Mar. 10, 1932.

2143. Hammond, Perry. New York Herald Tribune, Mar. 10, 1932.

2144. Herron, Ima Honaker. The Small Town in American Drama.
Dallas: Southern Methodist Univ. Press, 1969, pp. 132-
34, 423.

2145. Hutchens, John. Theatre Arts Monthly, XVI (May, 1932),
360-62.

2146. _____. Theatre Arts Monthly, XVI (June, 1932), 445.

2147. "Ibee" [signature]. Variety, CVI (Mar. 15, 1932), 50.

2148. Isaacs, Edith J. R. Theatre Arts Monthly, XXI (Oct., 1937),
763.

2149. Krutch, Joseph Wood. The Nation, CXXXIV (Mar. 30, 1932),
378.

2150. Lockridge, Richard. The New York Daily Sun, Mar. 10,
1932, p. 20.

2151. Mantle, Burns. New York Daily News, Mar. 10, 1932, p. 39.

2152. Miller, Jordan Y. "Maxwell Anderson: Gifted Technician,"
The Thirties: Fiction, Poetry, Drama. Edited by Warren
French. Deland, Fla.: Everett/Edwards, 1967, pp. 187-88.

2153. Nathan, George Jean. Vanity Fair, XXXVIII (May, 1932),
66, 76.

2154. Orlin, Lena Cowen. "Night Over Taos: Maxwell Anderson's
Sources and Artistry," North Dakota Quarterly, IIL (Summer, 1980), 12-25.

2155. Pollock, Arthur. Brooklyn Daily Eagle, Mar. 10, 1932, p. 22.

2156. Quinn, Arthur Hobson. A History of the American Drama
from the Civil War to the Present Day. New York: Appleton-Century-Crofts, 1936, p. 268.

2157. Rabkin, Gerald. Drama and Commitment Politics in the
       American Theatre of the Thirties. Bloomington: Indiana
       Univ. Press, 1964, pp. 276-77.

2158. Robinson, Cecil. With the Ears of Strangers; The Mexican
       in American Literature. Tucson: Univ. of Arizona Press,
       1963, pp. 103-05, 109-11.

2159. Ruhl, Arthur. New York Herald Tribune, Mar. 13, 1932,
       VII, 1, 6.

2160. Shivers, Alfred S. Maxwell Anderson. Boston: Twayne,
       1976, p. 30.

2161. _____. The Life of Maxwell Anderson. Briarcliff Manor,
       N.Y.: Stein and Day, 1983, pp. 123, 124.

2162. Sievers, W. David. Freud on Broadway. New York: Hermi-
       tage Press, 1955, pp. 174-75.

2163. Unsigned. Arts and Decoration, XXXVII (May, 1932), 56.

2164. _____. New York World-Telegram, Mar. 10, 1932.

2165. _____. Stage, IX (May, 1932), 32-35.

2166. _____. Theatre Guild, IX (May, 1932), 33.

2167. _____. The New York Times, Feb. 24, 1932, p. 24.

2168. Wyatt, Euphemia Van Rensselaer. Catholic World, CXXXV
       (Apr., 1932), 76.

2169. Young, Stark. "Hat-cha and Taos," New Republic, LXX
       (Mar. 30, 1932), 181-82.

OUTSIDE LOOKING IN

2170. Alms, Hawthorne. Survey, LV (Oct. 1, 1925), 46-47.

2171. Bailey, Mabel Driscoll. Maxwell Anderson[:] The Playwright
       as Prophet. New York: Abelard-Schuman, 1957, pp. 124-
       26.

2172. Benchley, Robert. Life, LXXXVI (Sept. 24, 1925), 20.

2173. Bromfield, Louis. Bookman, LXII (Nov., 1925), 321-22.

2174. Brown, John Mason. Theatre Arts Monthly, IX (Nov., 1925),
       710-11.

2175. Clark, Barrett H. Drama, XVI (Nov., 1925), 52.

2176. _____. Maxwell Anderson[:] The Man and His Plays.
       Ann Arbor, Mich.: University Microfilms, 1968 (originally
       published in 1933), pp. 15-16.

2177. Flexner, Eleanor. American Playwrights: 1918-1938 The
       Theatre Retreats from Reality. Freeport, N.Y.: Books
       for Libraries, 1969, pp. 81-82.

2178. Gabriel, Gilbert. The New York Daily Sun, Oct. 20, 1925.

2179. Hammond, Percy. New York Herald Tribune, Sept. 8, 1925.

2180. Hornblow, Arthur. Theatre Magazine, XXXXII (Nov., 1925),
       16.

2181. Krutch, Joseph Wood. "Liberty's Glories," The Nation, CXXI
       (Sept. 23, 1925), 338.

2182. Nathan, George Jean. American Mercury, VI (Nov., 1925),
       377.

2183. Quinn, Arthur Hobson. A History of the American Drama
       from the Civil War to the Present Day. New York: Apple-
       ton-Century-Crofts, 1936, p. 236.

2184. Shivers, Alfred S. Maxwell Anderson. Boston: Twayne,
       1976, p. 29.

2185. _____. The Life of Maxwell Anderson. Briarcliff Manor,
       N.Y.: Stein and Day, 1983, p. 104.

2186. Skinner, Richard Dana. Independent, CXV (Oct. 3, 1925),
       393.

2187. Taylor, Coley B. World Tomorrow, VIII (Oct., 1925), 310.

2188. Unsigned. Forward, Oct. 11, 1925.

2189. _____. New York World, Sept. 8, 1925.

2190. _____. New York World, Oct. 25, 1925.

2191. _____. The New York Daily News, Sept. 26, 1925.

2192. _____. The New York Daily News, Oct. 30, 1925.

2193. _____. The New York Times, Sept. 8, 1925.

2194. _____. The New York Times, Sept. 13, 1925, VIII, 1.

2195. _____. The New York Times, Oct. 4, 1925, IX, 2.

2196. _____. The New York Times, Oct. 11, 1925, VIII, 2.

2197. _____. The New York Times, Oct. 25, 1925, VIII, 2.

2198. _____. The New York Times, June 23, 1929, VIII, 2.

2199. Whipple, Leon. Survey, CV (Oct. 1, 1925), 46-47.

2200. Woollcott, Alexander. New York World, Sept. 13, 1925.

2201. Young, Stark. New Republic, XLIV (Sept. 23, 1925), 123-24.

SATURDAY'S CHILDREN

2202. Anderson, John. New York Evening Post, Jan. 27, 1927.

2203. Atkinson, Brooks. The New York Times, Jan. 27, 1927.

2204. Bailey, Mabel Driscoll. Maxwell Anderson[:]   The Playwright as Prophet. New York: Abelard-Schuman, 1957, pp. 126-28.

2205. Barretto, Larry. Bookman, LXV (Apr., 1927), 207.

2206. Benchley, Robert. Life, LXXXIX (Feb., 17, 1927), 19.

2207. Brown, John Mason. Theatre Arts Monthly, XI (Apr., 1927), 246-48.

2208. Carb, David. Vogue, LXIX (Apr. 1, 1927), 132.

2209. Clark, Barrett H. Drama, XVII (Apr., 1927), 200.

2210. _____. Maxwell Anderson[:]   The Man and His Plays. Ann Arbor, Mich.: University Microfilms, 1968 (originally published in 1933), pp. 16-17.

2211. Dale, Alan. New York American, Jan. 27, 1927.

2212. Darlington, W. A. The Daily Telegraph, Jan. 24, 1934.

2213. Disher, M. Willson. The Daily Mail, Jan. 24, 1934.

2214. "F. D. D." [signature]. Theatre World, XXI (Feb., 1934), 66.

2215. Flexner, Eleanor. American Playwrights: 1918-1938 The
       Theatre Retreats from Reality. Freeport, N.Y.: Books
       for Libraries, 1969, pp. 82-83.

2216. Foster, Edward. "Core of Belief: An Interpretation of the
       Plays of Maxwell Anderson," Sewanee Review, L (Jan.,
       1942), 88-89.

2217. Gabriel, Gilbert. The New York Daily Sun, Jan. 27, 1927.

2218. "Garrick" [signature]. New York Evening Journal, Jan. 27,
       1927.

2219. Hammond, Percy. New York Herald Tribune, Jan. 27, 1927.

2220. Hartung, Philip T. Commonweal, XXXII (May 10, 1940), 63.

2221. Heiney, Donald. Recent American Literature. Great Neck,
       N.Y.: Barron's Educational Series, 1958, pp. 272-73.

2222. _____, and Lenthiel H. Downs. Recent American Litera-
       ture After 1930. Woodbury, N.Y.: Barron's Educational
       Series, 1974, pp. 281-82.

2223. Krutch, Joseph Wood. The Nation, CXXIV (Feb. 16, 1924),
       194.

2224. _____. The Nation, CXXIV (Feb. 23, 1927), 194.

2225. Mantle, Burns. "Maxwell Anderson," American Playwrights
       of Today. New York: Dodd, Mead, 1930, pp. 69-70.

2226. Matlaw, Myron (ed.). Modern World Drama[:] An Encyclo-
       pedia. New York: E. P. Dutton, 1972, p. 680.

2227. Morris, Lloyd R. Postscript to Yesterday; America: The
       Last Fifty Years. New York: Random House, 1947, p.
       196.

2228. Nathan, George Jean. American Mercury, X (Apr., 1927),
       503-04.

2229. _____. Judge, XCII (Feb. 11, 1927), 16, 26.

2230. Parker, H. T. Boston Transcript, Mar. 6, 1938.

2231. Pollock, Arthur. Brooklyn Daily Eagle, Jan. 27, 1927.

2232. Quinn, Arthur Hobson. A History of the American Drama
       from the Civil War to the Present Day. New York: Apple-
       ton-Century-Crofts, 1936, p. 236.

2233. Riley, Wilfred J. Billboard, XXXIX (Feb. 5, 1927), 11.

2234. Shivers, Alfred S. Maxwell Anderson. Boston: Twayne, 1976, p. 29.

2235. _____. The Life of Maxwell Anderson. Briarcliff Manor, N.Y.: Stein and Day, 1983, pp. 106, 107.

2236. Sievers, W. David. Freud on Broadway. New York: Hermitage House, 1955, p. 172.

2237. Skinner, Richard Dana. Commonweal, V (Feb. 9, 1927), 382.

2238. Unsigned. American Magazine, LXXXXV (Mar., 1948), 114-15.

2239. _____. Boston Transcript, Feb. 2, 1927.

2240. _____. Boston Transcrpt, Mar. 21, 1927.

2241. _____. Scholastic, XXXVI (Apr. 22, 1940), 36.

2242. _____. New Statesman and Nation, VII (Feb. 3, 1934), 155.

2243. _____. The Illustrated Sporting and Dramatic News, Feb. 3, 1934, p. 216.

2244. _____. The Morning Post, Jan. 24, 1934.

2245. _____. The New York Daily Sun, Feb. 5, 1927.

2246. _____. The New York Times, Jan. 27, 1927, p. 13.

2247. _____. The New York Times, Feb. 6, 1927, VII, 1.

2248. _____. The New York Times, Aug. 30, 1927, p. 21.

2249. _____. The New York Times, Apr. 10, 1928, p. 32.

2250. _____. The New York Times, July 30, 1935, p. 17.

2251. _____. The New York Times, July 7, 1936, p. 22.

2252. _____. The New York Times, May 12, 1940, IX, 3.

2253. _____. The Times (London), Jan. 24, 1934.

2254. Waldman, Milton. London Mercury, XVII (Nov., 1927), 93.

2255. Wilson, A. E. The Star (London), Jan. 24, 1934. About a British production of Saturday's Children.

2256. Woollcott, Alexander. New York World, Jan. 27, 1927.

2257. Wyatt, Euphemia Van Rensselaer. Catholic World, CXXV
       (Apr., 1927), 93-94.

2258. Young, Stark. "Saturday's Children and Trelawney," New
       Republic, IL (Feb. 16, 1927), 357-58.

2259. Zilkin, Nathan. New York Telegraph, Jan. 28, 1927.

                        SECOND OVERTURE

2260. Bailey, Mabel Driscoll. Maxwell Anderson[:] The Playwright
       as Prophet. New York: Abelard-Schuman, 1957, pp. 25-
       30.

2261. Dunlap, Orrin E., Jr. "A Second Overture," The New York
       Times, Feb. 6, 1938.

2262. Shivers, Alfred S. Maxwell Anderson. Boston: Twayne,
       1976, p. 30.

                        STORM OPERATION

2263. Bailey, Mabel Driscoll. Maxwell Anderson[:] The Playwright
       as Prophet. New York: Abelard-Schuman, 1957, pp. 119-
       22.

2264. Barnes, Howard. New York Herald Tribune, Jan. 12, 1944.

2265. Chapman, John. New York Daily News, Jan. 12, 1944.

2266. _____. New York Daily News, Jan. 23, 1944.

2267. Colby, Ethel. New York Journal of Commerce, Jan. 2, 1944.

2268. Coleman, Robert. New York Daily Mirror, Jan. 12, 1944.

2269. Field, Rowland. Newark Evening News, Jan. 12, 1944.

2270. Foldes, Peggy. Daily Northside News (New York City), Jan.
       21, 1944.

2271. Freedley, George. New York Morning Telegram, Jan. 13,
       1944.

2272. Gibbs, Wolcott. The New Yorker, XIX (Jan. 22, 1944), 34.

2273. Gilder, Rosamond. Theatre Arts Monthly, XXVIII (Mar.,
      1944), 133-36.

2274. Jordan, Elizabeth. America, Feb. 5, 1944.

2275. Kronenberger, Louis. PM (New York City), Jan. 12, 1944.

2276. Krug, Karl. Pittsburgh Sun-Telegram, Dec. 21, 1943.

2277. Marshall, Margaret. The Nation, CLVIII (Jan. 22, 1944),
      105-07.

2278. Monahan, Kaspar. Pittsburgh Press, Dec. 21, 1943.

2279. Morehouse, Ward. New York Sun, Jan. 12, 1944.

2280. Nathan, George Jean. New York Journal-American, Jan. 17,
      1944.

2281. Nichols, Lewis. The New York Times, Jan. 12, 1944.

2282. Phelan, Kappo. Commonweal, XXXIX (Feb. 4, 1944), 398-99.

2283. Piet, Creighton. Los Angeles Daily, Jan. 29, 1943.

2284. Pollock, Arthur. Brooklyn Daily Eagle, Jan. 12, 1944.

2285. _____. Brooklyn Daily Eagle, Jan. 16, 1944.

2286. Price, Edgar. Brooklyn Citizen, Jan. 12, 1944.

2287. Rabkin, Gerald. Drama and Commitment Politics in the Amer-
      ican Theatre of the Thirties. Bloomington: Indiana Univ.
      Press, 1964, pp. 278-79.

2288. Rascoe, Burton. New York World Telegram, Jan. 12, 1944.

2289. Sherburne, E. C. The Christian Science Monitor, Jan. 12,
      1944.

2290. Shivers, Alfred S. Maxwell Anderson. Boston: Twayne,
      1976, pp. 62-63.

2291. _____. The Life of Maxwell Anderson. Briarcliff Manor,
      N.Y.: Stein and Day, 1983, pp. 214-16.

2292. Unsigned. The American Hebrew, Jan. 21, 1944, pp. 10, 15.

2293. _____. "Anderson Went to Front to Make 'Storm Opera-
      tion' Real," Brooklyn Daily Eagle, Jan. 2, 1944. MA
      visited Britain and North Africa during March-June of 1943.

It was in North Africa that he assembled most of the materials used in Storm Operation.

2294. _____. New York Herald Tribune, Dec. 17, 1943.

2295. _____. New York Herald Tribune, Jan. 11, 1944.

2296. _____. New York Journal-American, Jan. 23, 1944.

2297. _____. PM (New York City), Jan. 9, 1944.

2298. _____. Signal Corps Message, Jan. 21, 1944.

2299. _____. The New York Times, Dec. 26, 1943.

2300. _____. The New York Times Magazine, Dec. 26, 1943, 10-11.

2301. _____. Time, XLIII (Jan. 24, 1944), 40.

2302. Waldorf, Wilella. New York Post, Jan. 12, 1944.

2303. Wyatt, Euphemia Van Rensselaer. Catholic World, CLVIII (Feb., 1944), 489-90.

2304. Young, Stark. New Republic, CX (Jan. 31, 1944), 148.

THE BUCCANEER

2305. "Abel" [signature]. Variety, LXXX (Oct. 7, 1925), 78.

2306. Bailey, Mabel Driscoll. Maxwell Anderson[:]   The Playwright as Prophet. New York: Abelard-Schuman, 1957, p. 124.

2307. Benchley, Robert. Life, LXXXVI (Oct. 22, 1925), 20.

2308. Brown, John Mason. Theatre Arts Monthly, IX (Dec., 1925), 786, 789.

2309. Clark, Barrett H. Drama, XVI (Dec., 1925), 91.

2310. _____. Maxwell Anderson[:]   The Man and His Plays. Ann Arbor, Mich.: Univ. Microfilms, 1968, pp. 14-15. Contrary to what the title implies, this book is very thin on biography. MA refused to supply any vita when Clark requested it. Interesting as a pioneer study. First published in 1933.

2311. Coleman, Robert. New York Daily Mirror, Oct. 3, 1925.

2312. Dale, Alan. New York American, Oct. 3, 1925.

2313. Gabriel, Gilbert. The New York Daily Sun, Oct. 3, 1925.

2314. Gillette, Don Carle. Billboard, XXXVII (Oct. 10, 1925), 10.

2315. Hammond, Percy. New York Herald Tribune, Oct. 3, 1925.

2316. "H. J. M." [signature]. The New Yorker, I (Oct. 10, 1925), 17.

2317. Hornblow, Arthur. Theatre Magazine, XLII (Dec., 1925), 16.

2318. Jones, Robert Edmond. New York Morning Telegraph, Oct. 3, 1925.

2319. Krutch, Joseph Wood. The Nation, CXXI (Oct. 21, 1925), 469.

2320. Nathan, George Jean. Judge, LXXXIX (Oct. 31, 1925), 30.

2321. Osborn, E. W. New York Evening World, Oct. 3, 1925.

2322. Parker, H. T. Boston Transcript, Sept. 15, 1925.

2323. Quinn, Arthur Hobson. A History of the American Drama from the Civil War to the Present Day. Rev. ed. New York: Appleton-Century-Crofts, 1936, p. 235.

2324. Shivers, Alfred S. Maxwell Anderson. Boston: Twayne, 1976, p. 29.

2325. _____. The Life of Maxwell Anderson. Briarcliff Manor, N.Y.: Stein and Day, 1983, p. 104.

2326. Skinner, Richard Dana. Commonweal, II (Oct. 14, 1925), 567.

2327. Torres, H. Z. New York Commercial, Oct. 3, 1925.

2328. Unsigned. "Lord of the Spanish Main," The New York Times, Oct. 3, 1925, p. 10.

2329. Vreeland, Frank. New York Evening Telegram, Oct. 3, 1925.

2330. Woollcott, Alexander. New York World, Oct. 3, 1925.

THE DAY THE MONEY STOPPED

2331. Coleman, Robert. "Anderson's Play Not Up to Par," New
       York Daily Mirror, Feb. 21, 1958, p. 20.

2332. Gibbs, Wolcott. The New Yorker, XXXIV (Mar. 1, 1958),
       56, 58.

2333. Shivers, Alfred S. Maxwell Anderson. Boston: Twayne,
       1976, p. 31.

2334. _____. The Life of Maxwell Anderson. Briarcliff Manor,
       N.Y.: Stein and Day, 1983, p. 260.

2335. Unsigned. The New York Times, Feb. 21, 1958, p. 19.

2336. _____. Time, LXXI (Mar. 3, 1958), 74.

                THE ESSENCE OF TRAGEDY AND OTHER
                    FOOTNOTES AND PAPERS

2337. Halline, Allan G. "Maxwell Anderson's Dramatic Theory,"
       American Literature, XVI (May, 1944), 68-81.

2338. Knowlton, Edgar C. South Atlantic Quarterly, XXXVIII
       (Oct., 1939), 473.

2339. Morton, Frederick. Theatre Arts Monthly, XXIII (Aug.,
       1939), 612-13.

2340. Sampley, Arthur M. "Theory and Practice in Maxwell Ander-
       son's Poetic Tragedies," College English, V (May, 1944),
       412-18.

2341   Shivers, Alfred S. Maxwell Anderson. Boston: Twayne,
       1972, pp. 31-34.

2342. _____. The Life of Maxwell Anderson. Briarcliff Manor,
       N.Y.: Stein and Day, 1983, pp. 126-28.

                    THE EVE OF ST. MARK

2343. Allison, Gordon F. Newark Sunday Call, Oct. 11, 1942.

2344. Anderson, John. New York Journal-American, Oct. 8, 1942,
       p. 10.

2345. _____. New York Journal-American, Oct. 18, 1942, 7, 9.

2346. Atkinson, Brooks. The New York Times, Oct. 8, 1942.

2347. _____. The New York Times, Oct. 18, 1942, VIII, 1.

2348. Bailey, Mabel Driscoll. Maxwell Anderson[:] The Playwright as Prophet. New York: Abelard-Schuman, 1957, p. 119.

2349. Barnes, Howard. New York Herald Tribune, Oct. 8, 1942.

2350. _____. New York Herald Tribune, Oct. 18, 1942.

2351. Barron, Mark. Bee (Fresno, Calif.), Oct. 11, 1942.

2352. _____. Worcester Telegram (Worcester, Mass.), Oct. 18, 1942.

2353. Beaufort, John. The Christian Science Monitor, Oct. 8, 1942.

2354. _____. The Christian Science Monitor, Oct. 24, 1942.

2355. Bell, Nelson B. Washington Post, May 2, 1943.

2356. _____. Washington Post, May 4, 1943.

2357. Bellamy, Peter. New York Post, Mar. 16, 1943.

2358. _____. Cleveland News, Mar. 24, 1943.

2359. Bessie, Alvah. New Masses, Nov. 3, 1942.

2360. Bookman, William I. Central Aisle, Mar. 9, 1943.

2361. Bronson, Arthur. Philadelphia Record, May 16, 1943.

2362. Brown, John Mason. New York World Telegram, Oct. 8, 1942.

2363. Burnham, David. Commonweal, XXXVII (Oct. 23, 1942), 15.

2364. Carmody, Jay. "Anderson States Clearly Why Axis Cannot Win," Evening Star (Washington, D.C.), May 4, 1943.

2365. Clarke, George W. Boston Record, Sept. 26, 1942.

2366. _____. Boston Record, Sept. 29, 1942.

2367. Colby, Ethel. Journal of Commerce (New York City), Oct. 9, 1942.

2368. _____. Journal of Commerce, Oct. 19, 1942.

2369. Coleman, Robert. New York Daily Mirror, Oct. 8, 1942.

2370. _____. New York Daily Mirror, Oct. 9, 1942.

2371. Cooke, Richard P. The Wall Street Journal, Oct. 9, 1942.

2372. "C. W. D." [signature]. Boston Globe, Sept. 25, 1942.

2373. David, George L. Rochester Democrat and Chronicle, Jan. 1, 1943.

2374. Davis, Richard S. Milwaukee Journal, Mar. 11, 1943.

2375. Detzel, Helen. Cincinnati Times-Star, Apr. 2, 1943.

2376. Doyle, Peggy. Boston Evening American, Sept. 25, 1942.

2377. Eager, Helen. Boston Traveler, Sept. 25, 1942.

2378. Eaton, Hal. Newark Star Ledger, Oct. 8, 1942.

2379. "E. W. '43" [signature]. Wellesley College News, Dec. 3, 1942.

2380. Ferris, John. Meriden Daily Journal (Meriden, Conn.), Nov. 14, 1942.

2381. Field, Rowland. Newark Evening News, Nov. 6, 1942.

2382. _____. Newark Evening News, Feb. 23, 1943.

2383. Foldes, Peggy. North Side Daily News, Oct. 16, 1943.

2384. Frazer, Frank. Long Island Star Journal, Feb. 3, 1943.

2385. Freedley, George. New York Morning Telegraph, Oct. 9, 1942.

2386. Gaffney, Leo. Boston Record, Sept. 25, 1942.

2387. Gassner, John. Dramatic Soundings. New York: Crown Publishers, 1968, pp. 301-02.

2388. Gaver, Jack. San Francisco News, Oct. 24, 1942.

2389. _____. Newark Evening News, Oct. 26, 1942.

2390. _____. Waterbury Democrat (Waterbury, Conn.), Oct. 30, 1942.

2391. Gentry, Charles. Detroit Evening News, Jan. 5, 1943.

2392. Gibbs, Wolcott. The New Yorker, XVIII (Oct. 17, 1942),
       35-36.

2393. Gilbert, Don. Montreal Daily Star, Oct. 17, 1942.

2394. Gilder, Rosamond. Theatre Arts Monthly, XXVI (Dec.,
       1942), 735-37.

2395. _____. "A Job to Be Done," Theatre Arts Monthly, XXVII
       (July, 1943).

2396. Gilhagen, Evelyn. "The Curtain Rises," Independent Woman,
       XXI (Dec., 1942), 368.

2397. Gordon, Paul. Toronto Daily Star, Nov. 14, 1942.

2398. Gordon, Will. New York Morning Telegraph, Dec. 8, 1943.

2399. Halline, Edward P. Milwaukee Sentinel, Mar. 13, 1943.

2400. Harrison, Dale. Chicago News, Oct. 11, 1942.

2401. Hughes, Elinor. Boston Herald, Oct. 4, 1942.

2402. _____. Boston Herald, Sept. 25, 1942.

2403. _____. Boston Herald, Sept. 27, 1942.

2404. Jagendorf, M. South Norwalk Sentinel (South Norwalk,
       Conn.), Oct. 21, 1942.

2405. "J. F. M. L." [signature]. The World, Nov. 29, 1942.

2406. Jordan, Elizabeth. America, Oct. 24, 1942.

2407. Kelley, Andrew R. The Evening Star (Washington, D.C.),
       Jan. 25, 1943, p. B-16.

2408. Kilgallen, Dorothy. New York Journal-American, Oct. 10,
       1942.

2409. Klausner, Sam. Education Sun, Dec. 9, 1942.

2410. Kowalewsky, Ed. Buffalo Evening News, Mar. 28, 1943.

2411. Kronacher, Alwin. AUFBAU, Nov. 13, 1942. [In German.]

2412. Kronenberger, Louis. PM (New York City), Oct. 8, 1942.

2413. _____. PM (New York City), Oct. 19, 1942.

2414. _____. PM (New York City), Nov. 6, 1942.

2415. Krutch, Joseph Wood. The Nation, CLV (Oct. 24, 1942),
      425-26.

2416. Kuhl, Arthur. St. Louis Star-Times, Apr. 6, 1943.

2417. Kurlander, Regine. Plain Dealer (Cleveland, Ohio), Oct. 27,
      1942.

2418. Leonard, William. Chicago Journal of Commerce, Jan. 19,
      1943.

2419. _____. Chicago Journal of Commerce, Jan. 23, 1943.

2420. Levitt, Vic. Trade Union Courier, Oct. 17, 1942.

2421. Lewis, Lloyd. Chicago Daily News, Jan. 19, 1943, p. 11.

2422. Lewis, Richard. Indianapolis Times, Mar. 17, 1943.

2423. Leyendecker, Frank S. About Town, Oct. 17, 1943.

2424. Lightfoot, Jean. "Youthful Stars of Hit Play," St. Louis
      Post Dispatch, Mar. 8, 1943.

2425. Lockridge, Richard. The New York Daily Sun, Oct. 8, 1942.

2426. Lockridge, Sarah. South Bend Indiana Tribune, Oct. 29,
      1942.

2427. Logan, Floyd. The News-Sentinel (Fort Wayne, Ind.), Oct.
      2, 1942.

2428. Lowe, David. "Anderson's Play to Be Produced," New
      York Mirror, Nov. 23, 1942.

2429. McDermott, William F. Cleveland Plain Dealer, Oct. 25,
      1942.

2430. _____. Cleveland Plain Dealer, Mar. 10, 1943.

2431. _____. Cleveland Plain Dealer, Mar. 24, 1943.

2432. _____. Cleveland Plain Dealer, Aug. 10, 1943.

2433. McLauchlin, Russell. Detroit News, Dec. 5, 1943.

2434. Mantle, Burns. New York Daily News, Oct. 8, 1942.

2435. _____ . New York Sunday News, Oct. 18, 1942, p. 82.

2436. _____ . New York Sunday News, Oct. 25, 1942.

2437. Martin, Linton. Philadelphia Inquirer, May 18, 1943.

2438. _____ . Philadelphia Inquirer, May 23, 1943.

2439. Mizen, Walter. Knickerbocker News (Albany, N.Y.), Oct. 28, 1942.

2440. Monahan, Kaspar. Pittsburgh Press, Mar. 25, 1943.

2441. _____ . Pittsburgh Press, Mar. 26, 1943.

2442. Monk, Herbert L. St. Louis Daily Globe-Democrat, Apr. 6, 1943.

2443. Morehouse, Ward. The New York Daily Sun, Oct. 9, 1942.

2444. _____ . The New York Daily Sun, Feb. 24, 1943.

2445. Norton, Elliot. Boston Post, Sept. 25, 1942.

2446. _____ . Boston Post, Sept. 27, 1942.

2447. _____ . Boston Sunday Post, May 23, 1943.

2448. Parry, Florence Fisher. Pittsburgh Press, Oct. 14, 1942.

2449. Parton, Lemuel F. The New York Daily Sun, Dec. 3, 1942.

2450. Patrick, Corbin. Indianapolis Star, Mar. 17, 1943.

2451. _____ . Indianapolis Sunday Star, Mar. 18, 1943.

2452. Perry, Lawrence. The Sunday Star, June 27, 1943.

2453. _____ . Scranton Times (Scranton, Pa.), Oct. 23, 1942.

2454. "P. J. D." [signature]. Newark Star Ledger, July 29, 1943.

2455. Pollak, Robert. Chicago Daily Times, Jan. 19, 1943.

2456. _____ . Chicago Sunday Times, Jan. 31, 1943.

2457. Pollock, Arthur. Brooklyn Daily Eagle, Oct. 8, 1942, p. 4.

2458. _____ . Brooklyn Daily Eagle, Oct. 11, 1942.

2459. _____ . Brooklyn Daily Eagle, Oct. 21, 1942.

2460. Price, Edgar. Brooklyn Citizen, Oct. 8, 1942.

2461. Radcliffe, E. B. Cincinnati Enquirer, Apr. 2, 1943.

2462. Ranney, Omar. Cleveland Press, Oct. 8, 1942.

2463. _____. Cleveland Press, Mar. 24, 1943.

2464. Rice, Robert. PM (New York City), Oct. 18, 1942.

2465. Rodell, John S. "Maxwell Anderson: A Criticism," Kenyon
       Review, V (Spring, 1943), 272-77.

2466. Roosevelt, Eleanor. World Telegram [in "My Day" column],
       Dec. 7, 1942. She mentions having seen Eve of St. Mark
       produced. She found it "most absorbing."

2467. Rosenfield, John. Dallas Morning News, Oct. 20, 1942.

2468. Ryan, Dorothy D. Oregonian (Portland, Ore.), Oct. 18, 1942.

2469. Sasso, Joe. "The Playwrights Company," Italian Tribune,
       Mar. 19, 1943.

2470. Schloss, Edwin H. Philadelphia Record, May 18, 1943.

2471. _____. Philadelphia Record, May 23, 1943.

2472. Schreiber, Flora Rheta. Players Magazine, XIX (Dec., 1942),
       12.

2473. Sensenderfer, Robert. Philadelphia Bulletin, May 18, 1943.

2474. Shaw, Lena G. Detroit Free Press, Jan. 5, 1943.

2475. Shearer, Sgt. Lloyd. "Soldiers Author Met at Camp Find
       Selves in His 'Eve of St. Mark,'" Rochester Democrat and
       Chronicle, Dec. 20, 1942. MA openly used for his play the
       personalities of several soldiers, including Marion Hargrove,
       whom he had met at Ft. Bragg, S.C., earlier that year.

2476. Shipley, Joseph T. New Leader, Oct. 17, 1943.

2477. Shivers, Alfred S. Maxwell Anderson. Boston: Twayne,
       1976, pp. 57-61.

2478. _____. The Life of Maxwell Anderson. Briarcliff Manor,
       N.Y.: Stein and Day, 1983, pp. 193-98.

2479. Sievers, W. David. Freud on Broadway. New York: Hermi-
       tage House, 1955, p. 178.

2480. Sloper, L. A. The Christian Science Monitor, Sept. 25,
      1942.

2481. Smith, Ardis. Buffalo News, Nov. 24, 1942.

2482. Smith, Cecil. Chicago Daily Tribune, Jan. 19, 1943, p. 13.

2483. Smith, Katherine. Times-Herald (Washington, D.C.), Nov.
      2, 1942.

2484. _____. Times-Herald (Washington, D.C.), Jan. 25, 1943,
      p. 20.

2485. _____. Times-Herald (Washington, D.C.), May 4, 1943.

2486. Smith, William. Commercial and Financial Chronicle, Oct. 15,
      1942.

2487. Sobol, Louis. Santa Rosa Republican (Santa Rosa, Calif.),
      Oct. 17, 1942. In "New York Broadway Cavalcade" column.

2488. Solloway, Larry. "Topflight Cast to Present 'Eve of St.
      Mark,'" Service Parade, Mar. 6, 1943, p. 10.

2489. Starr, Ann. Columbus Citizen (Columbus, Ohio), Mar. 30,
      1943.

2490. Stephens, Anthony. Long Island Star Journal, Dec. 1, 1943.

2491. Stevens, Ashton. Chicago Herald American, Jan. 19, 1943.

2492. Stewart, Russell. Washington Daily News, Jan. 25, 1943,
      p. 22.

2493. _____. Washington Daily News, May 4, 1943.

2494. Stock, Ernest. City College of New York newspaper, Dec.
      15, 1942.

2495. Storm, Axel. Reporter (Two Rivers, Wisc.), Oct. 19, 1942.

2496. Unsigned. "Anderson Hit Booked Here," Rochester Times-
      Union, Dec. 12, 1942.

2497. _____. "Anderson's 'The Eve of St. Mark' Now Playing
      at the Cort Theatre," The Woodside Herald (New York
      City), Oct. 9, 1942.

2498. _____. Boston Daily Record, Sept. 7, 1942, p. 26.

2499. _____. Boston Globe, Sept. 13, 1942.

2500. _____. Boston Herald, Sept. 24, 1942.

2501. _____. Boston Herald, Sept. 25, 1942.

2502. _____. Boston Post, Sept. 13, 1942.

2503. _____. Boston Sunday Advertiser Pictorial Review, Sept. 27, 1942, p. 26.

2504. _____. "Command Performance for 'The Eve of St. Mark' for President's Birthday Ball," Broadway News, Dec. 8, 1943.

2505. _____. "Command Performance to Aid National Paralysis Foundation Attended by Mrs. Roosevelt and Federal Officials," The New York Times, Jan. 25, 1943, p. 8.

2506. _____. Buffalo Courier Express, Mar. 23, 1943.

2507. _____. Chicago Daily News, Feb. 6, 1943.

2508. _____. Cincinnati Post, Apr. 2, 1943.

2509. _____. Current History, III (Nov., 1942), 264-65.

2510. _____. "Dead Soldier 'Lives' Again in Play. Nephew Becomes Anderson's Model," Buffalo Evening News, Oct. [14], 1942.

2511. _____. Detroit Evening Times, Nov. 27, 1942.

2512. _____. "Eight Will Rogers Soldiers Have Roles in Sooner Show [sic]," Norman Transcript (Norman, Okla.), Oct. 18, 1942, p. 1.

2513. _____. Enbee Chips [publication of the New Britain (Conn.) Machine Co.], Nov. 28, 1942, Vol. I, p. 5.

2514. _____. "'Eve of St. Mark' Has Able Cast," Service Parade, Mar. 7, 1943. The play is to be presented with a soldier cast at Miami Beach High School. The patriotic fervor surrounding this play was such that soldier casts were commonly used all throughout the country and in Britain.

2515. _____. "'Eve of St. Mark' Sold for $300,000," The New York Times, Nov. 12, 1942. This refers to the sale of the film rights.

2516. "'Eve of St. Mark' to Give 'Command Performance,'" The New York Times, Jan. 6, 1943. This performance was finally given in the National Theatre in Washington, D.C., on Sun-

day evening, Jan. 24, 1943, in celebraiton of President
Roosevelt's birthday. MA and his wife were at the White
House for tea that day.

2517. _____. "Film Price Set at $200,000 for 'Eve of St. Mark,'"
The New York Times, Oct. 12, 1942. The price finally
settled on was $300,000. Twentieth Century-Fox bought
the rights.

2518. _____. "Friars Start Season Tonight," Tuscaloosa News,
Oct. 1, 1942, p. 2. This news notice concerns the presentation of Eve of St. Mark at the Univ. of Alabama.

2519. _____. Gotham Life, Oct. 18, 1942.

2520. _____. Greenville News (Greenville, N.J.), Feb. 12, 1943.

2521. _____. "Hargrove to Be Actor. Soldier-Author to Appear
in Anderson Play at Fort Knox," The New York Times,
Mar. 26, 1943. Marion Hargrove, the soldier-author that
MA met at Fort Bragg earlier that year, inspired the role
of Private Francis Marion in the play. Hargrove's book
about soldier life, See Here, Private Hargrove, became a
best-seller soon after publication late in 1942.

2522. _____. Hollywood Reporter, Oct. 8, 1942.

2523. _____. Home News, Oct. 8, 1942.

2524. _____. Houston Chronicle, Nov. 27, 1942.

2525. _____. Indianapolis News, Mar. 17, 1943.

2526. _____. Kansas City Star, Nov. 8, 1942.

2527. _____. Life, XIII (Oct. 19, 1942), 51-52, 54, 56.

2528. _____. "Maxwell Anderson Drama Gains N.Y. Accolades,"
Daily Herald (Montreal), Oct. 14, 1942.

2529. _____. "Two Companies Playing 'The Eve of St. Mark,'"
Milwaukee Sentinel Pictorial Review, Jan. 24, 1943. Actually there were numerous theatrical groups--professional as
well as amateur--that staged the play in America and in
England during WWII.

2530. _____. Newark Evening News, July 23, 1943.

2531. _____. Newark Star-Ledger, Dec. 13, 1942.

2532. _____. Newark Star-Ledger, May 30, 1943.

2533. _____. Newsweek, XX (Oct. 19, 1942), 76-78.

2534. _____. "Official Washington at 'Eve of St. Mark,'" The
New York Times, Jan. 25, 1943. This refers to a presentation of the drama at the National Theatre in Washington, D.C., on the evening of Jan. 24th.

2535. _____. "O. W. I. to Sponsor Presentation," The New
York Times, Jan. 10, 1943, VIII, 3. "O. W. I." is an ab-
breviation for Office of War Information.

2536. _____. New York World Tribune, Dec. 13, 1942.

2537. _____. New York Teacher News, Feb. 6, 1943.

2538. _____. Norwich Sun (Norwich, N.Y.), Oct. 21, 1942.

2539. _____. Ohio State Journal (Columbus, Ohio), Mar. 30,
1943.

2540. _____. Oswego Gazette (Oswego, N.Y.), Oct. 22, 1942.

2541. _____. Philadelphia Daily News, May 18, 1943.

2542. _____. PIC, Nov. 5, 1943, pp. 15-17.

2543. _____. Players Magazine, XIX (Nov., 1942).

2544. _____. Players Magazine, XIX (Dec., 1942), 12.

2545. _____. Post-Journal (Jamestown, N.Y.), Oct. 22, 1942.

2546. _____. "President Asks for 'Eve of St. Mark,'" Daily
Worker, Dec. 1, 1942. Roosevelt requested a presentation
in Washington. He saw it on the following Jan. 24th.

2547. _____. St. Louis Post Dispatch, Nov. 1, 1942.

2548. _____. Scholastic, XLI (Nov. 9, 1942), 20.

2549. _____. Sociology, XXVII (Jan., 1943), 250.

2550. _____. "'The Eve of St. Mark,'" The Stage (London),
July 8, 1943. About the staging of the play at the Scala
Theatre.

2551. _____. "'The Eve of St. Mark' Opens Tomorrow Night,"
St. Louis Globe-Democrat, May 4, 1943.

2552. _____. The New York Times, Oct. 4, 1942, VIII, 1.

2553. _____. The New York Times, Oct. 8, 1942, p. 30.

2554. _____. This Week in Philadelphia, Aug. 7, 1943.

2555. _____. This Week in Chicago, Jan. 16, 1943.

2556. _____. Time, XL (Oct. 19, 1942), 60.

2557. _____. Tuscaloosa News, Oct. 2, 1942. Eve of St. Mark is presented at the Univ. of Alabama.

2558. _____. "University Theatre to Present 'The Eve of St. Mark,'" Banner-Herald (Athens, Ga.), Oct. 18, 1942.

2559. _____. Variety, Oct. 7, 1942.

2560. _____. Washington Post Parade, Dec. 17, 1943, pp. 9-13.

2561. _____. Will Rogers Field News, Vol. II, no. 2 (Nov. 14, 1942).

2562. _____. Wilmington News (Wilmington, Dela.), Oct. 30, 1942.

2563. _____. Women's Wear Daily (New York City), Oct. 8, 1942.

2564. Waldorf, Wilella. New York Post, Oct. 8, 1942, p. 34.

2565. _____. New York Post, Oct. 17, 1942.

2566. _____. "The 'Eve of St. Mark' Company Plans Experimental Matinees," New York Post, Mar. 17, 1943.

2567. Warner, A. J. Rochester Times-Union, Jan. 2, 1943.

2568. Warner, Ralph. New York Worker, Oct. 18, 1942.

2569. Waterhouse, Helen. Akron Beacon Journal, Jan. 22, 1943.

2570. Weidenreich, Peter. The Reporter (New York City), Oct. 19, 1942.

2571. Whitney, Dwight. San Francisco Chronicle. Oct. 26, 1942.

2572. Wilson, Earl. New York Post, Nov. 18, 1942.

2573. Winchell, Walter. New York Mirror, Oct. 11, 1942.

2574. Wyatt, Euphemia Van Rensselaer. Catholic World, CLVI (Nov., 1942), 214-15.

2575. York, Tracy. The Chicago Sun, Jan. 19, 1943.

2576. Young, Stark. New Republic, CVII (Oct. 26, 1942), 546.

THE FEAST OF ORTOLANS

2577. Bailey, Mabel Driscoll. Maxwell Anderson[:] The Playwright as Prophet. New York: Abelard-Schuman, 1957, pp. 25-26, 30-34.

2578. Rabkin, Gerald. Drama and Commitment Politics in the American Theatre of the Thirties. Bloomington: Indiana Univ. Press, 1964, p. 277.

2579. Shivers, Alfred S. Maxwell Anderson. Boston: Twayne, 1976, p. 30.

2580. _____. The Life of Maxwell Anderson. Briarcliff Manor, N.Y.: Stein and Day, 1983, p. 155.

2581. Unsigned. "Poetic Drama Spun for Air by Anderson," New York Herald Tribune, Aug. 22, 1937.

2582. _____. The New York Daily Sun, Sept. 25, 1937.

2583. _____. The New York Times, Sept. 26, 1937, XI, 10.

THE GOLDEN SIX

2584. Coleman, Robert. New York Daily Mirror, Feb. 21, 1958, p. 20.

2585. Doyle, Peggy. Boston American, July 1, 1958.

2586. Durgin, Cyrus. Boston Globe, May 1, 1958.

2587. _____. Boston Sunday Globe, May 4, 1958.

2588. Hayes, Richard. "The Golden Six," Commonweal, LXIX (Nov. 14, 1958), 175-76.

2589. Hughes, Elinor. Boston Herald, May 13, 1958.

2590. Lewis, Allan. American Plays and Playwrights of the Contemporary Theatre. Rev. ed. New York: Crown, 1965, p. 140.

2591. Mahoney, Alta. "New Anderson Drama Done by B. U.
       School," Boston Traveler, May 1, 1958, p. 18. Refers to
       a production of the play by an amateur group at Boston
       Univ. Theatre.

2592. Malcolm, Donald. The New Yorker, XXXIV (Nov. 8, 1958),
       91-93.

2593. Melvin, Edwin F. The Christian Science Monitor, May 1,
       1958.

2594. Norton, Elliot. Boston Record, May 1, 1958.

2595. _____. Boston Record, May 19, 1958.

2596. Plasberg, Elaine. Boston University News, May 6, 1958.

2597. Shivers, Alfred S. Maxwell Anderson. Boston: Twayne,
       1976, pp. 71-73.

2598. _____. The Life of Maxwell Anderson. Briarcliff Manor,
       N.Y.: Stein and Day, 1983, p. 260.

2599. Unsigned. "Anderson's Play Opens," The New York Times,
       May 2, 1958, p. 31. Refers to the amateur production of
       the play at the Boston University Theatre, where it was
       to run for four days.

2600. _____. The New York Times, May 3, 1958.

2601. _____. The New York Times, Oct. 27, 1958, p. 31.

2602. _____. Theatre Arts Monthly, XXXXIII (Jan., 1959), 66.

2603. _____. Time, LXXII (Nov. 3, 1958), 50.

                        THE MASQUE OF KINGS

2604. Anderson, John. New York Evening Journal, Feb. 9, 1937.

2605. Atkinson, Brooks. The New York Times, Feb. 9, 1937, p.
       19.

2606. Bailey, Mabel Driscoll. Maxwell Anderson[:] The Playwright
       as Prophet. New York: Abelard-Schuman, 1957, pp. 67-
       76.

2607. Benet, Stephen Vincent. "New Grandeur in Our Theatre,"
       Stage, XIV (Jan., 1937), 38-39, 41.

2608. Coleman, Robert. New York Daily Mirror, Feb. 9, 1937.

2609. Downer, Alan Seymour. Fifty Years of American Drama.
       Chicago: Henry Regnery, 1951, p. 107.

2610. Dusenbury, Winifred L. "Myth in American Drama Between
       the Wars," Modern Drama, VI (Dec., 1963), pp. 298-99.

2611. Eaton, Walter Prichard. New York Herald Tribune, May 9,
       1937.

2612. Flexner, Eleanor. American Playwrights: 1918-1938 The
       Theatre Retreats from Reality. Freeport, N.Y.: Books
       for Libraries, 1969 (originally published in 1938), pp.
       120-25.

2613. Gabriel, Gilbert W. New York American, Feb. 9, 1937.

2614. _____. New York American, Feb. 21, 1937.

2615. Gagey, Edmond McAdoo. Revolution in American Drama.
       New York: Columbia Univ. Press, 1947, p. 79.

2616. Hall, Mordaunt. The Boston Evening Transcript. Jan. 26,
       1937.

2617. Himmelstein, Morgan Y. Drama Was a Weapon[:] The Left-
       Wing Theatre in New York 1929-1941. New Brunswick,
       N.J.: Rutgers Univ. Press, 1963, p. 140.

2618. "Ibee" [signature]. Variety, Feb. 10, 1937.

2619. Isaacs, Edith J. R. Theatre Arts Monthly, XXI (Apr.,
       1937), 260-61.

2620. Krutch, Joseph Wood. "The Death of Kings," The Nation,
       CXLIV (Feb. 20, 1937), 221-22.

2621. Lockridge, Richard. The New York Daily Sun, Jan. 20,
       1937.

2622. _____. The New York Daily Sun, Feb. 9, 1937.

2623. Mantle, Burns. New York Daily News, Feb. 9, 1937.

2624. Matlaw, Myron (ed.). Modern World Drama[:] An Encyclo-
       pedia. New York: E. P. Dutton, 1972, p. 512.

2625. Nathan, George Jean. Saturday Review of Literature, XV
       (Mar. 3, 1937), 23.

2626. Pollock, Arthur. Brooklyn Daily Eagle, Feb. 9, 1937.

2627. Rabkin, Gerald. Drama and Commitment Politics in the American Theatre of the Thirties. Bloomington: Indiana Univ. Press, 1964, pp. 279-81.

2628. Sedgwick, Ruth Woodbury. Stage, XIV (Mar., 1937), 80.

2629. Shivers, Alfred S. Maxwell Anderson. Boston: Twayne, 1976, pp. 93-96.

2630. _____. The Life of Maxwell Anderson. Briarcliff Manor, N.Y.: Stein and Day, 1983, p. 155.

2631. Unsigned. Booklist, XXXIII (May, 1937), 266.

2632. _____. "Dramatic Poets: Shakespeare and Anderson Lead: Mayerling Tragedy Replotted," Literary Digest, CXXIII (Feb. 20, 1937), 23-24.

2633. _____. "London Also Sees 'Masque of Kings'...," The New York Times, May 8, 1938, X, 1.

2634. _____. "Love Story: Maxwell Anderson Broods Over a Romance of Austrian Royalty," Newsweek, IX (Feb. 20, 1937), 24.

2635. _____. New York Herald Tribune, Feb. 7, 1937.

2636. _____. The Boston Globe, Jan. 26, 1937.

2637. _____. The New York Times, Jan. 19, 1937, p. 28.

2638. _____. The New York Times, Jan. 31, 1937, XI, 2.

2639. _____. The New York Times, Feb. 7, 1937, X, 2.

2640. _____. The New York Times, Feb. 21, 1937, X, 1.

2641. _____. Time, XXIX (Feb. 15, 1937), 39.

2642. Vernon, Grenville. Commonweal, XXV (Feb. 26, 1937), 502.

2643. _____. Commonweal, XXVI (June 18, 1937), 216.

2644. Wadeau, Roy S. Vintage Years of the Theatre Guild 1928-1939. Cleveland, Ohio: Case Western Reserve University, 1972, pp. 243-44.

2645. Waldorf, Wilella. New York Post, Feb. 9, 1937.

220   Part II: Secondary Works

2646. Wall, Vincent. "Maxwell Anderson: The Last Anarchist,"
American Drama and Its Critics. Edited by Alan Seymour
Downer. Chicago: Univ. of Chicago Press, 1965, pp.
169-71. [Originally published in Sewanee Review in 1941.]

2647. Watts, Richard, Jr. New York Herald Tribune, Feb. 9,
1937.

2648. _____. New York Herald Tribune, Feb. 21, 1937.

2649. Wilson, Edmund. New Republic, XCI (June 23, 1937), 193-94.

2650. Wyatt, Euphemia Van Rensselaer. Catholic World, CXXXXIV
(Mar., 1937), 731-32.

2651. Young, Stark. "Best American Play," New Republic, XC
(Mar. 3, 1937), 111-12.

THE MASQUE OF PEDAGOGUES

2652. Shivers, Alfred S. Maxwell Anderson. Boston: Twayne,
1976, pp. 22-23.

2653. _____. The Life of Maxwell Anderson. Briarcliff Manor,
N.Y.: Stein and Day, 1983, pp. 43-45.

THE MIRACLE OF THE DANUBE

2654. Shivers, Alfred S. The Life of Maxwell Anderson. Briarcliff
Manor, N.Y.: Stein and Day, 1983, p. 187.

THE STAR-WAGON

2655. Allen, Kelcey. Women's Wear Daily, Sept. 30, 1937.

2656. Anderson, John. New York Journal-American, Sept. 30,
1937.

2657. Atkinson, Brooks. The New York Times, Sept. 30, 1937, p.
18.

2658. _____. "Riding the Star Wagon," The New York Times,
Oct. 10, 1937, XI, 1.

2659. Bailey, Mabel Driscoll. Maxwell Anderson[:] The Playwright
as Prophet. New York: Abelard-Schuman, 1957, pp. 149-
51.

2660. Bolton, Whitney. New York Telegraph, Oct. 1, 1937.

2661. Brown, John Mason. New York Post, Sept. 30, 1937.

2662. _____. Two on the Aisle. Port Washington, N.Y.: Kennikat Press, 1969, pp. 155-59.

2663. Coleman, Robert. New York Daily Mirror, Sept. 30, 1937.

2664. Dusenbury, Winifred L. "Myth in American Drama Between
the Wars," Modern Drama, VI (Dec., 1963), 299.

2665. Dwyer, John P. Evening News (Rochester, N.Y.), Mar. 27,
1939.

2666. Flexner, Eleanor. American Playwrights: 1918-1938 The
Theatre Retreats from Reality. Freeport, N.Y.: Books
for Libraries Press, 1969, pp. 126-27, 129.

2667. Francis, Robert. Brooklyn Daily Eagle, Sept. 30, 1937.

2668. Gabriel, Gilbert W. "Time and Time Again," Stage, XV
(Nov., 1937), 55-57.

2669. Gassner, John. Forum, XCVIII (Dec., 1937), 335.

2670. Goldberg, Isaac. One Act Play Magazine, I (Jan., 1938),
857.

2671. Green, Mawbry. Theatre World, XXVIII (Nov., 1937), 236.

2672. "Ibee" [signature]. Variety, Oct. 6, 1937.

2673. Isaacs, Edith J. R. "Ring Out the Old," Theatre Arts
Monthly, XXI (Oct., 1937), 761. Contains drawings by
Jo Mielziner, the set designer for the play.

2674. _____. Theatre Arts Monthly, XXI (Nov., 1937), 838,
841-42. Illustrated on p. 834.

2675. Krutch, Joseph Wood. The Nation, CXXXXV (Oct. 16,
1937), 411-12.

2676. Lockridge, Richard. The New York Daily Sun, Sept. 30,
1937.

2677. McCarthy, Mary. Sights and Spectacles, 1937-1956. New
York: Farrar, Straus and Cudahy, 1956, pp. 6-8.

2678. _____. Theatre Chronicles, 1937-1962. New York: Farrar, Straus, 1963, pp. 6-7.

2679. Maney, Richard. "Maxwell Anderson's Cabin Cot Yields
       Another Play," New York World-Telegram, Aug. 21, 1937.
       During this period MA did much of his writing in a cabin
       behind the New House on South Mountain Road at New
       City, New York. But, contrary to some reports, he ap-
       parently did not write much in bed.

2680. Mantle, Burns. New York Daily News, Sept. 30, 1937.

2681. Nathan, George Jean. Encyclopedia of the Theatre. New
       York: Alfred A. Knopf, 1940, pp. 311-13.

2682. _____. The Morning After the First Night. New York:
       Alfred A. Knopf, 1938, pp. 116-20.

2683. _____. Newsweek, X (Oct. 11, 1937), 27.

2684. _____. The Saturday Review of Literature, XV (Mar. 3,
       1937), 23.

2685. _____. Scribner's Magazine, CII (Dec., 1937), 53-54.

2686. Quinn, Arthur Hobson. A History of the American Drama
       from the Civil War to the Present Day. New York: Apple-
       ton-Century-Crofts, 1936, p. 266.

2687. Shivers, Alfred S. Maxwell Anderson. Boston: Twayne,
       1976, pp. 122-25.

2688. _____. The Life of Maxwell Anderson. Briarcliff Manor,
       N.Y.: Stein and Day, 1983, pp. 155-57.

2689. Sievers, W. David. Freud on Broadway. New York: Hermi-
       tage House, 1955, p. 177.

2690. Talmey, Allene. Vogue, XC (Nov. 1, 1937), 90.

2691. Unsigned. The New York Times, Sept. 17, 1937, p. 28.

2692. _____. Time, XXX (Oct. 11, 1937), 52-53. Illustrated.

2693. Vernon, Grenville. Commonweal, XXVI (Oct. 15, 1937), 580.

2694. Watts, Richard, Jr. New York Herald Tribune, Sept. 30,
       1937.

2695. _____. New York Herald Tribune, Oct. 10, 1937.

2696. Whipple, Sidney B. New York World Telegram, Sept. 30,
       1937.

2697. Wyatt, Euphemia Van Rensselaer. Catholic World, CXLVI
      (Nov., 1937), 215-16.

2698. Young, Stark. New Republic, XCII (Oct. 20, 1937), 302-03.

THE WINGLESS VICTORY

2699. Anderson, John. New York Evening Journal, Dec. 24, 1936.

2700. Atkinson, Brooks. The New York Times, Jan. 3, 1937.

2701. _____. The New York Times, Dec. 24, 1936.

2702. Bailey, Mabel Driscoll. Maxwell Anderson[:] The Playwright
      as Prophet. New York: Abelard-Schuman, 1957, pp. 142-
      45.

2703. Bell, Nelson B. The Washington Post, Nov. 25, 1936.

2704. _____. The Washington Post, Nov. 26, 1936.

2705. Belli, Angeli. "Lenormand's 'Asie' and Anderson's 'The Wing-
      less Victory,'" Comparative Literature, XIX (Summer, 1967),
      226-39.

2706. Benet, Stephen Vincent. "New Grandeur in Our Theatre,"
      Stage, XIV (Jan., 1937), 38-41.

2707. Brown, John Mason. New York Evening Post, Dec. 24, 1936.

2708. Carmody, Jay. The Evening Star (Washington, D.C.), Nov.
      25, 1936.

2709. Coleman, Robert. New York Daily Mirror, Dec. 24, 1936.

2710. Colum, Mary M. "The Drama," Forum, XCVII (June, 1937),
      353-54.

2711. Dusenbury, Winifred L. The Theme of Loneliness in Modern
      American Drama. Gainesville: Univ. of Florida Press,
      1960, pp. 124-25.

2712. Flexner, Eleanor. American Playwrights: 1918-1938 The
      Theatre Retreats from Reality. Freeport, N.Y.: Books
      for Libraries, 1969, pp. 116-20.

2713. Gabriel, Gilbert W. New York American, Nov. 24, 1936.

2714. _____. New York American, Dec. 24, 1936.

2715. _____. New York American. Jan. 3, 1937.

2716. Gagey, Edmond McAdoo. Revolution in American Drama.
      New York: Columbia Univ. Press, 1947, pp. 81-83.

2717. Gilbert, Douglas. New York World-Telegram, Dec. 24, 1936.

2718. Gloss, Edward E. Akron Beacon Journal, Feb. 21, 1941.
      The Weathervane Players are staging the play in Akron.

2719. Gassner, John. "The Theatre at the Crossroads," One Act
      Play Magazine, I (July, 1937), 275.

2720. Goldstein, Malcolm. The Political Stage[:] American Drama
      and Theater of the Great Depression. New York: Oxford
      Univ. Press, 1974, p. 394.

2721. Herron, Ima Honaker. The Small Town in American Drama.
      Dallas: Southern Methodist University Press, 1969, pp.
      423-25.

2722. Hynes, Betty. The Washington Herald, Nov. 25, 1936.

2723. "Ibee" [signature]. Variety, Dec. 30, 1936.

2724. Isaacs, Edith J. R. "Coat of Many Colors," Theatre Arts
      Monthly, XXI (Feb. 1937), 89-95.

2725. Krutch, Joseph Wood. "More Matter and Less Art," The
      Nation, CXXXIV (Jan. 9, 1937), 53-54.

2726. Lockridge, Richard. The New York Daily Sun, Dec. 24,
      1936.

2727. _____. The New York Daily Sun, Jan. 9, 1937.

2728. MacCarthy, Desmond. "A Tragedy of Race," New Statesman
      and Nation, XXVI (Sept. 18, 1943), 184.

2729. McLauchlin, Russell. The Detroit News, Dec. 15, 1936.

2730. Mantle, Burns. The New York Daily News, Dec. 24, 1936.

2731. Nathan, George Jean. Saturday Review of Literature, XV
      (Jan. 30, 1937), 19.

2732. Norma, Sister Mary. "The Many Faces of Medea," Classical
      Bulletin, XXXXV (Dec. 1968), 17-20.

2733. Pollock, Arthur. Brooklyn Daily Eagle, Dec. 24, 1936.

2734. Rabkin, Gerald. Drama and Commitment Politics in the American Theatre of the Thirties. Bloomington: Indiana Univ. Press, 1964, p. 277.

2735. Seldes, Gilbert. Scribner's Magazine, CI (Mar., 1937), 69-70.

2736. Shivers, Alfred S. Maxwell Anderson. Boston: Twayne, 1976, pp. 103-105.

2737. _____. The Life of Maxwell Anderson. Briarcliff Manor, N.Y.: Stein and Day, 1983, pp. 119, 150.

2738. Sievers, W. David. Freud on Broadway. New York: Hermitage House, 1955, p. 176.

2739. Talmey, Allene. Vogue, LXXXIX (Feb. 1, 1937), 64.

2740. Unsigned. "Cheers for Cornell in 'Wingless Victory,'" The New York Times, Nov. 25, 1936, p. 17. Katharine Cornell played the lead role in the first stage production.

2741. _____. New Statesman and Nation, XXVI (Sept. 18, 1943), 184.

2742. _____. Newsweek, IX (Jan. 2, 1937), 22.

2743. _____. New York World Telegram, Sept. 9, 1934.

2744. _____. Theatre Arts Monthly, XXIX (May, 1945), 309. Refers to Stockholm production of Wingless Victory.

2745. _____. The New York Times, Dec. 24, 1936, p. 20.

2746. _____. The New York Times, Jan. 3, 1937, X, 1.

2747. _____. The New York Times, Jan. 17, 1937.

2748. _____. The New York Times, Feb. 21, 1937, X, 1.

2749. _____. Time, XXIX (Jan. 4, 1937), 29.

2750. Vernon, Grenville. Commonweal, XXV (Jan. 8, 1937), 304.

2751. Watts, Richard, Jr. New York Herald Tribune, Dec. 24, 1936.

2752. White, Rosalind. Baltimore News-Post, Nov. 26, 1936.

2753. Wyatt, Euphemia Van Rensselaer. Catholic World, CXXXXIV (Feb., 1937), 598-99.

2754. Young, Stark. New Republic, LXXXIX (Feb. 3, 1937), 411.

2755. _____. Immortal Shadows. New York: Charles Scribner's
       Sons, 1948, pp. 185-87.

THREE AMERICAN PLAYS

2756. Eaton, Walter Prichard. New York Herald Tribune Books,
       III (Dec. 26, 1926), 2.

2757. Footner, Hulbert. Saturday Review of Literature, III (Dec.,
       1926), 417-18.

2758. Gilder, Rosamond. Theatre Arts Monthly, X (Dec., 1926),
       868, 871.

2759. Unsigned. Time, VIII (Nov. 15, 1926), 39-40.

2760. Van Doren, Carl. Century, CXIII, new series XCI (Dec.,
       1926), 255.

TRUCKLINE CAFE

2761. Barnes, Howard. New York Herald Tribune, Feb. 28, 1946.

2762. Burton, Rascoe. "Anderson in 'Truckline Cafe' Writes an
       Agony Column," New York World-Telegram, Feb. 28, 1946.

2763. Chapman, John. "Maxwell Anderson Hits His Low with a
       Dreadful 'Truckline Cafe,'" New York Daily News, Feb. 28,
       1946.

2764. Clurman, Harold, and Elia Kazan. "To the Theatre Going
       Public," The New York Times, Mar. 1, 1946, p. 17. In a
       response to the negative reviews given to their production
       of Truckline Cafe, Clurman and Kazan said that they had
       some things to get off their chests. They charged that
       the New York critics were ruining the stage there because
       they were assuming powers which they had neither the
       training nor the taste to exercise. Three days later, MA,
       as part of his own war against the New York critics, as-
       sailed them in another paper along the same grounds.

2765. Finch, Everett L. Schenectady Union Star, Feb. 16, 1946.

2766. "Fredi" [signature]. People's Voice, Mar. 6, 1946, p. 22.

2767. Garland, Robert. New York Journal-American, Feb. 28, 1946.

2768. Gassner, John. Forum, CV (Apr., 1946), 753-55.

2769. Gibbs, Wolcott. The New Yorker, XXII (Mar. 9, 1946), 43-44.

2770. Gilder, Rosamond. Theatre Arts Monthly, XXX (May, 1946), 260, 263.

2771. Johnson, Malcolm. "Critics' Reply to Producers," The New York Sun, Mar. 1, 1946.

2772. Kronenberger, Louis. PM (New York City), Mar. 1, 1946.

2773. Krutch, Joseph Wood. The Nation, CLXII (Mar. 16, 1946), 324.

2774. Morehouse, Ward. "'Truckline Cafe' Is a Hopelessly Jumbled Play, Its Author Badly Off Form," The New York Sun, Feb. 28, 1946.

2775. Nichols, Lewis. The New York Times, Feb. 28, 1946, p. 19.

2776. Phelan, Kappo. Commonweal, XLIII (Mar. 15, 1946), 553-54.

2777. Pollock, Arthur. Brooklyn Daily Eagle, Mar. 10, 1946.

2778. Rice, Vernon. "'Truckline Cafe' a Confused Study of the Post-War Period," New York Post, Feb. 28, 1946.

2779. Shivers, Alfred S. Maxwell Anderson. Boston: Twayne, 1976, pp. 64-65.

2780. _____. The Life of Maxwell Anderson. Briarcliff Manor, N.Y.: Stein and Day, 1983, pp. 220-21.

2781. Sievers, W. David. Freud on Broadway. New York: Heritage House, 1955, p. 178.

2782. Unsigned. "Cafe Brawl," Time, XXXXVII (Mar. 11, 1946), 86.

2783. _____. Newsweek, XXVII (Mar. 11, 1946), 82.

2784. _____. New York Herald Tribune, Mar. 2, 1946.

2785. _____. Schenectady Gazette, Feb. 16, 1946.

2786. _____. The New York Daily Sun, Feb. 27, 1946, p. 29.

2787. _____. The New York Daily Sun, Mar. 8, 1946.

2788. _____. The New York Times, Feb. 24, 1946, II, 1.

2789. Young, Stark. New Republic, CXIV (Mar. 11, 1946), 349.

VALLEY FORGE

2790. Anderson, John. New York Herald Tribune, Dec. 11, 1934.

2791. Atkinson, Brooks. "Philip Merivale in Valley Forge," The
       New York Times, Dec. 11, 1934, p. 28.

2792. _____. "Washington at Valley Forge," The New York
       Times, Dec. 23, 1934, IX, 1.

2793. Bailey, Mabel Driscoll. Maxwell Anderson[:] The Playwright
       as Prophet. New York: Abelard-Schuman, 1957, pp. 61-
       67.

2794. Crouse, Russel. "Maxwell Anderson's Play of the Revolu-
       tion," New York American, Dec. 9, 1934.

2795. Dusenbury, Winifred L. "Myth in American Drama Between
       the Wars," Modern Drama, VI (Dec., 1963), 298.

2796. Eaton, Walter Prichard. New York Herald Tribune, XI
       (May 26, 1935), 16.

2797. Flexner, Eleanor. American Playwrights: 1918-1938 The
       Theatre Retreats from Reality. Freeport, N.Y.: Books
       for Libraries, 1969, pp. 98-102.

2798. Gabriel, Gilbert. New York American, Dec. 11, 1934.

2799. Gagey, Edmond McAdoo. Revolution in American Drama.
       New York: Columbia Univ. Press, 1947, pp. 80-81.

2800. Garland, Robert. New York World-Telegram, Dec. 11, 1934.

2801. Graber, Ida. Golden Book, XXI (Feb., 1935), 30a.

2802. Hammond, Percy. New York Herald Tribune, Dec. 11, 1934.

2803. Hansen, Harry. New York World-Telegram, Dec. 28, 1934.

2804. Himmelstein, Morgan Yale. Drama Was a Weapon[:] The
       Left-Wing Theatre in New York 1929-1941. New Brunswick,
       N.J.: Rutgers Univ. Press, 1963, p. 133.

2805. "Ibee" [signature]. Variety, Dec. 18, 1934.

2806. Isaacs, Edith J. R. Theatre Arts Monthly, XIX (Feb.,
       1935), 94-96.

2807. Krutch, Joseph Wood. "Red--and White and Blue," The Na-
       tion, CXXXIX (Dec. 26, 1934), 750.

2808. Lawson, John H. Theory and Technique of Playwriting and
       Screenwriting. New York: G. P. Putnam's Sons, 1949,
       p. 151.

2809. Lockridge, Richard. The New York Sun, Dec. 11, 1934.

2810. _____. The New York Sun, Dec. 13, 1934.

2811. McCalmon, George, and Christian Moe. Creating Historical
       Drama. Carbondale: Southern Illinois Univ. Press, 1965,
       pp. 204-06.

2812. Mantle, Burns. New York Daily News, Dec. 11, 1934.

2813. Matlaw, Myron (ed.). Modern World Drama[:] An Encyclo-
       pedia. New York: E. P. Dutton, 1972, p. 789.

2814. Mersand, Joseph E. The American Drama Since 1930[:] Es-
       says on Playwrights and Plays. Port Washington, N.Y.:
       Kennikat Press, 1968 (originally published in 1949), p. 122.

2815. Mok, Michel. New York Evening Post, Dec. 11, 1934.

2816. Nathan, George Jean. The Theatre of the Moment. Cran-
       bury, N.J.: Fairleigh Dickinson Univ. Press, 1970 (orig-
       inally published in 1936), pp. 235-36.

2817. Pollock, Arthur. Brooklyn Daily Eagle, Dec. 11, 1934.

2818. Quinn, Arthur Hobson. A History of the American Drama
       from the Civil War to the Present Day. New York: Apple-
       ton-Century-Crofts, 1936, p. 270.

2819. Rabkin, Gerald. Drama and Commitment Politics in the Amer-
       ican Theatre of the Thirties. Bloomington: Indiana Univ.
       Press, 1964, pp. 281-84.

2820. Ruhl, Arthur. New York Herald Tribune, Dec. 16, 1934.

2821. Shirk, Samuel Blaine. The Characterizations of George Wash-
       ington in American Drama Since 1875. Easton, Pa.: J. S.
       Correll, 1949, pp. 39-43.

2822. Shivers, Alfred S. Maxwell Anderson. Boston: Twayne, 1976, pp. 44-49.

2823. _____. The Life of Maxwell Anderson. Briarcliff Manor, N.Y.: Stein and Day, 1983, p. 146.

2824. Unsigned. Literary Digest, CXVIII (Dec. 22, 1934), 22.

2825. _____. Newsweek, IV (Dec. 22, 1934), 24.

2826. _____. New York World-Telegram, Dec. 15, 1934.

2827. _____. Scholastic, XXVI (Feb. 16, 1935), 11.

2828. _____. Stage, XII (Jan., 1935), 24-27.

2829. _____. The New York Times, Nov. 27, 1934, p. 26.

2830. _____. The New York Times, Dec. 11, 1934, p. 28.

2831. _____. The New York Times, Dec. 23, 1934, IV, 4. Editorial statement on the kind of liberty as found expressed in Valley Forge.

2832. _____. Time, XXIV (Dec. 10, 1934), 46-48.

2833. _____. Vanity Fair, XXXXIII (Feb., 1935), 37-38.

2834. Vernon, Grenville. Commonweal, XXI (Dec. 28, 1934), 264.

2835. Wadeau, Roy S. Vintage Years of the Theatre Guild 1928-1939. Cleveland, Ohio: Case Western Reserve Univ., 1972, pp. 194-95, 199.

2836. Wall, Vincent. "Maxwell Anderson: The Last Anarchist," American Drama and Its Critics. Edited by Alan S. Downer. Chicago: Univ. of Chicago Press, 1965, p. 165. [Originally published in Sewanee Review in 1941.]

2837. Wyatt, Catharine Van Rensselaer. Catholic World, CXXXX (Feb., 1935), 596-97.

2838. Young, Stark. "Valley Forge," Immortal Shadows. New York: Charles Scribner's Sons, 1948, pp. 165-68.

2839. _____. New Republic, LXXXI (Dec. 26, 1934), 196.

WHAT PRICE GLORY

2840. Atkinson, Brooks, and Albert Hirschfeld. The Lively Years
1920-1973. New York: Association Press, 1973, pp. 30-33.

2841. Avery, Laurence G. "Maxwell Anderson," Twentieth-Century
American Dramatists. Part I: A-J. Edited by John Mac-
Nicholas. Detroit: Gale Research Co., 1981, pp. 27-28.

2842. Bailey, Mabel Driscoll. Maxwell Anderson[:] The Playwright
as Prophet. New York: Abelard-Schuman, 1957, pp. 98-
102.

2843. Benchley, Robert. Life, LXXXIV (Sept. 25, 1924), 18.

2844. Bird, Carol. "The Men Who Write the Hits," Theatre Magazine, XL (Dec., 1924), 28, 50.

2845. Block, Anita. The Changing World in Plays and Theatre.
Boston: Little, Brown, 1939, pp. 306-10.

2846. Broun, Heywood. New York World, Sept. 6, 1924.

2847. Brown, John Mason. Still Seeing Things. New York: Mc-
Graw-Hill, 1950, pp. 227-32.

2848. Cartmell, Van H. (ed.). "What Price Glory," Plot Outlines
of 100 Famous Plays. Gloucester, Mass.: Peter Smith,
1975, pp. 33-37.

2849. Clark, Barrett H. Maxwell Anderson[:] The Man and His
Plays. Ann Arbor, Mich.: University Microfilms, 1968
(originally published in 1933), pp. 12-14.

2850. _____. "Stallings and Anderson," An Hour of American
Drama. Philadelphia: J. P. Lippincott, 1930, pp. 89-90.

2851. Couch, M. B. "A Soldier's Right to Curse" [letter to editor],
The New York Times, Oct. 6, 1924, p. 18.

2852. DeVany, Ione. "What Price Glory Again" [letter to editor],
The New York Times, Nov. 16, 1924, VIII, 2.

2853. Dickinson, Thomas H. Theatre Arts Monthly, VIII (Nov.,
1924), 723-25.

2854. _____. "The Theatrical Interpreter," American Review,
III (Mar., 1925), 220.

2855. Dusenbury, Winifred L. "Myth in American Drama Between
the Wars," Modern Drama, VI (Dec., 1963), 296-97.

2856. Flexner, Eleanor. American Playwrights: 1918-1938 The
Theatre Retreats from Reality. Freeport, N.Y.: Books
for Libraries, 1969, pp. 80-81.

2857. Fort, Alice Buchanan, and Herbert S. Kates. Minute History
of the Drama. New York: Grosset & Dunlap, 1935, p.
137.

2858. Gassner, John. "Laurence Stallings [and] Maxwell Anderson," A Treasury of the Theatre. Vol. 3, rev. ed.
New York: Simon and Schuster, 1951, pp. 837-38.

2859. Hammond, Percy. New York Herald Tribune, Sept. 6, 1924.

2860. Hart, James D. (ed.). Oxford Companion to American Literature. 5th ed. New York: Oxford Univ. Press, 1983,
p. 815.

2861. Heiney, Donald. Recent American Literature. Great Neck,
N.Y.: Barron's Educational Series, 1958, pp. 371-72.

2862. _____, and Lenthiel H. Downs. Recent American Literature After 1930. Woodbury, N.Y.: Barron's Educational
Series, 1974, pp. 280-81.

2863. Hewitt, Barnard. Theatre U.S.A.[:] 1665-1957. New
York: McGraw-Hill, 1959, pp. 358-60.

2864. Hinckley, Theodore B. "War and the Drama: A Broadway
Review," Drama Magazine, XV (Oct., 1924), 4.

2865. Hockman, Stanley, et al. (eds.). McGraw-Hill Encyclopedia
of World Drama. 2nd ed. New York: McGraw-Hill Book
Co., 1984, Vol. I, p. 139.

2866. Hopkins, Arthur. "The Theatre Seeks the Rhythm of the
Times," Literary Digest, CXVII (June 30, 1934), 21, 35.

2867. _____. To a Lonely Boy. Garden City, N.Y.: Double-
day, Doran, 1937, pp. 235-43. Hopkins was the director
of the premiere production of What Price Glory.

2868. Hornblow, Arthur. Theatre Magazine, XXXX (Nov., 1924),
14-15.

2869. _____. Theatre Magazine, XXXXI (Jan., 1925), 19.

2870. Krutch, Joseph Wood. "An American Drama," Literary History of the United States. Edited by Robert E. Spiller et
al. Rev. ed. New York: Macmillan, 1955, pp. 1317,
1318, 1320.

2871. _____. New York Herald Tribune, Aug. 28, 1949.

2872. _____. The American Drama Since 1918. New York:
George Braziller, 1957, pp. 29-44.

2873. _____. The Nation, CXIX (Sept. 24, 1924), 316-17.

2874. _____. The Nation, CXX (Jan. 7, 1925), 22-23.

2875. _____. The Nation, CXXIV (June 15, 1927), 676.

2876. _____. "Three New Realists," American Drama Since 1918;
An Informal History. New York: George Braziller, 1957
(originally published in 1939), pp. 26-72.

2877. _____. "'What Price Glory?' Is 25, but Still New," New
York Herald Tribune, Aug. 2, 1949, V, 1-2. The question
mark after "Glory" is an error; none of the published editions of the play carry it.

2878. Littell, Robert. "What Price Glory," Read America First.
New York: Harcourt, 1926, pp. 233-37.

2879. _____. "What Price Glory?" New Republic, XL (Sept. 24,
1924), p. 98.

2880. MacGowan, Kenneth (ed.). Famous American Plays of the
1920's. New York: Dell Publishing Co., 1967, pp. 18-19.

2881. Marx, Milton. The Enjoyment of Drama. New York: F. S.
Crofts, 1940, pp. 52-53.

2882. Matlaw, Myron (ed.). Modern World Drama[:] An Encyclopedia. New York: E. P. Dutton, 1972, pp. 815-16.

2883. Miller, Jordan Y. "Maxwell Anderson: Gifted Technician,"
The Thirties: Fiction, Poetry, Drama. Edited by Warren
French. Deland, Fla.: Everett/Edwards, 1967, pp. 185-86.

2884. Mordden, Ethan. The American Theatre. New York: Oxford Univ. Press, 1981, pp. 106-07.

2885. Morehouse, Ward. Matinee Tomorrow[:] Fifty Years of Our
Theatre. New York: Whittlesey House, 1949, pp. 197-99.

2886. Nathan, George Jean. Review of What Price Glory in Read-
ings from the American Mercury. Edited by G. C. Knight.
Freeport, N.Y.: Books for Libraries, 1968 (first published in 1926) pp. 138-42.

2887. _____. American Mercury, III (Nov., 1924), 372-73.
Reprinted in Knight's book, above.

2888. _____. Theatre Book of the Year 1948-1949[:] An Inter-
       pretation. New York: Alfred A. Knopf, 1949, p. 203.

2889. _____. Judge, LXXXVII (Oct. 4, 1924), 16.

2890. O'Hara, Frank Hurbert. Today in American Drama. New
      York: Greenwood Press, 1969, pp. 263-64. First pub-
      lished in 1939.

2891. Quinn, Arthur Hobson. A History of the American Drama
      from the Civil War to the Present Day. New York: Apple-
      ton-Century-Crofts, 1936, pp. 234-35.

2892. Runchey, Geraldine. "Mr. Hopkins and the Army," Canadian
      Magazine, LXIV (Apr., 1925), 74.

2893. Seldes, Gilbert. Dial, LXXVII (Nov., 1924), 440.

2894. Shivers, Alfred S. Maxwell Anderson. Boston: Twayne,
      1976, pp. 49-52.

2895. _____. The Life of Maxwell Anderson. Briarcliff Manor,
       N.Y.: Stein and Day, 1983, pp. 85-102. A detailed study
       of the writing of the play, the problems of getting the work
       produced, the staging, the attempts at censorship, and
       other related matters.

2896. Sievers, W. David. Freud on Broadway. New York: Hermi-
      tage House, 1955, p. 172.

2897. Skinner, Richard Dana. Commonweal, I (Nov. 12, 1924), 2.

2898. _____. "Glory and Claptrap," Independent, CXIII (Nov.
       15, 1924), 403.

2899. Steiner, Pauline, and Horst Frenz. "Anderson and Stallings'
      What Price Glory? and Carl Zuckmayer's Rivalen," German
      Quarterly, XX (Nov., 1947), 239-51.

2900. Unsigned. American Review, III (Mar., 1925), 220.

2901. _____. "Arms and the--Baby," New Republic, XL (Oct.
       15, 1924), 160-61.

2902. _____. "British Comments on 'What Price Glory,'" Literary
       Digest, LXXXIV (Jan. 10, 1925), 30-31.

2903. _____. "Car Kills Original 'Captain Flagg,'" New York
       Herald Tribune, Dec. 11, 1933, pp. 1, 32. Philip Town-
       send Case, former captain of the 5th Marine Regiment in
       which Stallings had served in France, died in an automobile
       accident.

2904. _____. "Censors of 'Glory' Hit from Pulpit," New York
        World, Oct. 27, 1924, p. 28.

2905. _____. "1800 Authors Censure Hylan," New York World,
        Oct. 10, 1924. New York City's Mayor John F.
        Hylan had made attempts to expurgate the indecent language from
        What Price Glory.

2906. _____. "Hayward Considers What Price Glory," The New
        York Times, Sept. 27, 1924, I, 17. The United States
        District Attorney, Colonel William Hayward, was called
        upon to rule on whether What Price Glory contained lan-
        guage that was offensive to the honor of the armed forces.
        He finally ruled that he found nothing disturbing about
        the language, and declined to prosecute.

2907. _____. "How a Great Play Is Written," Current Opinion,
        LXXVII (Nov., 1924), 617-18.

2908. _____. Life, LXXXIV (Sept. 24, 1924), 18.

2909. _____. Literary Digest, LXXXXII (Mar. 5, 1927), 24-25.
        About the first movie version starring Edmund Lowe as
        Sergeant Quirt and Victor McLagen as Captain Flagg.

2910. _____. Living Age, CCCXXIV (Jan. 3, 1925), 68.

2911. _____. "Maxwell Anderson--Record Maker," Vogue, CI
        (Feb. 1, 1943), 80-83.

2912. _____. New York Herald Tribune, Sept. 6, 1924.

2913. _____. New York Herald Tribune, Sept. 21, 1924.

2914. _____. New York World, Sept. 29, 1924.

2915. _____. Outlook, CXXXVIII (Nov. 19, 1924), 439-41.

2916. _____. "Stage Marines Soften 'Damns'; 'Vanities' Balks,"
        New York Herald Tribune, Sept. 24, 1924. The play's
        director, Arthur Hopkins, consented to the censorship.
        But the management of Earl Carroll's pulchritudinous and
        erotic show called Vanities resisted such interference.

2917. _____. The New York Times, Sept. 14, 1924, VIII, 1.

2918. _____. The New York Times, Sept. 21, 1924, VII, 1.

2919. _____. The New York Times, Sept. 24, 1924, p. 1.
        New York City's Mayor John F. Hylan wrote a joint letter
        to the Commander of the Brooklyn Navy Yard, Rear Ad-

miral Charles P. Plunkett, to the ranking Army officer in
New York City, Major General Robert Lee Bullard, and to
the city's police commissioner, requesting a conference with
these men in order to eliminate the objectionable language
in What Price Glory. Of these three summoned officials,
only the police commissioner was to take any action.

2920.   _____. The New York Times, Sept. 25, 1924, I, 1, 6.

2921.   _____. The New York Times, Sept. 25, 1924, 1. More
about New York City's attempts to censor the play.

2922.   _____. The New York Times, Sept. 25, 1924, 1. Under
threat of official investigation, the theater director Arthur
Hopkins agreed to excise from the play the words that the
police had found objectionable.

2923.   _____. The New York Times, Sept. 26, 1924, p. 22.

2924.   _____. The New York Times, Sept. 27, 1924, VII, 1.

2925.   _____. The New York Times, Sept. 27, 1924, p. 14. An
editorial dealing with Mayor John F. Hylan's criticism of
What Price Glory.

2926.   _____. The New York Times, Sept. 29, 1924, p. 14.
Major General Robert Lee Bullard, the ranking Army officer in the city, refused to assist in removing the offensive
content in the play.

2927.   _____. The New York Times, Oct. 2, 1924, p. 22.

2928.   _____. The New York Times, Oct. 11, 1924, p. 17. The
Author's League of America sent a resolution to President
Coolidge and to the Secretaries of War and the Navy cen-
suring Mayor John F. Hylan for having asked the military
to pass judgement on the play.

2929.   _____. The New York Times, Oct. 12, 1924, IV, 7.

2930.   _____. The New York Times, June 28, 1925, VIII, 1.

2931.   _____. The New York Times, Sept. 25, 1925, p. 21.
Faced with a staging of What Price Glory in Boston, the
mayor there has required that all profanity be cut from
the play.

2932.   _____. The New York Times, Apr. 28, 1929, IX, 2.

2933.   _____. The New York Times, Oct. 30, 1936, p. 25.

2934. _____. The New York Times, Mar. 3, 1949, p. 33.

2935. _____. "The Stage Captured by a Hard-Boiled War," Literary Digest, LXXXIII (Oct. 4, 1924), 30-31.

2936. _____. Theatre, XXXIX (Dec., 1924), 28.

2937. _____. Theatre Arts Monthly, XI (Sept., 1927), 659.

2938. _____. Theatre Arts Monthly, XVIII (Aug., 1934), 601-06.

2939. _____. Theatre Arts Monthly, XXV (Aug., 1941),578.

2940. _____. Time, IV (Sept. 15, 1924), 15.

2941. _____. "U.S. Prosecutor Takes No Action Against War Play," New York World, Sept. 27, 1924.

2942. _____. "'What Price Glory' and Its Authors," The New York Times, Sept. 14, 1924, VIII, 1.

2943. _____. "Wilbur Criticizes 'What Price Glory,'" The New York Times, Sept. 28, 1924, I, 9. The Secretary of the Navy, Curtis D. Wilbur, who had never attended the play, branded What Price Glory as shameful for its use of "gutter language," and said that men in today's Navy did not speak such filthy language as Captain Flagg did.

2944. _____. "Wilbur Silent on 'What Price Glory' Until Judge Reports," New York Herald Tribune, Sept. 21, 1924.

2945. _____. World Tomorrow, VII (Oct., 1924), 309-10.

2946. Wall, Vincent. "Maxwell Anderson: The Last Anarchist," American Drama and Its Critics. Edited by Alan S. Downer. Chicago: Univ. of Chicago Press, 1965. Pp. 149-50.

2947. Whyte, Gordon. Billboard, XXXV (Sept. 13, 1924), 10.

2948. Williams, Valentine. "Americans at the Front," The New York Times, Dec. 26, 1924, p. 14. In this letter to the editor, a British officer protests that What Price Glory does his country an injustice.

2949. Woollcott, Alexander. Review of What Price Glory in The American Theatre as Seen by Its Critics 1752-1934. Edited by Montrose J. Moses and John Mason Brown. New York: W. W. Norton, 1934, pp. 245-47. First published in The New York Evening Sun, Sept. 6, 1924.

2950. _____. Portable Woollcott. New York: Viking, 1946, pp. 441-43.

2951. _____. Vanity Fair, XXIII (Nov., 1924), 38, 110.

2952. Young, Stark. The New York Times, Sept. 6, 1924, p. 14.

2953. _____. The New York Times, Sept. 28, 1924, VII, 1.

2954. _____. Immortal Shadows. New York: Charles Scribner's
      Sons, 1948, pp. 185-88.

WHITE DESERT

2955. Allen, Kelcey. Women's Wear Daily, Oct. 19, 1923.

2956. Block, Anita. New York Leader, Oct. 19, 1923.

2957. Broun, Heywood. New York Herald Tribune, Oct. 19, 1923.

2958. Clark, Barrett H. Maxwell Anderson[:] The Man and His
      Plays. Ann Arbor, Mich.: University Microfilms, 1968,
      pp. 10-11. Originally published in 1933.

2959. Corbin, John. "The Play," The New York Times, Oct. 19,
      1923, p. 17.

2960. Craig, James. New York Mail, Oct. 19, 1923.

2961. Dale, Alan. New York American, Oct. 19, 1923.

2962. Hammond, Percy. New York Herald Tribune, Oct. 19, 1923.

2963. Mantle, Burns. "Maxwell Anderson," American Playwrights
      of Today. New York: Dodd, Mead, 1930, pp. 67-68.

2964. Quinn, Arthur Hobson. A History of the American Drama
      from the Civil War to the Present Day. New York: Apple-
      ton-Century-Crofts, 1936, pp. 233-34.

2965. Shivers, Alfred S. Maxwell Anderson. Boston: Twayne,
      1976, pp. 28-29.

2966. _____. The Life of Maxwell Anderson. Briarcliff Manor,
      N.Y.: Stein and Day, 1983, pp. 81-83.

2967. Sievers, W. David. Freud on Broadway. New York: Hermi-
      tage House, 1955, pp. 171-72.

2968. Torres, H. Z. New York Commercial, Oct. 19, 1923.

2969. Unsigned. Brooklyn Times, Oct. 19, 1923.

2970. _____. New York Evening World, Oct. 19, 1923.

2971. _____. New York Journal of Commerce, Oct. 19, 1923.

2972. _____. New York World, Oct. 20, 1923.

2973. _____. New York Telegraph, Oct. 19, 1923.

2974. _____. The New York Daily Sun, Oct. 19, 1923.

2975. _____. Time, II (Oct. 29, 1923), 16.

2976. Whyte, Gordon. Billboard, XXXIV (Oct. 27, 1923), 10, 128.

2977. Woollcott, Alexander. New York Herald Tribune, Oct. 19, 1923.

WINTERSET

2978. "Abel" [signature]. Variety, Oct. 2, 1935.

2979. Abernethy, Francis E. "Winterset: A Modern Revenge Tragedy," Modern Drama, VII (Sept., 1964), 185-89.

2980. Adler, Jacob H. "Shakespeare in Winterset," Educational Theatre Journal, VI (Oct., 1954), 241-48.

2981. Anderson, John. New York Evening Journal, Sept. 26, 1935.

2982. _____. New York Evening Journal, June 3, 1936.

2983. Anderson, Maxwell. "In Which the Author of Winterset Sets Forth His Reasons for Attempting a Modern Theme in Verse," The New York Times, Oct. 6, 1935, XI, 6.

2984. Atkinson, Brooks. The New York Times, Sept. 26, 1935, p. 19.

2985. _____. "Winterset and Mr. Anderson," The New York Times, Oct. 6, 1935, XI, 1.

2986. _____, and Albert Hirschfeld. The Lively Years 1920-1973. New York: Association Press, 1973, pp. 103-06.

2987. Avery, Laurence G. "Maxwell Anderson," Twentieth-Century American Dramatists. Part I: A-J. Edited by John Mac-Nicholas. Detroit: Gale Research Co., 1981, pp. 30, 32.

2988. Bailey, Mabel Driscoll. Maxwell Anderson[:] The Playwright
       as Prophet. New York: Abelard-Schuman, 1957, pp. 132-
       42.

2989. Barnes, Howard. New York Herald Tribune, June 7, 1936.

2990. Benet, William Rose. Review of Winterset in Saturday Review
       of Literature, XII (Oct. 12, 1935), 16.

2991. Block, Anita. The Changing World in Plays and Theatre
       Boston: Little, Brown, 1939, pp. 239-45.

2992. Bolton, Whitney. New York Morning Telegraph, Sept. 26,
       1935.

2993. Borden, Gail. Times (Chicago), Apr. 14, 1936.

2994. Boyce, Benjamin. "Anderson's 'Winterset,'" Explicator, II,
       (Feb., 1944), item 32.

2995. Brown, John Mason. Dramatis Personae[:] A Retrospective
       Show. New York: Viking Press, 1963, pp. 73-76.

2996. _____. New York Evening Post, Sept. 26, 1935.

2997. _____. New York Evening Post, Oct. 26, 1935.

2998. _____. Two on the Aisle. Port Washington, N.Y.: Ken-
       nikat Press, 1969, pp. 148-52.

2999. Burton, David. The New York Times [letter to the editor].
       Nov. 10, 1935, IX, 2.

3000. Coleman, Robert. New York Mirror, Sept. 26, 1935.

3001. _____. New York Mirror, Sept. 27, 1935.

3002. Collins, Charles. New York Herald Tribune, Apr. 15, 1936.

3003. Colum, Mary Maguire. Forum, VC (June, 1936), 344-46.

3004. _____. Forum, XCVII (June, 1937), 352-53.

3005. Craig, Don. Washington Daily News, Mar. 31, 1936.

3006. Davenport, William H. "Anderson's Winterset," Explicator, X
       (Apr., 1952), 41.

3007. Downer, Alan Seymour. Fifty Years of American Drama.
       Chicago: Henry Regner, 1951.

3008. Drake, Herbert. New York Herald Tribune, June 2, 1936.

3009. Dusenbury, Winifred L. "Myth in American Drama Between
       the Wars," Modern Drama, VI (Dec., 1963), 295-96.

3010. _____. The Theme of Loneliness in Modern American
       Drama. Gainesville, Fla.: Univ. of Florida Press, 1960,
       pp. 119-124.

3011. Eager, Helen. Boston Traveler, Mar. 3, 1936.

3012. Eaton, Walter Prichard. New York Herald Tribune, May 15,
       1936.

3013. Farm, William J. Players Magazine, XII (Jan.-Feb., 1936),
       12-13.

3014. Ferguson, Otis. "East River Hamlet: I," New Republic,
       LXXXIX (Jan. 13, 1937), 328-29. First of two parts re-
       viewing film version of Winterset.

3015. _____. "East River Hamlet: II," New Republic, LXXXIX
       (Jan. 27, 1937), 386. Concluding review of the film made
       from Winterset.

3016. Field, Rowland. The Brooklyn Times Union, Sept. 26, 1935.

3017. Foster, Edward. "Core of Belief: An Interpretation of the
       Plays of Maxwell Anderson," Sewanee Review, L (Jan.,
       1942), 93-95.

3018. Flexner, Eleanor. American Playwrights: 1918-1938 The
       Theatre Retreats from Reality. Freeport, N.Y.: Books
       for Libraries, 1969, pp. 102-115.

3019. Fox, R. M. Theatre Arts Monthly, XXXI (Nov., 1947), 30.
       About the production of Winterset in Dublin, Ireland, star-
       ring Paulette Goddard and Burgess Meredith.

3020. Gabriel, Gilbert W. New York American, Sept. 26, 1935.

3021. _____. "Maxwell Anderson's Magnificent Poetry in 'Winter-
       set,'" Theatre Arts Monthly, XX (June, 1936), 465.

3022. Gagey, Edmond McAdoo. Revolution in American Drama.
       New York: Columbia Univ. Press, 1947, pp. 83-85.

3023. Garland, Robert. New York Evening Telegram, Sept. 26,
       1935.

3024. _____. "Winterset Improves Upon Acquaintance," New
       York World-Telegram, Oct. 10, 1935, p. 34.

3025.   _____. New York World-Telegram, Oct. 18, 1935.

3026.   _____. New York World-Telegram, Mar. 28, 1936.

3027.   _____. New York World-Telegram, Apr. 6, 1936.

3028.   Gassner, John. "Maxwell Anderson, Realist and Romancer,"
         Masters of the Drama. 3rd ed. New York: Dover Pub-
         lications, 1954, p. 682.

3029.   Gilbert, Robert L. "Mio Romagna: A New View of Maxwell
         Anderson's Winterset," North Dakota Quarterly, XXXVIII
         (Winter, 1970), 33-43.

3030.   Gilder, Rosamond, et al. (eds.). Theatre Arts Anthology[:]
         A Record and a Prophecy. New York: Theatre Arts
         Books, 1948, pp. 632-34.

3031.   Gregory, Horace. "Poets in the Theatre," Poetry, XLVIII
         (July, 1936), 221-28.

3032.   Hammond, Percy. New York Herald Tribune, Sept. 26, 1935.

3033.   _____. New York Herald Tribune, Sept. 29, 1935.

3034.   Harris, Ainslie. "Maxwell Anderson," Madison Quarterly, IV
         (Jan., 1944), 30-44.

3035.   Hart, James D. (ed.). Oxford Companion to American Lit-
         erature. 5th ed. New York: Oxford Univ. Press, 1983,
         pp. 838-39.

3036.   Hatcher, Harlan (ed.). Modern American Dramas. New edi-
         tion. New York: Harcourt, Brace, 1949, pp. 72-122.

3037.   Heilman, Robert Bechtold. Tragedy and Melodrama. Seattle:
         Univ. of Washington Press, 1968, pp. 276-78.

3038.   Heiney, Donald. Recent American Literature. Great Neck,
         N.Y.: Barron's Educational Series, 1958, pp. 374-75.

3039.   _____, and Lenthiel H. Downs. Recent American Litera-
         ture After 1930. Woodbury, N.Y.: Barron's Educational
         Series, 1974, pp. 283-84.

3040.   Hewitt, Barnard. Theatre U.S.A.[:] 1668-1957. New York:
         McGraw-Hill, 1959, pp. 394-96.

3041.   Hochman, Stanley, et al. (eds.). McGraw-Hill Encyclopedia
         of World Drama. 2nd ed. New York: McGraw-Hill Book
         Co., 1984, Vol. I, p. 142.

3042. Isaacs, Edith J. R. Theatre Arts Monthly, XIX (Nov.,
      1935), 815-18.

3043. Jones, John Bush. "Shakespeare as Myth and the Structure
      of Winterset," Educational Theatre Journal, XXV (Mar.,
      1973), 34-45.

3044. Kernodle, George R. "Playwrights and Ancestors," College
      English, II (Jan., 1941), 330-31.

3045. Kliger, Samuel. "Hebraic Lore in Maxwell Anderson's Winter-
      set," American Literature, XVIII (Nov., 1946), 219-32.

3046. Krutch, Joseph Wood. The American Drama Since 1918. New
      York: George Braziller, 1957, pp. 295-301.

3047. _____. "Modernism" in Modern Drama. New York: Cor-
      nell University, 1966, pp. 120-22.

3048. _____. "An American Tragedy," The Nation, CXXXXI
      (Oct. 9, 1935), 420.

3049. _____. "'Winterset'--Critics' Prize-Winner," The Nation,
      CXLII (Apr. 15, 1936), 484-85. Winterset won the first
      Drama Critics Circle award ever presented.

3050. _____. "An American Drama," Literary History of the
      United States. Edited by Robert E. Spiller et al. New
      York: Macmillan, 1955, pp. 1321-22.

3051. Lockridge, Richard. The New York Evening Sun, Sept. 26,
      1935.

3052. Luckett, Perry D. "Winterset and Some Early Eliot Poems,"
      North Dakota Quarterly, IIL (Fall, 1960), 26-37.

3053. McCullen, J. T., Jr. "Two Quests for Truth: King Oedipus
      and Winterset," Laurel Review (West Va. Wesleyan College),
      V (1965), 28-35.

3054. McDermott, William F. Cleveland Plain Dealer, Mar. 10, 1936.

3055. McGee, Betty Ruth. "A Production Book for Maxwell Ander-
      son's Winterset." Unpublished master's thesis. Stanford,
      1948.

3056. Magill, Frank N. (ed.). "Winterset" (synopsis), Master-
      pieces of World Literature in Digest Form. First Series.
      New York: Harper & Brothers, 1952, pp. 1123-25.

3057. Maney, Richard. "Maxwell Anderson's Cabin Cot Yields

Another Play," New York World Telegram, Aug. 21, 1937.
MA did much of his writing in a cabin in the woods back
of the New House in New City, N.Y.

3058. Mantle, Burns. New York Daily News, Sept. 26, 1935.

3059. _____. New York Sunday News, Oct. 6, 1935.

3060. _____. New York Daily News, June 4, 1936, p. 49.

3061. Marx, Milton. The Enjoyment of Drama. New York: F. S.
       Crofts, 1940, pp. 124-28.

3062. Matlaw, Myron (ed.). Modern World Drama[:] An Encyclo-
       pedia. New York: E. P. Dutton, 1972, pp. 834-36.

3063. Melcher, E. de S. The Evening Star (Washington, D.C.),
       Mar. 31, 1936.

3064. Melvin, Edwin. Boston Transcript, Mar. 3, 1936.

3065. Meredith, Burgess. "On the Set with Winterset," Stage, XIV
       (Dec., 1936), 45-46. Meredith, who had played the lead
       role in the premiere Broadway production of Winterset, was
       now the star of the motion picture version too.

3066. Miller, Jordan Y. "Maxwell Anderson: Gifted Technician,"
       The Thirties: Fiction, Poetry, Drama. Edited by Warren
       French. Deland, Fla.: Everett/Edwards, 1967, pp. 188-89.

3067. Mordden, Ethan. The American Theatre. New York: Ox-
       ford Univ. Press, 1981, pp. 151-53.

3068. Morris, Lloyd R. Postscript to Yesterday; America: The
       Last Fifty Years. New York: Random House, 1947, pp.
       198-99.

3069. Nannes, Caspar Harold. Politics in the American Drama.
       Washington, D.C.: Catholic Univ. of America Press, 1960,
       pp. 94-96.

3070. Nathan, George Jean. Saturday Review of Literature, XIII
       (Mar. 14, 1936), 3-4.

3071. _____. The Theatre of the Moment. Cranbury, N.J.:
       Fairleigh Dickinson Univ. Press, 1970, pp. 236-38.

3072. _____. Vanity Fair, VL (Dec., 1935), 39.

3073. Nicoll, Allardyce. "The Lyric Drama," The New York Times,
       Feb. 16, 1936, IX, 1, 3.

3074. _____. World Drama. Rev. ed. New York: Harper &
Row, 1976, pp. 737-38.

3075. Norton, Elliot. Boston Post, Mar. 3, 1936.

3076. O'Hara, Frank Hurbert. Today in American Drama. New
York: Greenwood Press, 1969 (first published in 1939),
pp. 25-33.

3077. Pearce, Howard D. "Job in Anderson's Winterset," Modern
Drama, VI (May, 1963), 32-41.

3078. Pollock, Arthur. Brooklyn Daily Eagle, Sept. 26, 1935.

3079. _____. Brooklyn Daily Eagle, Sept. 29, 1935.

3080. _____. Brooklyn Daily Eagle, Apr. 6, 1936.

3081. _____. Brooklyn Daily Eagle, June 2, 1936.

3082. Price, Edgar. Brooklyn Daily Eagle, Sept. 26, 1935.

3083. Prior, Moody E. The Language of Tragedy. New York:
Columbia Univ. Press, 1947, pp. 320-25.

3084. Quinn, Arthur Hobson. A History of the American Drama
from the Civil War to the Present Day. New York: Appleton-Century-Crofts, 1936, p. 271.

3085. _____. The New York Times, Oct. 20, 1935.

3086. _____ (ed.). Introduction to Winterset in Representative
American Plays from 1767 to the Present Day. 7th ed.
New York: Appleton-Century-Crofts, 1953, pp. 1103-07.

3087. Rabkin, Gerald. Drama and Commitment Politics in the American Theatre of the Thirties. Bloomington: Indiana Univ.
Press, 1964, pp. 268-70.

3088. Roby, Robert C. "Two Worlds: Maxwell Anderson's Winterset," College English, XVIII (Jan., 1957), 195-202.

3089. Rave, Kenneth Thorpe. A Theatre in Your Head. New
York: Funk & Wagnalls, 1960, pp. 146-47, 151-52.

3090. Rodell, John S. "Maxwell Anderson: A Criticism," Kenyon
Review, V (Spring, 1943), 274-75.

3091. Sata, Masanori. "Maxwell Anderson No Winterset," Eigo
Seinen [The Rising Generation] (Tokyo), CXVI (1970),
206-08.

3092. _____. "Superstition (1824) to Winterset (1935): Romeo-
      Juliet theme kara no kosatsu," English Language and Lit-
      erature (Tokyo), VI (1969), 131-46.

3093. Sedgwick, Ruth W. Stage, XIII (May, 1936), 32.

3094. Shank, Theodore J. (ed.). A Digest of 500 Plays[:] Plot
      Outlines and Production Notes. New York: Crowell-
      Collier Press, 1963, pp. 300-01.

3095. Sharpe, Robert Boris. "Nine Steps to the Tragic Triumph,"
      University of North Carolina Extension Bulletin, Vol.
      XXXVI, No. 3 (Mar., 1957), 37-38.

3096. Shivers, Alfred S. Maxwell Anderson. Boston: Twayne,
      1976, pp. 107-114.

3097. _____. The Life of Maxwell Anderson. Briarcliff Manor,
      N.Y.: Stein and Day, 1983, pp. 146-49.

3098. Sievers, W. David. Freud on Broadway. New York: Hermi-
      tage House, 1955, pp. 175-76.

3099. Silver, Lee. "Revival of Winterset Falls Short in Poetry,"
      New York Daily News, Feb. 10, 1966.

3100. Spaeth, Arthur. Cleveland News, Mar. 10, 1936.

3101. Sprinchorn, Evert. "Winterset," 20th Century Plays in Syn-
      opsis. New York: Thomas Y. Crowell, 1965, pp. 19-22.

3102. Stevenson, Philip. "Maxwell Anderson: Thursday's Child,"
      New Theatre, III (Sept. 3, 1936), 25-27.

3103. Tees, Arthur. "Winterset: Four Influences on Mio," Modern
      Drama, XIV (Feb., 1972), 408-12.

3104. Thompson, Alan Reynolds. The Anatomy of Drama. Berke-
      ley: Univ. of California Press, 1946, pp. 385-91.

3105. Thomsen, Christian W. "Maxwell Anderson: Winterset," Das
      Amerikanische Drama. Edited by Paul Goetsch. Dussel-
      dorf: Bagel, 1974, pp. 127-48.

3106. Unsigned. "Critics Pick Winterset Lest the Pulitzer Judges
      Miss It," Newsweek, VII (Apr. 4, 1936), 32.

3107. _____. "Do Gangsters Speak Verse?" The Nation, CXLI
      (Dec. 4, 1935), 638.

3108. _____. Literary Digest, CXX (Oct. 5, 1935), 20.

3109. _____. London News, CXC (Apr. 17, 1937), 675.

3110. _____. Newsweek, VI (Oct. 5, 1935), 32-33.

3111. _____. Newsweek, VII (Apr. 4, 1936), 32.

3112. _____. Newsweek, VIII (Dec. 5, 1936), 20.

3113. _____. New York Evening Post, Dec. 7, 1935.

3114. _____. New York Evening Post, Mar. 31, 1936.

3115. _____. New York Morning Telegraph, Sept. 22, 1935.

3116. _____. Saturday Review of Literature, XXXII (Aug. 6, 1949), 127-28.

3117. _____. Theatre Arts Monthly, XX (May, 1936), 326.

3118. _____. The New York Times, June 2, 1936, p. 35. About a return engagement of Winterset in New York City.

3119. _____. The Times (London), Oct. 30, 1935.

3120. _____. Time, XXVI (Oct. 7, 1935), 38, 40.

3121. _____. The Wall Street Journal, June 28, 1935.

3122. _____. "'Winterset' Selected as Prize Play," New York World-Telegram, Mar. 27, 1936.

3123. _____. Women's Wear Daily, Sept. 26, 1935.

3124. Van Doren, Mark. The Nation, CXXXXIII (Dec. 19, 1936), 741-42.

3125. Vernon, Grenville. Commonweal, XXII (Oct. 11, 1935), 585.

3126. _____. Commonweal, XXIV (June 19, 1936), 218.

3127. Wall, Vincent. "Maxwell Anderson: The Last Anarchist," American Drama and Its Critics[:] A Collection of Critical Essays. Edited by Alan S. Downer. Chicago: Univ. of Chicago Press, 1965, pp. 156-62, 166-67. [Essay originally published in Sewanee Review in 1941.]

3128. Weathers, Winston. "Winterset: The Archetypal Stage," The Archetype and the Psyche: Essays in World Literature. Univ. of Tulsa Dept. of English Monograph Series #4. Tulsa: Univ. of Tulsa, 1968, pp. 97-102.

3129. Wilson, Edmund. New Republic, LXXXXI (June 23, 1937),
       193.

3130. _____. "Prize Winning Blank Verse," The Shores of Light.
       New York: Farrar, Straus & Young, 1952, pp. 674-80.

3131. Wilward, Burton. Lexington [Ky.] Leader, Mar. 29, 1939.

3132. Wyatt, Catherine Van Rensselaer. "Farce and Tragedy--
       Winterset," Catholic World, CXXXXII (Nov., 1935), 211-12.

3133. Young, Stark. "American Drama in Production: Winterset
       by Maxwell Anderson," Literary Opinion in America.
       Edited by Morton Dauwen Zabel. New York: Harper &
       Brothers, 1937, pp. 292-95.

3134. _____. New Republic, LXXXIV (Oct. 16, 1935), 274.

3135. _____. New Republic, LXXXIV (Nov. 6, 1935), 365.

3136. _____. New Republic, LXXXV (Jan. 8, 1936), 257. Re-
       view of the book.

YOU WHO HAVE DREAMS

3137. Auslander, Joseph. New York World, Sept. 27, 1925.

3138. Deutsch, Babette. New Republic, XXXXV (Feb. 10, 1926),
       338-39.

3139. Monroe, Harriet. "Quiet Music," Poetry: A Magazine of
       Verse, XXVII (Mar., 1926), 337-38.

■ DOCTORAL DISSERTATIONS AND MASTER'S THESES

3140. Artz, Lloyd Charles. "An Aristotelian Critique of Maxwell Anderson's Dramas." M.A. Univ. of Illinois, 1946.

3141. Avery, Laurence Green. "Maxwell Anderson: An Analytic Catalogue." Ph.D. Univ. of Texas, 1966.

3142. Bailey, Mabel Driscoll. "Maxwell Anderson[:] The Playwright as Prophet." Ph.D. Univ. of Iowa, 1955. Published under this title in 1957 by Abelard-Schuman.

3143. Bartlett, Patricia Ann. "The Use of History in the Plays of Maxwell Anderson." M.A. Univ. of Idaho, 1957.

3144. Bassett, Clyde Harold. "The Playwrights' Producing Company, Inc., 1938-1960." Ph.D. Univ. of Wisconsin, 1965.

3145. Bay, Marjorie C. "Idealism in the Writings of Maxwell Anderson." M.A. Baylor University, 1964.

3146. Bell, Joanna A. "Themes in the Plays of Maxwell Anderson." M.A. Baylor University, 1953.

3147. Bell, Raynal. "The Love Motif in the Plays of Maxwell Anderson." M.A. Texas Christian University, 1959.

3148. Bergland, Maurine. "A Critical Study of the Plays of Maxwell Anderson." M.A. Ft. Hays Kansas State College, 1941.

3149. Blanchard, Fred C. "The Place of Maxwell Anderson in the American Theatre." Ph.D. New York University, 1939.

3150. Boughton, Donald James, Jr. "The Broadway Plays of Maxwell Anderson." Ph.D. Univ. of California at Santa Barbara, 1974.

3151. Bourque, Joseph H. "Maxwell Anderson's Political Philosophy: A Reevaluation." M.A. Washington State University at Pullman, 1968.

3152. Buchanan, Randall J. "Maxwell Anderson's Rules for Playwrights and Their Application to His Plays." Ph.D. Univ. of Louisiana, 1964.

3153. Chambers, Mary L. "The Plays of Maxwell Anderson, 1923-
       1936." M.A. Washington Univ. at St. Louis, 1939.

3154. Chase, Marion C. "An Analysis and Production Book on
       High Tor by Maxwell Anderson." M.A. Ohio State Uni-
       versity, 1951.

3155. Comer, Richard. "The Individual and Democracy in Maxwell
       Anderson's Plays." M.A. Univ. of North Carolina, 1982.

3156. Covington, W. P., III. "A Maxwell Anderson Bibliography
       with Annotations." M.A. Univ. of North Carolina, 1950.

3157. Cox, Martha H. "Maxwell Anderson and His Critics," Ph.D.
       Univ. of Arkansas, 1955.

3158. Crouch, Isabel M. "Joan of Arc and Four Playwrights: A
       Rhetorical Analysis for Oral Interpretation." Ph.D. South-
       ern Illinois University, 1972. The playwrights are Shake-
       speare, G. B. Shaw, Maxwell Anderson, and Jean
       Anouilh.

3159. Dwelle, Ronald. "The Politics of Maxwell Anderson." M.A.
       Univ. of Kansas, 1962.

3160. Dykes, Charlotte J. "Maxwell Anderson's Theory of Tragedy."
       M.A. Oklahoma State University, 1957.

3161. Fallan, Richard G. "The Quest for Tragedy by O'Neill and
       Anderson as Evidenced by Their Plays Beyond the Horizon
       and Winterset." M.A. Columbia University, 1952.

3162. Foote, Ronald C. "The Verse Dramas of Maxwell Anderson
       in the Modern Theatre." Ph.D. Tulane University, 1956.

3163. Frenz, Horst. "The Contributions of Maxwell Anderson to
       the American Drama." M.A. Univ. of Illinois, 1939.

3164. Gilbert, Robert Lewis. "The Thirties Verse Tragedies of
       Maxwell Anderson." Ph.D. Univ. of Washington, 1967.

3165. Gilbert, Vedder M. "Maxwell Anderson[:] His Interpreta-
       tion of Tragedy in Six Poetical Dramas." M.A. Cornell
       University, 1938.

3166. Gordon, Albert Claude. "A Critical Study of the History
       and Development of the Playwrights' Producing Company."
       Ph.D. Tulane University, 1965.

3167. Graves, Eleanore. "Maxwell Anderson." M.A. State Univ.
       of New York at Buffalo, 1939.

3168. Gross, James R. "Maxwell Anderson and the Renascence of
      Verse Drama." M.A. Univ. of North Carolina at Chapel
      Hill, 1960.

3169. Harris, Kenneth E. "Maxwell Anderson's Critical Theories
      and Their Application to His Verse Dramas." M.A. Univ.
      of Pittsburgh, 1948.

3170. Hensley, Jack Alton. "The Playwrights' Company." M.S.
      Univ. of Wisconsin, 1952. This is the only master's or
      doctoral study based on interviews with members of the
      Playwrights Company.

3171. Herring, Victoria Ann. "The Making of a Tragic Heroine."
      M.A. Univ. of North Carolina, 1979.

3172. Hobson, Henry E. "An Essay on Character Portrayal, Style
      and Technique of Writing in Maxwell Anderson's Biograph-
      ical Plays in Verse." M.A. Univ. of the Pacific, 1942.

3173. Hynes, Carolyn. "An Analysis of Nine Tragedies by Ameri-
      can Playwrights: Eugene O'Neill, Maxwell Anderson and
      Lillian Hellman." M.A. Univ. of Houston, 1954.

3174. Johnson, Kay Irene. "Playwrights as Patriots: A History
      of the Playwrights Producing Company, 1938-1960."
      Ph.D., Univ. of Wisconsin, 1974. Like the other disser-
      tations about the Playwrights Company, this one is based
      on a study of the Company's papers that are filed at the
      Wisconsin State Historical Society, Madison, Wisconsin.

3175. Lancaster, Ray H. "Irony in Maxwell Anderson's Elizabeth
      the Queen, Mary of Scotland and Anne of the Thousand
      Days." M.A. Univ. of North Carolina at Chapel Hill,
      1966.

3176. Landauer, A. "Maxwell Anderson: Defeatist or Man of Vi-
      sion?" M.A. Univ. of Connecticut, 1940.

3177. Larrabee, Ruth. "Maxwell Anderson's Theory and Practice
      of Tragedy in Relation to the Aristotelian Tradition."
      M.A. Fresno State College, 1951.

3178. Lauterbach, Charles Everett. "A Descriptive Study of
      Trends in Dramatic Styles in the Successful Serious Amer-
      ican Drama of the Broadway Stage in the 1920's." Ph.D.
      Michigan State University, 1966.

3179. Lee, Henry G. "The Use of History in the Historical Plays
      of Maxwell Anderson." Ph.D. Tulane University, 1967.

3180.   Lewis, Mary P.   "The Free Spirit: Some Aspects of the Con-
        cept of Man in Maxwell Anderson."   M.A.   Univ. of San
        Diego, 1963.

3181.   Lewis, Wesley L.   "The Complete Design for a Production of
        Maxwell Anderson's Journey to Jerusalem, Together with a
        Critical Essay Upon the Problems of Interpretation and
        Production."   M.A.   Whittier College, n.d.

3182.   Luckett, Perry D.   "The Mind and Matter of Maxwell Ander-
        son."   Ph.D.   Univ. of North Carolina at Chapel Hill, 1979.

3183.   McCarty, Mary.   "Maxwell Anderson's Poetic Tragedies."
        M.A.   Univ. of Texas at El Paso, 1946.

3184.   McGee, Betty Ruth.   "A Production Book for Maxwell Ander-
        son's Winterset."   M.A.   Stanford University, 1948.

3185.   MacGowan, Mary Lou.   "Sunlight and Hours[:]   A Brief Dis-
        cussion of Folk Drama Elements in the Pulitzer Prize
        Plays."   M.A.   Univ. of North Carolina, 1946.

3186.   McNiven, Kathleen E.   "Idealism in the Plays of Maxwell
        Anderson."   M.A.   Cornell University, 1943.

3187.   Maik, Anna J.   "A Study of the Tragic Vision in Maxwell
        Anderson's Plays."   M.A.   Univ. of Oklahoma, 1964.

3188.   Maloney, Martin J.   "Maxwell Anderson's Debt to Shake-
        speare."   M.A.   Univ. of Kansas, 1938.

3189.   Marley, Mary C.   "Study of Maxwell Anderson's Theory and
        Practice of Making Blank Verse Drama."   M.A.   Boston
        College, 1939.

3190.   Meyer, Marilyn G.   "Maxwell Anderson's Dramatic Conception
        of the Historical Personage."   M.A.   Texas Christian Uni-
        versity, 1960.

3191.   Mills, Ronald E.   "Research for Technical Production and Di-
        rection of the Following Plays: Of Mice and Men by Stein-
        beck, High Tor by Anderson and Beautiful People by
        Saroyan."   M.A.   Eastern New Mexico University, 1963.

3192.   Milstead, Marian M.   "A Study and Presentation of Character,
        Queen Elizabeth in Maxwell Anderson's Play, Elizabeth the
        Queen."   M.A.   Univ. of Wyoming, 1955.

3193.   Mitchell, Albert O.   "A Study of Irony in the Plays of Max-
        well Anderson."   Ph.D.   Univ. of Wisconsin, 1939.

3194.   Mitchell, Roger E.   "Maxwell Anderson and His Critics."

M.A.   Univ. of Maine, 1954.

3195. Mordoff, Helen Lee. "Dramatic Theories of Maxwell Anderson."
       M.A. Cornell University, 1942.

3196. Mouton, Janice Malsten. "Joan of Arc on the Twentieth-
       Century Stage: Dramatic Treatments of the Joan of Arc
       Story by Bertolt Brecht, George Bernard Shaw, Jean
       Anouilh, Georg Kaiser, Paul Claudel, and Maxwell Ander-
       son." Ph.D. Northwestern University, 1974.

3197. Nardin, James T. "Maxwell Anderson: A Critical Estimate."
       M.A. Lehigh University, 1947.

3198. Newland, Paul D. "Joan of Lorraine: A Play in Two Acts
       by Maxwell Anderson." M.A. Ohio State University,
       1947.

3199. Norgress, Ben. "Maxwell Anderson as a Dramatic Poet."
       M.A. Louisiana State University, 1941.

3200. Paxton, Patricia M. "An Analysis of the American Criticism
       of Maxwell Anderson as Playwright and Poet." M.A.
       Washington State Univ. at Pullman, 1960.

3200a. Pearce, Bee. "An Exhibition of Original Designs Created for
       the Premiere Performances of Plays by Maxwell Anderson."
       M.A. Univ. of North Dakota, 1984.

3201. Pinckney, Elizabeth R. "The Theme of War in the Plays of
       Maxwell Anderson." M.A. Univ. of North Carolina at
       Chapel Hill, 1946.

3202. Plouffe, J. B. "The Poetic Drama of Maxwell Anderson."
       M.A. Boston University, 1941.

3203. Potter, Marian L. "Protest and Criticism in the Plays of
       Maxwell Anderson." M.A. Univ. of Rhode Island, n.d.

3204. Reveaux, Edward C. "A Study of Contemporary Verse Drama
       with Especial Emphasis on Maxwell Anderson." M.A. Univ.
       of Arizona, 1938.

3205. Rice, Patrick J. "Maxwell Anderson and Tragic Drama."
       M.A. Loyola University, 1950.

3206. Robbins, Buren E. "A Prompt Book and Production of Max-
       well Anderson's Saturday's Children." M.A. Univ. of
       Iowa, 1935.

3207. Robinson, Doris Martha. "Maxwell Anderson's Tragedies: A
       Study in Theory and Practice." M.A. Univ. of Arkansas,
       1951.

3208. Sanders, Melba Frances. "Maxwell Anderson and His
       Dramas." M.A. Univ. of Southern California, 1941.

3209. Schmerl, Rudolf B. "An Examination of the Social, Political
       and Economic Content in the Plays of Maxwell Anderson."
       M.A. Univ. of Toledo, 1952.

3210. Schooley, Bill J. "Production Notebook for Maxwell Ander-
       son's Elizabeth the Queen." M.F.A. Univ. of Oklahoma,
       1968.

3211. Seabury, Lorna. "Study of Imagery in Maxwell Anderson."
       M.A. Univ. of Wisconsin, 1937.

3212. Shelton, John. "A Study of Maxwell Anderson's Conception
       of Tragedy." M.A. Univ. of Texas at Austin, 1941.

3213. Shields, James Christie. "Dramatic Irony, an Essential Sup-
       plement of Maxwell Anderson's Views on Recognition in
       Tragedy." M.A. Univ. of Pittsburgh, 1951.

3214. Shular, Mary. "The Development of Maxwell Anderson as a
       Dramatist." M.S. Kansas State College at Pittsburg,
       1944.

3215. Siegel, Gerald. "The Individual as Idealist in Maxwell Ander-
       son's Plays." M.A. Texas Christian University, 1966.

3216. Sollnar, William J. "Modern Playwrights on Dramatic Theory:
       Anderson, Eliot and Fry." M.A. Univ. of Kansas, 1951.

3217. Stanley, Aurora M. "Maxwell Anderson as a Historical Drama-
       tist." M.A. Univ. of Texas at Austin, 1941.

3218. Tees, Arthur Thomas. "Maxwell Anderson: An Attitude
       Toward Man." Ph.D. Univ. of Kansas, 1967.

3219. Thomas, Harriett K. "Maxwell Anderson's Concept of Man."
       M.A. Baylor University, 1955.

3220. Tidwell, Lois G. "Theme of Social Justice in the Dramas of
       Maxwell Anderson." M.A. Texas Arts and Industries
       University, 1952.

3221. Toran, William B. "A Study of Maxwell Anderson's Theory
       of Drama as Found in His Own Criticism and the Practice
       of It as Found in His Poetic Plays on Contemporary
       Themes." M.A. Univ. of Kentucky, 1947.

3222. Tout, Dorothy J. "Maxwell Anderson: His Theories and
       His Plays." M.A. West Texas State University, 1950.

3223. Weinman, Richard Jay. "The 'Core of Belief' of Maxwell
       Anderson and the Structure of His Tragedies." Ph.D.
       Indiana University, 1965.

3224. Weshinsky, Roy K. "Maxwell Anderson's Application of His
       Own Theory of Verse Tragedy: 1930-1939." M.A. South-
       ern Illinois University, 1950.

3225. White, Susan Jere. "Corruption of Power in the Plays of
       Maxwell Anderson." M.A. Stephen F. Austin State Uni-
       versity, 1974.

3226. Williams, Richard Arthur. "A Critical Study of Religious
       Ideas in Five Plays of Maxwell Anderson." Ph.D. Univ.
       of Illinois at Urbana-Champaign, 1976.

3227. Yeazell, Paul G. "Maxwell Anderson's Treatment of Historical
       Material in Gods of the Lightning and Winterset." M.A.
       Univ. of Arizona, 1954.

■ BIBLIOGRAPHIES AND CHECK-LISTS

3228. Adelman, Irving, and Rita Dworkin. Modern Drama[:] A
Checklist of Critical Literature on 20th Century Plays.
Metuchen, N.J.: The Scarecrow Press, 1967, pp. 22-27.

3229. Avery, Laurence G. "Addenda to the Maxwell Anderson Bibliography: Monro's Chapbook," Papers of the Bibliographical Society of America, LXV (Fourth Quarter, 1971), 408-
11.

3230. _____. "Addenda to the Maxwell Anderson Bibliography:
The Measure," Papers of the Bibliographical Society of
America, LXIII (First Quarter, 1969), 31-36.

3231. _____. A Catalogue of the Maxwell Anderson Collection at
the University of Texas. Austin: Univ. of Texas Press,
1968. 175 pp. An indispensable guide to the world's
largest collection of Andersonia.

3232. Breed, Paul F., and Florence M. Sniderman. Dramatic Criticism Index. Detroit: Gale Research Co., 1972, pp. 19-30.

3233. Coleman, Arthur, and Gary R. Tyler. Drama Criticism[:]
A Checklist of Interpretations Since 1940 of English and
American Plays. Denver: Alan Swallow, 1966, Vol. I,
pp. 21-23.

3234. Covington, W. P., III. "A Maxwell Anderson Bibliography
with Annotations." Master's thesis. Univ. of North Carolina, 1950.

3235. Cox, Martha. Maxwell Anderson Bibliography. Charlottes-
ville: Bibliographical Society at the University of Virginia,
1958. 117 pp. Includes newspaper and magazine reviews
under the separate play titles. There is a section on
books and articles of a general nature. No listing of the
unpublished works nor of master's theses and doctoral dissertations.

3236. Curley, Dorothy Nyren; Maurice Kramer; and Elaine F. Kramer (eds.). A Library of Literary Criticism. New York:
Frederick Ungar, 1969, Vol. I, pp. 32-35.

3237. Eddleman, Floyd Eugene. American Drama Criticism 1890-
       1977. 2nd edition. Hamden, Conn.: The Shoe String
       Press, 1979, pp. 20-30.

3238. Gilbert, Vedder M. "The Career of Maxwell Anderson: A
       Check List of Books and Articles," Modern Drama, II
       (Feb., 1960), 386-94.

3239. Harris, Richard H. Modern Drama in England and America
       1950-1970. Detroit: Gale Research Co., 1982, pp. 66-67.

3240. Hochman, Stanley, et al. (eds.). McGraw-Hill Encyclopedia
       of World Drama. Rev. edition. New York: McGraw-Hill,
       1984, Vol. I, pp. 142-43.

3241. Howard, Patsy C. Theses in American Literature 1896-1971.
       Ann Arbor, Mich.: The Pierian Press, 1973, pp. 5-6.
       The entries here are by no means complete for the time
       period represented, for most schools do not publish lists
       of their theses.

3242. Klink, William. Maxwell Anderson and S. N. Behrman: A
       Reference Guide. Boston: G. K. Hall, 1977. The MA
       section runs to 48 pages. Useful for its annotated entries
       on literary criticism. The items included are highly selec-
       tive and are grouped by the year published rather than
       by subject matter--a most awkward procedure. Unless the
       year of the play's production is known, the reader is
       handicapped.

3243. Leary, Lewis. Articles in American Literature 1900-1950.
       Durham, N.C.: Duke Univ. Press, 1954, p. 11.

3244. _____. Articles in American Literature 1950-1967. Dur-
       ham, N.C.: Duke Univ. Press, 1970, pp. 14-15.

3245. _____. Articles in American Literature 1968-1975. Dur-
       ham, N.C.: Duke Univ. Press, 1979, p. 13.

3246. Literary Writings in America: A Bibliography. Millwood,
       New York: KTO Press, 1977, Vol. I, pp. 276-83. No
       editor is cited on the cover or the title page, but E. H.
       O'Neill was the project supervisor during the five years
       of preparing this most useful bibliography. Covers only
       primary source material.

3247. Magill, Frank N. Magill's Bibliography of Literary Criticism.
       Englewood Cliffs, N.J.: Salem Press, 1979, Vol. I, pp.
       38-43.

3248. Millett, Fred B. Contemporary American Authors. New
       York: Harcourt, Brace & Co., 1940, pp. 219-21.

3249. Moses, Montrose J. (ed.). Dramas of Modernism and Their
       Forerunners. Boston: D. C. Heath, 1941, pp. 931-33.

3250. Palmer, Helen H., and Jane Anne Dyson. American Drama
       Criticism[:] Interpretations, 1890-1965, Inclusive, of
       American Drama Since the First Play Produced in America.
       Hamden, Conn.: The Shoe String Press, 1957, pp. 8-17.

3251. Perkins, Barbara M.; James Vinson; and D. L. Kirkpatrick.
       Great Writers of the English Language[:] Dramatists.
       New York: St. Martin's Press, 1979, pp. 10-11.

3252. Salem, J. M. A Guide to Critical Reviews. Part I, 2nd edi-
       tion. Metuchen, N.J.: The Scarecrow Press, 1973, pp.
       18-30.

3253. _____. A Guide to Critical Reviews. Part II: The Musi-
       cal. 2nd edition. Metuchen, N.J.: The Scarecrow Press,
       1976, pp. 254-55, 282-83. Covers Knickerbocker Holiday
       and Lost in the Stars.

3254. Shivers, Alfred S. Maxwell Anderson. Boston: Twayne,
       1976, pp. 163-70.

3255. _____. The Life of Maxwell Anderson. Briarcliff Manor,
       N.Y.: Stein and Day, 1983, pp. 359-76.

3256. Smeall, J. F. S. "Additions to the Maxwell Anderson Bibli-
       ography." North Dakota Quarterly, IIL (Summer, 1980),
       60-63.

3257. Spiller, Robert E., et al. (eds.). Literary History of the
       United States: Bibliography. 4th edition. New York:
       Macmillan, 1974, pp. 386-88, 870, 1143.

3258. Tanselle, G. Thomas. "Additions to the Bibliography of
       Maxwell Anderson," Papers of the Bibliographical Society
       of America, LVII (First Quarter, 1963), 90-91.

3259. Woodress, James Leslie, and Marian Koritz. Dissertations in
       American Literature 1891-1966. Rev. edition. Durham,
       N.C.: Duke Univ. Press, 1968. Items 61-69. Must be
       supplemented with other reference works, such as Disserta-
       tion Abstracts International and American Doctoral Disserta-
       tions.

■ RECORDED INTERVIEWS CONDUCTED BY ALFRED SHIVERS

These interviews, which are valuable for the study of
the playwright's life, were conducted with MA's relatives, friends, and neighbors for the purpose of writing
my The Life of Maxwell Anderson. The original cassette
recordings and their typed transcripts are presently in
my possession, but after the publication of this book
they will be turned over to some university library for
safekeeping.

3260. Anderson, Alan Haskett (1917-), (second son of MA by
his marriage to Margaret E. Haskett). Interview conducted
on May 14, 1978, at his home at 170 S. Mountain Rd., New
City, N.Y. 31 pp. More remarks by Alan are found at
the end of the Quentin Anderson interview (see below).

3261. Anderson, Hesper (1934-), (daughter of MA's union with
Mab Maynard). Five interviews conducted at her apartment
at 12400 Moorpark St., Studio City, Calif., and at restaur-
ants in the area, on Jan. 4-5, 1980. 63pp.

3262. Anderson, John Kenneth (1902-), (younger brother of
MA's, and business manager of Anderson House, which
had published some of MA's books). Interview conducted
at the apartment of his sister Lela Chambers, 703 W. Sulli-
van St., Olean, N.Y., on May 12, 1978, in the presence
of Lela, who speaks also. 16 pp.

3263. Anderson, Lawrence (1913-), (MA's youngest brother).
Interview conducted at his apartment at Lakeside 1-0,
Shrewville Rd., Ledyard, Conn., on May 18, 1978, in the
presence of his life, Lillian, who speaks a little also. 29
pp.

3264. Anderson, Margaret Elizabeth (née Margaret Elizabeth Pickett;
nicknamed Meg), (became MA's daughter-in-law and neighbor in 1933 by marrying his son Quentin; divorced in 1946).
Interview conducted at her house at Craryville, N.Y., on
May 16, 1978. 21 pp. Present at the interview and sometimes commenting is her daughter by Quentin, named Martha
Haskett.

3265. Anderson, Mrs. Terence (née Anastasia Sadowsky, nick-
       named Lulu; became MA's daughter-in-law in 1949). A
       painter. Interview conducted at her home at 160 S. Moun-
       tain Road, New City, N.Y., on May 15, 1978. 10 pp.
       In the middle of the interview are remarks by Terence
       on his father's love of music.

3266. Anderson, Mrs. Alan Haskett (née Nancy Swan; became MA's
       daughter-in-law in 1941). Interview conducted at her
       home at 170 S. Mountain Rd., New City, N.Y., on May
       15, 1978. 19 pp.

3267. Anderson, Quentin Maxwell (1912-), (first son by MA's
       marriage to Margaret E. Haskett). Interview conducted
       at his apartment at 29 Claremont Ave., New York, N.Y.,
       on May 19, 1978. 29 pp. Alan Anderson, after listening
       to the taped interviews with Quentin and Meg, respective-
       ly, furnished some corrections; these are found at the end
       of this tape.

3268. Anderson, Terence (1921-), (MA's third son by his mar-
       riage to Margaret E. Haskett). Interview conducted in
       his home at 160 S. Mountain Rd., New City, N.Y., on
       May 14, 1978. 19 pp. More remarks by Terence are found
       in the middle of the interview with his wife, Lulu.

3269. Chambers, Glen Avery (1920-), (the third of four sons by
       Lela Blanch Chambers, who is MA's sister). Interview
       conducted at his house at 703 W. Sullivan St., Olean,
       N.Y., on May 12, 1978. 24 pp. This interview followed
       the one with Lela and preceded those with Blanche and
       Kenneth, all at the same address.

3270. Chambers, Mrs. Glen Avery (wife of the above; called
       Blanche). Interview conducted at her home at 703 W.
       Sullivan St., Olean, N.Y., on May 12, 1978. 5 pp.
       Blanche was one of MA's typists during his last years.

3271. Chambers, Mrs. Lela Blanch (1891-), (MA's sister). In-
       terview conducted at her apartment at 703 W. Sullivan St.,
       Olean, N.Y., on May 11, 1978. 41 pp.

3272. Hargrove, Marion Lawton (1919-), (journalist and film
       script writer; author of best-selling soldier book See
       Here, Private Hargrove during WWII; protégé and neighbor
       of MA's in New City; intimate with MA's daughter Hesper).
       Interview conducted at his home at 130 Adelaide Dr.,
       Santa Monica, Calif., on Jan. 6, 1980. 19 pp.

3273. Green, Mrs. Paul E. (called Elizabeth). Interview conducted
       at her house on the outskirts of Chapel Hill, N.C., on

May 22, 1978. 6 pp. Both she and her husband had been
students of Prof. Frederick Henry Koch, who years earlier
had been one of MA's professors at the Univ. of North
Dakota. Also, MA had been a friend of theirs.

3274. Green, Paul E. (1894-1981), (playwright and friend of MA's;
both men had been students under Prof. Frederick Henry
Koch, who was a nationally known teacher of playwriting
and an exponent of folk plays). Interview conducted at
his home on the outskirts of Chapel Hill, N.C., on May
22, 1978. 11 pp.

3275. Lenya, Lotte (1898-1981), (née Karoline Blamauer in Vienna,
Austria; wife of Kurt Weill, who was one of MA's closest
friends and associates; friend and neighbor of MA's for
many years; actress, dancer, and singer--she took the
role of Jenny in the original production of Weill's <u>Die</u>
<u>Dreigroschenoper</u>). Interview conducted in her home at
116 S. Mountain Rd., New City, N.Y., on May 15, 1978.
29 pp. At the end is Alan Anderson's response after lis-
tening to the cassette recording of the Lenya interview.

3276. Sloane, Mrs. Julie (wife of MA's publisher William M. Sloane;
friend and neighbor of MA's for several years). Interview
conducted in her home at 44 S. Mountain Rd., New City,
N.Y. 15 pp.

■ INDEX TO WORKS BY ANDERSON